THE HOUSE OF
WISDOM

How the Arabs Transformed Western Civilization

JONATHAN LYONS

BLOOMSBURY PRESS

NEW YORK BERLIN LONDON

Copie de la Carte de L'EDRISI, tirée de l'Ouvrage du Docteur Vincent Sur le periple d'Arrien.

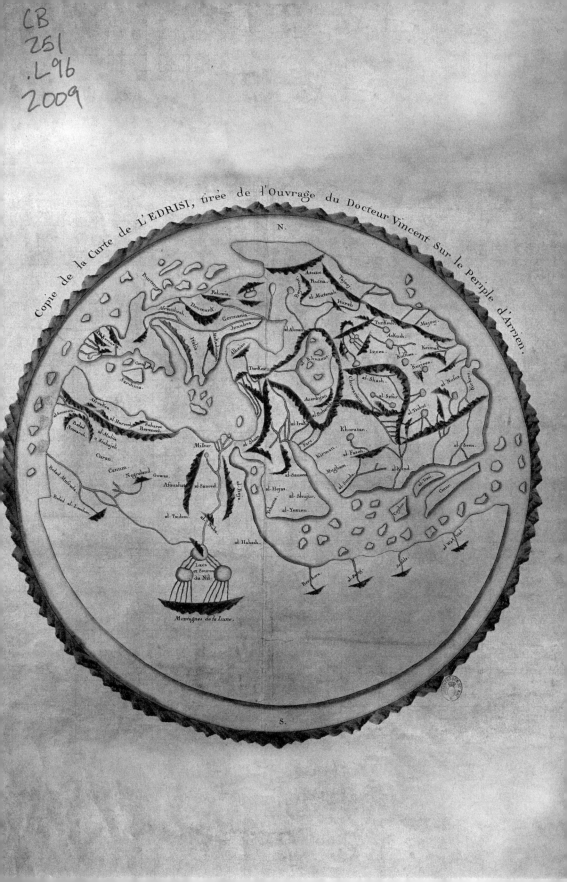

Copie de la Carte de L'EDRISI, tirée de l'Ouvrage du Docteur Vincent sur le Periple d'Arrien.

Montagnes de la Lune.

Published by Bloomsbury Press, New York

All papers used by Bloomsbury Press are natural, recyclable products made
from wood grown in well-managed forests. The manufacturing processes
conform to the environmental regulations of the country of origin.

ISBN-13: 978-1-59691-459-9

Printed in the United States of America

To the memory of my father, Will Lyons,
who introduced me to the power of ideas.

CONTENTS

NOTE TO READERS

DEFINITIONS OF TERMS and concepts are rarely associated with works for the general reader, no matter how serious or weighty the subject, and I have deliberately kept these to a minimum. Nonetheless, a few words are in order at the outset about my choice of "Arab science"—or words to that effect—to convey the complex cultural milieu of the medieval Islamic world, rather than "Islamic science." As many readers will already be aware, much of the cultural flowering in this time and place was not exclusively the work of ethnic Arabs. Nor was it strictly the work of Muslims. Persians—including Zoroastrians and Christians—Jews, Greeks, Syriac Christians, Turks, Kurds, and others played crucial roles in all aspects of science, theology, and philosophy.

However, this work was almost always conducted in Arabic and frequently under the aegis of Arab rulers, most notably the Umayyad and Abbasid caliphs, first in Damascus and then in Baghdad. In one notable case, as we shall see, an ethnic Persian scholar produced a major work in his native language but then rewrote it in Arabic, which he found far more precise and more effective for his purposes. Throughout much of the period in question, Arabic served as the global language of scholarship, and learned men of all stripes could travel widely and hold serious and nuanced discussions in this lingua franca. Medieval Western scholars who wanted access to the latest findings also needed to master the Arabic tongue, or work from translations by those who had done so. It is also worth noting that such labels, today largely associated with nation-states and the demands for distinct cultural identity, were far more fluid in the era under discussion.

This is not to say that Islam and the unique culture of the Muslims are not important elements of our story. I refer to the great importance of Islam to the development of Arab science throughout the text and have devoted an entire chapter to this vital relationship between faith and reason. Yet much of the research during this period went well beyond specific questions relating to the Islamic faith and was not generally carried out with an eye to establishing theological or doctrinal truths. At the same time, it is worth avoiding any confusion with the established notion of the "Islamic sciences," which generally refers to strictly religious disciplines: jurisprudence, Koranic exegesis, the study of the hadith, or the collected sayings of the Prophet Muhammad, and so on.

A few words on my use of names and dates and my system of transliteration will also be useful. This work presents the enormous impact of Arab learning on the West—that is, on the lands of medieval Christendom and the states and societies they later produced. It seemed only sensible to use the Latinized forms instead of the Arabic names in the case of figures widely known to the Western world. Thus, I have used the Latin Averroes, not the Arabic Ibn Rushd, and Avicenna, not Ibn Sina. Less familiar figures have retained their Arabic names. For similar reasons, dates are presented in the traditional "Western" fashion— that is, anno Domini (A.D.) and before Christ (B.C.) In transliterating, I have chosen readability, familiarity, and convention over linguistic purity or consistency.

Finally, a reference to the structure of *The House of Wisdom*, which pays tribute to the success of Arab scholars in measuring out the ever-changing pattern of night and day that determines the times of the five daily Muslim prayers. The book begins at sunset (*al-maghrib* prayer), the traditional start of the day in the Middle East; then moves through the nightfall (*al-isha*) of the Christian Middle Ages; recounts the dawn (*al-fajr*) of the great age of Arab learning; soars toward the glory of midday (*al-zuhr*) with our central hero, Adelard of Bath, in the Near East; and concludes with the rich colors of afternoon (*al-asr*) that mark the end of the Age of Faith in the West and the seemingly unstoppable triumph of Reason.

SIGNIFICANT EVENTS

These are some of the most important events surrounding the story of *The House of Wisdom*. By necessity, several of the dates are only approximate. More details can be found in the narrative that follows.

622   Prophet Muhammad leads a migration of his followers from Mecca to Medina, the *hijra*. It marks the start of the Muslim epoch.

632   The death of Muhammad.

732   An Arab raiding party is defeated near Tours, in southern France, effectively ending Muslim penetration of Western Europe from Spain.

750   The victory of the Abbasid revolution against the Umayyad caliphs.

756   Abd al-Rahman proclaims himself master of Muslim Spain, known as al-Andalus.

762   Caliph al-Mansur founds Baghdad as the new Abbasid capital.

771   Hindu sages bring Sanskrit scientific texts to Baghdad.

813–833   The reign of Caliph al-Mamun, an enthusiastic promoter of science and philosophy.

825   Muhammad ibn Musa al-Khwarizmi produces his famous star tables, the *zij al-Sindhind*.

848   Albumazar (Abu Mashar) completes *The Introduction to Astrology* in Baghdad.

948   Byzantines send Dioscorides's medical encyclopedia to the Arab court of Cordoba.

967   Gerbert d'Aurillac, the future Pope Sylvester II, is sent to
           Catalonia for advanced schooling in basic knowledge gleaned
           from the nearby Arabs.

1009   Muslims destroy the Holy Sepulcher, aggravating tensions with
           the Christian world.

1066   The Normans conquer England.

Ca. 1080   Adelard of Bath is born.

1088   John de Villula, Adelard's future patron, is named bishop of
           Wells. He moves his see to Bath.

1091   The Normans complete the conquest of Muslim Sicily.

1092   Walcher of Malvern, an English cleric, carries out the first known
           Western experiment to improve astronomical predictions.

1095   Pope Urban II issues the call to crusade in Clermont, France.

1096   The People's Crusade is crushed by Turkish troops at Civetot,
           near Constantinople, before the arrival of the main crusader
           host from Europe.

1099   Forces of the First Crusade capture Jerusalem from the Muslims.

Ca. 1100   Adelard leaves Bath to attend the cathedral school in Tours, France.

1109   Adelard heads for the East, in pursuit of Arab learning.

1114   Adelard is caught in an earthquake near Antioch, in modern-day
           Turkey.

1126   First Latin introduction to Euclid's *Elements*, attributed to
           Adelard of Bath.

1138   King Roger II of Sicily invites al-Idrisi to create a new map of
           the world. The king also mints the first European coins to use
           the Hindu-Arabic numeral system.

1142   Peter the Venerable commissions the first Latin translation of
           the Koran.

1146   The Berber dynasty of the Almohads takes control of al-Andalus.

1149   Adelard completes *On the Use of the Astrolabe.* Some experts date
or 1150 it as early as 1142.

Ca. 1152 The death of Adelard.

1175   Gerard of Cremona completes a translation from the Arabic of
        the *Almagest.*

1187   Saladin retakes Jerusalem from the crusaders.

1210   Aristotle's natural philosophy is officially banned at the
        University of Paris.

1229   Frederick II takes control of Jerusalem after months of
        negotiations with the Arabs.

Ca. 1230 Michael Scot's translations of Averroes reach Paris.

1236   Cordoba, once the imperial capital of al-Andalus, falls to
        Christian forces.

1258   The Mongols, under Hulegu, the grandson of Genghis Khan,
        conquer and sack Baghdad.

1259   Hulegu orders the construction of an observatory at Maragha,
        in what is today northwest Iran, and staffs it with prominent
        astronomers.

1260   Nasir al-Din Tusi, director of the Maragha observatory,
        publishes an important revision to Ptolemaic astronomy. This
        appears in Copernicus's work three centuries later.

1270   Thomas Aquinas writes *On the Eternity of the World,* arguing that
        the Arab case for eternity cannot be disproved but must be
        rejected on the grounds of religious faith.

1270   The church issues thirteen "condemnations" at the University of
        Paris. These ban the teaching of the Eternity of the World and
        God's indifference to particulars. Most are ignored.

1277   The bishop of Paris issues two hundred and nineteen condemnations, including some linked to the teachings of Thomas Aquinas.

1323   Thomas Aquinas is canonized.

1453   Constantinople falls to the Ottoman Turks.

1492   The Muslim kingdom of Granada, the last holdout in Spain, falls to the Christians.

1497   Portuguese explorer Vasco da Gama completes a voyage around Africa. He later reaches India, apparently with the help of a Muslim navigator.

1543   The publication of Copernicus's *De Revolutionibus*, which proposes a sun-centered universe. The work includes two key Arab contributions.

1592   An abridged Arabic version of al-Idrisi's Map of the World is printed in the West.

1633   Galileo is convicted of heresy for upholding Copernicus's ideas.

1687   Isaac Newton's theory of gravitation "completes" the Copernican revolution, establishing the preeminence of science in the Western world.

LEADING FIGURES

The following figures are central to the rise of Arab science and its reception in the West. Few are household names, and they are included here as a handy reference for the reader.

Adelard of Bath—Early pioneer of Arab teaching who brought the wonders of geometry, astronomy, astrology, and other fields to the medieval West.

Albumazar—Leading Arab authority on astrology who grounded his art in the natural philosophy of Aristotle. He was known in Arabic as Ja'far ibn Muhammad Abu Mashar al-Balkhi.

Augustine of Hippo—Incorporated Greek philosophy into church teachings but de-emphasized its concerns with natural science. He died in 430 and was later recognized as a saint.

Averroes—Muslim philosopher who exerted enormous influence on Western thought, primarily as a commentator on Aristotle. He was known in Arabic as Abu al-Walid ibn Rushd.

Avicenna—Persian philosopher and physician. His influence on the West exceeded that of Averroes up until the mid-thirteenth century, while his import as an authority in medicine continued for several more centuries. In Arabic, Ibn Sina.

Bede—Eighth-century monk and intellectual in northern England. His work was advanced for its time and place.

Boethius—Sixth-century Roman patrician whose translations into Latin of Aristotle's logical system, treatises on music, and a few basics of geometry provided much of European learning before the arrival of Arabic science and philosophy.

Copernicus, Nicolaus—Polish astronomer whose proposition of a sun-centered universe eventually replaced the notion that the earth stood at the center of all celestial movements.

Frederick II—Holy Roman emperor and proponent of Arabic learning. He was the patron of Michael Scot and underwrote translations of Averroes, Avicenna, and Maimonides.

Gerard of Cremona—The most prolific of the Latin translators based in Spain. He is credited with more than seventy translations from the Arabic.

Gerbert d'Aurillac—Later Pope Sylvester II, Gerbert was exposed to basic Arab science and technology as a student in Spain. He spread his knowledge to the rest of Europe.

Al-Ghazali—Muslim theologian whose masterful *The Incoherence of the Philosophers* posed a significant challenge to the philosophers on their own terms. Also known in the West as Algazel.

Hermann of Carinthia—Major translator of Arab science. He contributed to the first translation of the Koran into Latin.

al-Idrisi—Arab geographer and director of King Roger II of Sicily's Map of the World project.

Isidore of Seville—Medieval bishop and "encyclopedist" who taught that the world was flat, like "a wheel."

John de Villula—Named bishop of Wells in 1088, he moved his see to nearby Bath. He was the patron of Adelard.

Al-Khwarizmi—Mathematician and astronomer, born in modern-day Uzbekistan. He was affiliated with the House of Wisdom, and his star tables and works on arithmetic, algebra, the astrolabe, and Arabic numerals greatly influenced the West.

Al-Kindi—Called the first Arab philosopher, he sought to harmonize Plato and Aristotle.

Leonardo of Pisa—Learned mathematics from the Arabs of North Africa and became one of the greatest mathematicians of the Western world. Also known as Fibonacci.

Maimonides, Moses—Jewish scholar from al-Andalus. A contemporary of

Averroes, he helped introduce Christian thinkers to the Arab philosophical tradition. His philosophical works were written in Arabic and were widely translated into Latin.

Al-Mamun, Abdallah—Seventh Abbasid caliph. He took a direct interest in science and philosophy and actively promoted scholars at the House of Wisdom and elsewhere.

Maslama al-Majriti—Eleventh-century Spanish mathematician and astronomer whose local edition of the Arab star tables Adelard later translated into Latin.

Michael Scot—Translator of Averroes and the greatest public intellectual of his day. He served as science adviser and court astrologer to Frederick II.

Peter the Hermit—Charismatic leader of the disastrous People's Crusade. Peter survived and lived to see Jerusalem under crusader control.

Ptolemy—Preeminent astronomer of classical times. His *Almagest* was the leading textbook on the heavens from the second century A.D. until its final overthrow in the Copernican revolution fourteen hundred years later.

Robert of Ketton—Latin translator of Arab science. He worked on the first Western translation of the Koran, together with Hermann of Carinthia.

Roger II—Norman king of Sicily, known as the "baptized sultan" for his adoption of Arab high culture at his court. He was the patron of al-Idrisi's Map of the World.

Roger Bacon—Thirteenth-century philosopher, scientist, and teacher. An early proponent of Arab philosophy, he once noted, "Philosophy is drawn from the Muslims."

Siger de Brabant—Leader of the secular philosophers at Paris. He was hounded by the Inquisition and was murdered at the papal court.

Thomas Aquinas—Catholic theologian and philosopher who proposed a "truce" between faith and reason. He was canonized in 1323.

Urban II—As pope, he proclaimed the First Crusade, in 1095.

AL-MAGHRIB/SUNSET

FEW HAD ANY doubts that God had sent the earthquake to punish Antioch for its wanton and profligate ways. The residents of this Christian outpost not far from the eastern shores of the Mediterranean were notoriously corrupt and flouted their solemn obligations to God. "Certain men who hated fasting and loved lavish banquets, slaves to gluttony for enticing foods, were eager to copy the life and life-style not of those who lived well but those who ate well," scoffs Walter the Chancellor, a cleric and longtime Antioch functionary whose firsthand account of life in Antioch is dotted with references to Christian scripture and well-worn quotations from Ovid and Virgil.[1] The women reveled in scandalous, low-cut tunics and draped themselves in unseemly adornment. Some—"or so gossip has it," Walter says with a wink—even commissioned local artisans to have "coverings carefully made in Arab gold and a manifold of precious jewels for their shameful parts, not to clothe the appearance of their shame or to restrain the flame of lust, but so that that which was forbidden might inflame more hotly those people who did not desire legitimate pleasures."[2] Others prostituted themselves for sport, soliciting friends and neighbors alike from the town streets.

If a plague of locusts two years earlier had failed to stem this tide of dissolution among these Western newcomers to the Near East, then perhaps the very tremor of the earth would command the attention of the wayward populace. On November 13, 1114, an earthquake struck the outlying town of Mamistra, inflicting great damage and foreshadowing the destruction to come. Sixteen days later, "in the silence at the dead of night, when human frailty was accustomed more suitably and sweetly to sleep," Antioch itself felt the wrath of the Lord. "The city was a scene of destruction," Walter tells us, "with many killed in their homes. Others, indeed, were terrified; they abandoned their homes, scorned their wealth, left everything, and behaved as if demented in the streets and squares of the town. They stretched their hands towards the heavens because of their manifold fear and powerlessness, and cried tearfully without ceasing in different languages: 'Spare us, Lord, spare your people.'"[3] The next morning, chastened survivors filed into the central St. Peter's Church, miraculously untouched by the violent swaying of the ground, and forswore the pursuit of earthly pleasure.

The Antiochenes were not the only ones to have their world turned upside down. Huddling for shelter on a stone bridge in Mamistra was a young country gentleman far from home. Adelard of Bath had not made the arduous journey from England's West Country for the celebrated wedding of King Baldwin of Jerusalem to Adelaide of Sicily. He was not interested in the debaucheries of his fellow Europeans. Nor had he followed in the footsteps of the conquering crusaders sixteen years before him to *Outremer*, literally "the lands beyond the sea." Unlike those fearsome holy warriors—that "race of Franks" unleashed by Pope Urban II—who had raped and pillaged their way across Central Europe even before they had gotten to the Holy Land, Adelard was determined to learn from the Muslims rather than kill them under the sign of the cross. Where the crusaders had seen only evil in the Muslim infidel, Adelard sought the light of Arab wisdom.

Antioch—today the provincial Turkish town of Antakya—must have been irresistible for the restless Adelard, who as a young scholar had already decreed the value of traveling far and wide in the pursuit of learning: "It will be worthwhile to approach teachers of different people, to commit to memory what you may find is most finely expressed among each of them. For what the French studies are ignorant of, those across the Alps will unlock; what you will not learn amongst the Latins, eloquent Greece will teach you."[4] The city, founded in the fourth century B.C., had once been the leading metropolis of Asia. Its memory was particularly dear to the Christian world: Here the name "Christian" had first been applied, and Saint Peter had served as the city's first bishop, a point the ever-touchy, status-conscious popes of Rome preferred to overlook.[5] It had once flourished under Muslim rule but was now controlled by crusading Normans. This new principality of Antioch comprised the fortified central town, the surrounding plain, and the seaports of Alexandretta and St. Simeon. The land was very rich, its fortunes resting on the manufacture of fine silks, carpets, pottery, and glass.

Like Adelard himself, the city that awaited him stood on the cusp between East and West. Antioch had long been an important stopover on the lucrative caravan trade route from Mesopotamia, traditional commerce that scrupulously ignored the inconvenient religious warfare of the Crusades and carried on much as before. Most of the city's inhabitants were Christians—Eastern Orthodox, Jacobites, Nestorians, and Armenians. The predominant language was Arabic, but religious and cultural affinities also ensured a place for Greek and Latin, creating a living Rosetta stone that eased the exchange of books and ideas across sectarian, cultural, and ethnic lines. Now, the principality found itself a vital link between opposing worlds, thrust together by the religious and political struggle for control of the holy city of Jerusalem, almost three hundred miles to the south.

A few years before Adelard's arrival, combined Norman and Genoese forces had captured the nearby city of Tripoli from the Banu Ammar, its refined Muslim princes. *The Damascus Chronicle of the Crusades*, a contemporary Arab account, recorded that among the booty carted off from Tripoli by the victorious Christians were "the books of its college and libraries of private collectors."[6] Thousands of these works ended up in the hands of Antioch's merchants, now within easy reach of the man from Bath.

Still, nothing had prepared Adelard for what he found in his dogged pursuit of what he called the *studia Arabum*, the learning of the Arabs. Here at last were the secrets of the ages, buried for six centuries beneath the chaos of western Christendom. This peripatetic Englishman immediately grasped the power of Arab knowledge to remake the world as he knew it. Adelard left his native England a young scholar thirsting for wisdom only the Arabs could supply. He would return as the first Western man of science and help change his world forever.

If, as Adelard now learned from his Arab teachers, the heavens moved to regular and immutable rhythms, then what role remained for God Almighty? Could he suspend these laws of nature? Did the universe have a beginning and an end, as written in the Bible and the Koran? Or was it eternal, neither created in time nor subject to change, as the Muslim philosophers said? If this "new logic" was correct, then what was one to make of the sacred teaching of creation? To Adelard, the world suddenly seemed a new and unfamiliar place. Such questions had engaged Arab thinkers for centuries, as they struggled to fit their own monotheistic faith into a growing understanding of the universe around them. This great struggle between faith and reason was about to come crashing down on an unsuspecting Europe.

The arrival of Arab science and philosophy, the legacy of the pioneering Adelard and of those who hurried to follow his example, transmuted the backward West into a scientific and technological superpower. Like the elusive "elixir"—from the alchemists' *al-iksir*—for changing base metal into gold, Arab science altered medieval Christendom beyond recognition. For the first time in centuries, Europe's eyes opened to the world around it. This encounter with Arab science even restored the art of telling time, lost to the western Christians of the early Middle Ages. Without accurate control over clock and calendar, the rational organization of society was unthinkable. And so was the development of science, technology, and industry, as well as the liberation of man from the thrall of nature. Arab science and philosophy helped rescue the Christian world from ignorance and made possible the very idea of the West.

Yet how many among us today stop to acknowledge our enormous debt to the Arabs, let alone endeavor to repay it? How many recognize their invaluable bequest of much of our modern technical lexicon: from *azimuth* to *zenith*, from *algebra* to *zero*? Or the more mundane Arab influence in everything from the foods we eat—apricots, oranges, and artichokes, to name a few—to such common nautical terms as *admiral, sloop,* and *monsoon*? Even the quintessentially English tradition of the Morris folk dance is really a corruption of *Moorish* dancing, harkening back to a time when Arab minstrels entertained the nobility of Muslim Spain.

The names al-Khwarizmi, Avicenna, al-Idrisi, and Averroes—giants of Arab learning and dominant figures in medieval Europe for centuries—today invoke little if any response from the educated lay reader. Most are forgotten, little more than distant memories from a bygone era. Yet these were just a few of the players in an extraordinary Arab scientific and philosophical tradition that lies hidden under centuries of Western ignorance and outright anti-Muslim prejudice. A recent public opinion survey found that a majority of Americans see "little" or "nothing" to admire in Islam or the Muslim world.[7] But turn back the pages of time and it is impossible to envision Western civilization without the fruits of Arab science: al-Khwarizmi's art of algebra, the comprehensive medical teachings and philosophy of Avicenna, the lasting geography and cartography of al-Idrisi, or the rigorous rationalism of Averroes.

Even more important than any individual work was the Arabs' overall contribution that lies at the very heart of the contemporary West—the realization that science can grant man power over nature.

The power of Arab learning, championed by Adelard of Bath, refashioned Europe's intellectual landscape. Its reach extended into the sixteenth century and beyond, shaping the groundbreaking work of Copernicus and Galileo. This brought Christian Europe face-to-face with the fact that the sun—not the earthly home of God's creature, man—stood at the center of the universe. Averroes, the philosopher-judge from Muslim Spain, explained classical philosophy to the West and first introduced it to rationalist thought. Avicenna's *Canon of Medicine* remained a standard European text into the 1600s. Arab books on optics, chemistry, and geography were equally long-lived.

The West's willful forgetting of the Arab legacy began centuries ago, as anti-Muslim propaganda crafted in the shadow of the Crusades began to obscure any recognition of Arab culture's profound role in the development of modern science. This message comprised four central themes, a number of which still resonate today: Islam distorts the word of God; it is spread solely by violence; it perverts human sexuality, either by encouraging the practice of polygamy, as in the famed harems of the sultans, or through repressive or excessively prudish attitudes; and its prophet, Muhammad, was a charlatan, a tool of the Devil, or even the Antichrist.

The thirteenth-century philosopher Roger Bacon, one of the earliest Western proponents of the scientific method, praised the Muslims for their intellectual innovations, a subject he knew well: "Philosophy is drawn from the Muslims."[8] Yet the same Roger Bacon was just as enthusiastic in denouncing aspects of Muslim life of which he had no real knowledge or experience: The Arabs, he asserted confidently, "are absorbed in sensual pleasures because of their polygamy."[9] Soon such fanciful notions completely displaced all others in the popular imagination.

These views gained further currency in the Renaissance, when the West increasingly looked for inspiration to an idealized notion of classical Greece.[10] Eager to claim direct descent from the likes of Aristotle, Pythagoras, and Archimedes, Western thinkers deliberately marginalized the role of Arab learning. "I shall scarcely be persuaded that anything good can come from Arabia," wrote Petrarch, the most prominent of the early humanists, in the fourteenth century.[11] Western historians of science have largely carried on in this vein; many cast the Arabs as benign but effectively neutral caretakers of Greek knowledge who did little or nothing to advance the work of the ancients.

Such accounts are grounded in the persistent notion of the West's "recovery" of classical learning, with the clear implication that this knowledge was somehow the natural birthright of Christian Europe and was merely misplaced during the Middle Ages. They are also profoundly colored by a Western consensus, often invoked to explain the state of the Muslim world today, that Islam is inherently hostile to innovation and became all the more so from the early twelfth century onward.[12]

PART I

Al-Isha/Nightfall

Chapter One

THE WARRIORS OF GOD

THEY COULDN'T EVEN tell the time—this uncountable army of believers.

The warriors of God pushed on to the gates of the imperial city of Constantinople, their arrival heralded by a plague of locusts that destroyed the vines but left the wheat untouched. Their leader, an implacable cleric who had appeared from nowhere to great popular acclaim, exhorted his charges to holy war against the infidel with promises of a home in paradise. Disease and malnutrition were rife. Medical care often involved exorcism or the amputation of injured limbs. Torture and other ordeals settled criminal cases.

Few had any learning at all. What education there was back home consisted of memorizing outdated texts under the watchful eyes of hidebound doctors of religion. They had no understanding of basic technology, science, or mathematics. They could not date their most important holy days, nor chart the regular movements of the sun, the moon, and the planets. They knew nothing of papermaking or the use of lenses and mirrors, and they had no inkling of the prince of contemporary scientific instruments—the astrolabe. Natural phenomena, such as an eclipse of the moon or a sudden change in weather, terrified them. They thought it was black magic.

The arrival of this fanatical army horrified the locals. Who were these pale-skinned, blue-eyed barbarians, marching under the sign of the cross, and what did they want on Arab shores at the dawn of the twelfth Christian century?

"The whole West, and much of the land of barbarian peoples as lies beyond the Adriatic Sea up to the Pillars of Hercules—all this . . . was bursting forth into Asia in a solid mass, with all its belongings, taking its march through the intervening portion of Europe," records Princess Anna Comnena, daughter of the Byzantine emperor, in Constantinople, the empire's capital.[1] Among their ranks were true believers and righteous folk, notes the chronicler Albert of Aix, but also "adulterers, homicides, thieves, perjurers, and robbers."[2] Their leader,

Peter the Hermit, rode a white mule and promised the remission of sins for all who joined the cause.

A small, ugly man, Peter effortlessly touched the hearts of the common people, who snatched hairs from his lowly mount to preserve as holy relics as he preached the Crusade across northern France. Many sold what meager possessions they had and set out behind him for the ends of the earth. Some brought their entire families; others simply abandoned wives, children, and aging parents. Crops were left untended and chores unfinished in the haste to follow Peter's call. The hermit kept his arms and feet bare, and he wore a rough wool shirt, covered by a mantle that reached to his ankles. "He lived on wine and fish; he hardly ever, never, ate bread," reports Guibert of Nogent, in one of the earliest accounts of the Crusades.[3]

The diminutive monk appeared suddenly, voicing a populist echo of the great call to arms by Pope Urban II, who appealed to the princes of Christendom on November 27, 1095, in the French town of Clermont to end their ceaseless warring and turn their murderous energies on the un-believers of the East. "Let those who have been accustomed unjustly to wage private warfare against the faithful now go against the infidels and end with victory. Let those who have been fighting against their brothers and relatives now fight in a proper way against the barbarians," the pope told an overflowing crowd gathered to hear his sermon. "Let those who have been serving as mercenaries for small pay now obtain the eternal reward."[4] Within months of Urban's summons, as many as eighty thousand people, city residents and country dwellers alike, left for the East.[5]

A combustible mixture of church politics, theological dispute, domestic concerns, and world affairs fueled Urban's call to crusade. In recent decades the church had struggled with Europe's secular rulers over rights and privileges, most notably the power to invest new bishops and outfit them with the symbols of office, the ring and staff. Urban and his supporters within the church saw the Crusade as a way to restore the authority of Rome at the head of the Christian world, without reliance on unruly monarchs.

For some time now, a number of religious thinkers had been arguing that religious violence was both permissible and justified. Pope Gregory VII—Urban the Crusader's mentor—had had a long-standing interest in warfare on behalf of the church, and he had even proposed the creation of a Militia of St. Peter composed of European knights, the need for which was made all the more pressing by the emerging struggle between secular kings and the papacy. Bishop Anselm II of Lucca, a loyal partisan of the pope, had collated the writings of St. Augustine on theories of just war in support of Gregory's endeavors.[6] These reformers were also influenced by the notion that the church had to bring itself closer to the people; this in turn supported the phenomenon of papal armies that could provide believers with the chance to defend the faith in return for the remission of sins.[7]

Global events played their part, too. In 1074, Gregory wrote a series of letters calling for the liberation of the Eastern Orthodox Christians, who had suffered a major military defeat three years before at the hands of the Muslim Turks at Manzikert, in eastern Asia Minor. Establishing a clear link between fighting for the church and the practice of indulgence, Gregory promised "eternal reward" for those who took part.[8] The West's anxieties were further heightened by reports—largely untrue but widely accepted as fact—that the modest but steady flow of Christian pilgrims to Jerusalem was being systematically impeded, or worse, by the strict Seljuk Turks, who had taken control of the holy city in 1070 from the more relaxed Fatimids of Egypt.

Peter the Hermit himself may have been manhandled by the local Muslims as he attempted without success to reach Jerusalem on a personal pilgrimage some years before the Crusades. Anna Comnena, the Byzantine princess, says Peter "suffered much at the hands of the Turks and Saracens," before making his way back to Europe only "with difficulty."[9] In some versions of the story, Jesus appears to Peter in a dream and commands him to return home, gather an army of believers, and liberate the Church of the Holy Sepulcher from Muslim control; in others, the patriarch of Jerusalem deputizes Peter to make his way to Europe to summon help for embattled eastern Christians. The late twelfth-century Song of Antioch depicts Peter, "whom God made messenger," as the sole survivor of an earlier campaign who then returns to Europe to raise a great army and lead the Crusade.[10]

Peter's exact role in launching the Crusade remains uncertain, although later medieval chronicles are notable for the increasing prominence they give the hermit as inspiration and even prime mover behind the entire enterprise. Popular accounts celebrate Peter for aiding the poor and providing dowries for prostitutes so that they might marry. One twelfth-century text, The Rosenfeld Annals, says the hermit's arrival on the scene was foreshadowed by an impressive celestial display: "One evening . . . with not a cloud in the air, balls of fire, as it seemed, shone forth in different places and reconstituted themselves in another part of the sky. It was observed that this was no fire but angelic powers which, by their migration, were signifying the movement and foreshadowing the departure of people from their places, which later seized nearly all the Western world."[11]

With Urban II, protégé of the bellicose Gregory VII, on the throne of St. Peter, there was no more holding back the disparate forces pulling the church toward war. Reformers grouped around the pope were locked in battle for influence and power with both internal and secular rivals. A long and varied history of Christian teachings on permissible war in defense of the faith and the growing popularity of martial metaphors in religious writings eased the way. As those around the pontiff recognized, the call to Christian arms would allow the pope to exercise enormous personal authority and help unite his fractious flock in a sacred mission; it seemed like the answer to their prayers. The result was Christian holy war on a massive scale, an attempt by an atavistic West to remake a changing world in its own image. Although they would ultimately end in failure, the Crusades nonetheless paid significant dividends by bringing the Latin world face-to-face with the scientific and technological prowess of the Arab East. They also fired the imagination regarding things Eastern among many in Europe, including Adelard, who was in his teens at the time of Urban's momentous appeal.

The pope had envisioned a long, careful buildup to a proper military campaign under the command of his appointed lieutenant, the papal legate, and backed by the ruling families of the West. But the tide of humanity that quickly fell in behind Peter the Hermit and a handful of other populist leaders had no interest in the prelate's cautious timetable, or the church's broader political, social, and theological goals. This People's Crusade, a prelude to the main military effort, would wait for no man. *"Deus vult!"* the crowds had chanted in Clermont in response to the pope's fighting words. "God wills it!" The faithful, eager to escape lives of degradation, violence, and disease, soon set off by the tens of thousands without waiting for their betters. "Therefore, while the princes, who felt in the need of many expenses and great services from their attendants, made their preparations slowly and carefully, the common people who had little property, but were very numerous, joined . . . Peter the Hermit, and obeyed him as a master while these affairs were going on among us," says the account of Guibert of Nogent.[12]

The majority comprised simple peasants, but there were townspeople, too, and even some impoverished knights, renegades, debtors, and outright criminals. For many, the quest for the Holy Land was guided more by superstition and popular frenzy than by any true understanding of the faith or the goals of church leaders. "They asserted that a certain goose was inspired by the Holy Spirit, and that a she-goat was not less filled by this same Spirit," records Albert of Aix, clearly mortified by the very words he is writing. "These they made their guides on this holy journey to Jerusalem; these they worshipped excessively; and most of the people following them, like beasts, believed with their whole minds that this was the true course."[13] Sexual license also ran rampant among the crusaders. "These people . . . joined up in one force, but did not abstain at all from illicit unions and the pleasures of the flesh; they gave themselves up to gluttonous excess without interruption and amused themselves without interruption with women and young girls who had also emigrated from their homes to give themselves to the same follies."[14]

By the spring of 1096, the ill-disciplined mobs that constituted this People's Crusade were sweeping through the unfamiliar lands of Central and Eastern Europe with predictably disastrous results. The Jews of the Rhineland, forewarned by their brethren in France who had successfully bribed Peter and other leaders to leave them alone, braced for the worst. "At this time arrogant people, a people of strange speech, a nation bitter and impetuous, Frenchmen and Germans, set out for the holy city, which had been desecrated by barbaric nations, there to seek their house of idolatry and banish the Ishmaelites [the Muslims] and other denizens of the land and conquer the land for themselves," recounts *The Chronicle of Solomon bar Simson*, left behind by a little-known Jewish writer. "Their ranks swelled until the numbers of men, women and children exceeded a locust horde covering the earth."[15] Another account, written by an anonymous Jewish author from Mainz, then a center of learning, was recorded shortly after the events. It tells us that Jews all along the Rhine began to fast, to repent their sins, and to beseech God for help. Some sought the protection of the local Catholic bishops, while others tried to emulate their French brethren and pay the crusaders to go away. Their appeals, sacred and profane, went unheeded.

The worst depredations were carried out by the forces under the local German count Emicho as they marched eastward up the Rhine. At Worms, in May 1096, they killed five hundred Jews who had sought the protection of local Catholic leaders. Another thousand were killed in Mainz, amid anti-

Jewish rioting in the city. Again, the local church leadership failed to restrain its flocks or honor earlier promises to the Jews of sanctuary.[16] Jewish leaders organized mass suicides rather than let their charges fall into the hands of the attacking crusaders and face the prospect of forced conversion. "They all cried out together in a loud voice, . . . 'Whoever has a knife, come kill us for the honor of the unique eternal God, and then pierce himself with his sword in the neck or belly, slaughter himself,'" the anonymous chronicler reports. "And the pure women were throwing money out [the windows] to delay the enemies a bit, until the women could slaughter their own children; the hands of merciful women were strangling their own children, to do the will of the Creator, and were turning their children's tender faces to the Gentiles."[17]

Pope Urban's call to crusade had fired the religious zeal of Christians across Europe with its appeal to battle the "enemies" of Christ. This was a dangerous development at a time of growing tensions in the Rhineland between Jews, long seen in the European imagination as Christ's tormentors, and non-Jews over access to expanding trade and commerce.[18] Popular Christian tracts accusing the Jews of scheming with the far-off Muslims, often in fantastic ways, only aggravated matters further. "Emicho the wicked, enemy of the Jews, came with his whole army against the city gate, and the citizens opened it up for him. Emicho, a German noble, led a band of plundering German and French crusaders. The enemies of the Lord said to each other: 'See, they have opened the gate for us; now let us avenge the blood of the crucified one,'" writes Solomon bar Simson.[19] Volkmar, another populist leader, attacked the Jews of Prague at the end of June, while more massacres took place near the Hungarian border. By the summer, the crusaders had left the Rhineland and were headed for Constantinople, much to the relief of the local Christian rulers who wanted them out of their lands as quickly as possible.[20]

No wonder Anna Comnena recounts with awe the fanatical tide of humanity—dirty, ill fed, sick, and exhausted—that poured into the realm in the summer of 1096, on the way to battle the Muslim infidel to the south. It was, she notes gravely, "a matter greater and more terrible than famine."[21] Most of Peter's loyal followers were slaughtered by the Turks on October 21 at Civetot, not far from Constantinople. They had set off against the counsel of Emperor Alexius—Anna's father—and without the protection of the organized armies of Christendom that were still in transit from Europe. The hermit, however, was not present at the disastrous end to this People's

Crusade. Contemporary European accounts are contradictory: Either he remonstrated unsuccessfully with his followers not to take on the well-trained Turkish forces, or he cowered in the safety of Constantinople to avoid the slaughter he knew was inevitable. Anna's version has him whisked to safety by Byzantine forces. In any event, Peter eventually reached his beloved Jerusalem with the main contingent of knights three years later. One of Peter's chief lieutenants was less fortunate. His coat of mail pierced by seven arrows, he died at Civetot at the head of his fanatical army.

Along the eastern Mediterranean and into the Syrian heartland, the arrival of the crusaders appeared to confirm the worst fears of the local Arabs and their Jewish and Christian subjects. Medieval Arab geography customarily divided the world into seven zones, or climates. The central third and fourth zones—the Arab world, North Africa, Iran, and parts of China—enjoyed the greatest balance and harmony. The northerly sixth zone was home to the Slavs, the Turks, and the European Christians, the latter known among the Arabs simply as al-Ifranj, or the Franks. All three were warlike, filthy, and inclined toward treachery.[22] In the case of the Franks, their northerly provenance also made them unstable. Other notable qualities included profligate sexuality, a lack of jealousy, and a general propensity for violence.[23]

The Arab geographer al-Masudi blamed the absence of sunlight for these personal shortcomings. At the same time, his assessment betrayed a grasp of astronomy—if not, perhaps, of meteorology—that was well beyond that of his subjects, the crusading Franks:

> As regards the people of the northern quadrant, they are the one for whom the sun is distant from the zenith . . . The power of the sun is weak among them because of their distance from it; cold and damp prevail in their regions, and snow and ice follow one another in endless succession. The warm humor is lacking among them; their bodies are large; their natures gross, their manners harsh, their understanding dull, and their tongues heavy . . . Their religious beliefs lack solidity, and this is because of the nature of cold and the lack of warmth.[24]

The debacle of Peter and his populist campaign was soon eclipsed by the arrival outside Constantinople of the main Christian fighting force. Here were trained military men, led by members of Europe's royal houses and subject to both the new religious zeal of the day and more traditional political and economic interests of their own. This jumble of kings, princes, and other nobility from across Europe often left the fortunes of the First Crusade hostage to internal rivalries, personal ambition, and the lack of a single recognized authority or commander. At first Emperor Alexius successfully exploited these differences and used the crusaders' military prowess and enthusiasm to reestablish his own grip over western Asia Minor, which he had lost earlier to the Muslims. In one such campaign, Raymond of Saint-Gilles, Count of Toulouse, captured the Syrian port of Latakia from the Arabs and then handed it to the Byzantine ruler in line with an oath he and other crusader lords had taken at Alexius's insistence.

But the princes of western Christendom were not all so pliable. Many were intent on performing their religious and military duty as quickly as possible before hurrying back to their dominions at home. But a select handful, including some of the leading lights of the First Crusade, such as Godfrey of Bouillon and the wily Norman commander Bohemond of Taranto, had ill-disguised territorial designs of their own. Pope Urban had, at least in part, used the First Crusade to export the endless bickering and warring of such minor princelings from an exhausted and violence-racked Europe. He had said as much at Clermont. Both the church's higher ambitions for the Crusades and Alexius's own dream of restoring Constantinople's hold over Asia Minor and the eastern Mediterranean with the help of the zealous arrivals had to compete with the more mundane and secular concerns of the individual crusaders.

Almost immediately, fissures opened in the Latin ranks. The push south from Constantinople to the Holy Land—the stated objective of the entire venture, after all—was threatened by the decision of Baldwin of Boulogne, a prominent French nobleman, and a handful of others to split off temporarily from the main body in search of territory they could call their own. Baldwin had carefully studied the social and political complexities of the Armenian lands along the nearby Euphrates. He and his men, accompanied by Armenian political advisers, headed eastward to make their fortune. They may have taken some comfort in the notion that such a campaign would further the crusaders' mission by protecting the eastern flank of the drive for Jerusalem. But it was clear that Baldwin, as astute a diplomatic and military operator as any of the crusader commanders, had sensed opportunity amid the traditional political and religious intrigues of the region, particularly in Edessa, then a predominantly Armenian town in what is today southern Turkey. He was not about to let the demands of Christian holy war stand in his way.

As Baldwin and his aides had been led to expect, the local Armenian Christian population at once welcomed the crusading Franks with open arms. They had grown tired of constant Turkish military raids and were restive under the rule of the former Byzantine official Thoros, a fellow Armenian who followed the Eastern Orthodox Church of hated Byzantium rather than the national rite. Unpopular at home, increasingly unsuccessful at war, and childless in marriage, the aging Thoros offered to adopt the popular Baldwin as his heir and immediately made him coruler. The pair even underwent an adoption ritual, clearly designed for young children, in which they both wriggled into a single oversize shirt or tunic and rubbed their chests together; Baldwin then repeated the process with Thoros's wife, now his adoptive "mother." *The Chronicle of Matthew of Armenia* reports that a plot to remove Thoros was soon hatched and that Baldwin was informed, although his overt role as instigator, if any, remains murky. On March 7, 1098, the conspirators whipped the population into a frenzy of rioting and brought down the hapless Thoros. Three days later, the town notables invited Baldwin to take his place. Thoros, we are told, was caught trying to escape and was torn to pieces by the mob.[25]

Edessa, the first territory to fall to the crusaders and the first to slip from their grasp again, was little more than a sideshow to the West's campaign for control of the Holy Land. Yet it played an outsize role in the early history of the so-called Latin East. First, it showed how skillful diplomacy and a healthy dose of intrigue could easily tip the region's fragile balance among competing ethnic, linguistic, and sectarian factions, groups, and nations. Second, it created a powerful if fleeting example of what an ambitious prince and a handful of knights—Baldwin's initial force was said to number just sixty horsemen—could accomplish, inspiring acquisitive rivals to strike out on their own rather than struggle on toward the holy city.

Most important, it saw the emergence under Baldwin, who had proclaimed himself Count of Edessa, of a model of state and society for the rest of the Latin East, one that the irrepressible Norman would later implement more widely as king of Jerusalem. According to this approach, Frankish princes and their vassals were allocated the top positions of government, but plenty of room was left for the talents and ambitions of the locals, whether Christian or

Muslim. This would prove a successful system, well adapted to the ethnic and sectarian mosaic of the Middle East, but it stood at odds with the militant notions of crusading as preached by Pope Urban two and a half years earlier.

Like the future Count of Edessa, Bohemond of Taranto seemed more concerned with immediate earthly pursuit than future heavenly reward. One of the ablest commanders of the First Crusade, this Norman adventurer from southern Italy took no direct role in the march to Jerusalem in 1099. Instead, he overrode the objections of his colleagues and ignored his own oath to Emperor Alexius by setting out to take Antioch, gateway to the Holy Land, from the Muslims and keep it for himself and his heirs. Once outside its walls, he repeatedly thwarted joint crusader efforts to seize the city, whose defenders soon recovered from their initial dismay at the arrival of the large Christian army. Bohemond's tactic cost the crusaders the chance to seize the city immediately and forced many months of delay in the main host's push for Jerusalem, but it successfully ensured that the spoils of victory would ultimately accrue to him alone.

The city and its surrounding lands were a rich prize. It sat at the crossroads of lucrative East-West trade and had periodically changed hands among the Arabs, Byzantines, and Seljuk Turks. The Arab physician Ibn Butlan, far from his native Baghdad, found the bazaars of Antioch overflowing with goods, while residents enjoyed civic water supplies and other conveniences, including a public clepsydra, or water clock, near one of the city gates.[26] Now, with the Byzantine emperor helpless back in Constantinople and the local Muslims deeply divided, Antioch's impressive defenses were all that stood between the ambitious Bohemond and his dream of establishing his own royal line. "So fortified was it with walls and towers and barbicans, that it had no need to fear assault of any machine or the attack of any man, not even if all mankind were to come together against it," says the Frenchman Raymond of Aguilers in his firsthand account of the First Crusade.[27]

After a long and ineffectual siege, Bohemond's agents managed to bribe a disgruntled tower guard to look the other way as a small force of crusaders climbed one of the walls and then threw open Antioch's massive gate. The local garrison fled to the city's impressive citadel, while a considerable Muslim relief force under the command of the Turkish general Kerbogha approached menacingly from the east. The crusaders, by now tired and suffering from a lack of supplies, mounting desertion, and general low morale, found themselves unable to take the citadel and faced with the mortal threat of Kerbogha's looming counterattack. Food supplies soon ran low, and the depleted countryside had little left to offer the hordes of scavenging crusaders. Fulcher of Chartres, loyal chaplain to Baldwin of Edessa, describes how many were reduced to subsisting on barely cooked thistles, bean shoots, and the meat of horses, donkeys, dogs, and rats. "We believed that these misfortunes befell the Franks, and that they were not able for so long a time to take the city, because of their sins. Not only dissipation, but also avarice or pride or rapaciousness corrupted them." An army council resolved to send the women away "lest they, stained by the defilement of dissipation, displease the Lord."[28]

It is emblematic of the Crusades that a religious vision, even one doubted by almost all of the prominent figures present, saved the day for the Christians. Peter Bartholomew, a lowly pilgrim, claimed divine inspiration had revealed the location in the city of the Holy Lance, which tradition said had pierced Christ's side as he hung from the cross. The pilgrim directed the increasingly desperate crusaders to the local cathedral of St. Peter, patron saint of Antioch and its first bishop. Sure enough, a little digging in the floor of the cathedral uncovered what the searchers were convinced was the tip of this valued relic. The discovery transformed the morale in the crusader camp, inspiring a remarkable victory on June 28, 1098, against the much larger attacking force of Kerbogha, which had already been weakened along the way by a failed attempt to retake Edessa from Baldwin. The Muslim armies fled in disgrace.

Bohemond, who had skillfully outmaneuvered all his European and Byzantine rivals, including Emperor Alexius and his top generals, now controlled Antioch. The local Arab princes, chiefly the rulers of the nearby towns of Aleppo and Shaizar, were unprepared to set aside their own long-standing feud to challenge the establishment of this crusader statelet. Instead, they saw Christian Antioch as just one more player in a crowded geopolitical field that also included Sunni and Shi'ite Muslim factions, as well as their mutual rivals of long standing, the Byzantines.[29]

In the far-off Muslim capital of Baghdad—three weeks' ride by camel under the desert sun—the caliph was not impressed by accounts of murder and mayhem at the hands of these cold-blooded crusaders. Not even the fall of Jerusalem, on July 15, 1099, and its attendant slaughter of Muslims, Jews, and eastern Christians, could stir the court. "How dare you slumber in the shade of complacent safety, leading lives as frivolous as garden flowers, while your brothers in Syria have no dwelling place save the saddles of camels and the bellies of vultures?" demanded Abu Saad al-Harawi, who had made the long journey from Damascus to warn the caliph of the danger posed by al-Ifranj.[30] Al-Harawi, who had discarded his traditional judge's turban and shaved his head as a sign of mourning, got nowhere.

There was, the caliph's court concluded, little cause for alarm, but those in the direct path of the marauding Ifranj were appalled by what they saw and heard of the barbarians from the West. One learned Arab knight, Usama ibn Munqidh, summed up local reaction to these Christian interlopers, setting a tone that still strikes a chord across the Muslim world: "Glory be to the Creator, the Maker! Indeed, when a person relates matters concerning the Franks, he *should* give glory to God and sanctify Him! For he will see them to be mere beasts possessing no other virtues but courage and fighting, just as beasts have only the virtues of strength and the ability to carry loads."[31]

The Christians' reliance on trial by ordeal offended the sensibilities of the Muslims, with their highly evolved system of legal disputation and formal schools of religious law. Western notions of medicine were based largely on superstition and exorcism, in sharp contrast to the Arabs' advanced clinical training and understanding of surgery, pharmacology, and epidemiology. The newcomers lacked any real knowledge of hygiene and sanitation, a deep affront to Muslims who performed ritual ablutions before each of the five daily prayers. Muslim observers thought very little of what they saw of Frankish culture. From their perspective, the Ifranj had no understanding of even basic technology, except perhaps for the engines of war, no proper science, medicine, or mathematics, and no real philosophical inquiry. Moreover, the crusaders' reputation for cruelty was sealed by an outbreak of cannibalism after the sack of the Syrian town of Mara, in the winter of 1098. "Our troops boiled pagan adults whole in cooking pots; they impaled children on spits and devoured them grilled," writes Radulph of Caen, a witness to the atrocities at Mara.[32] Fellow chronicler Albert of Aix captures the full horror of the incident in a single, banal aside: "Not only did our troops not shrink from eating dead Turks and Saracens, they also ate dogs."[33]

Usama, scion of the local Muslim dynasty the Banu Munqidh, came to know the crusaders intimately, fighting with some and befriending others. His highly personable memoir, *The Book of Contemplation*, condemns the Christians for the barbarity of trial by ordeal and chastises them for their loose morals, poor diet, and general bad habits. As the title suggests, the book falls within the classical Arabic genre of *adab*, works designed to instruct the reader more than to convey literal truths.[34] Still, *The Book of Contemplation* provides a fascinating window on the crusaders' world as seen by the Arabs. In one passage, Usama recounts an Arab doctor's tale of two Christian patients who died needlessly after the physician's sage advice was spurned and more primitive Western techniques applied. Ignoring the Arab's pleas, the Franks lopped off a knight's mildly infected leg with an ax and made an incision in the shape of a cross into an ill woman's head, before rubbing her skull with salt; both died on the spot. At this point, the doctor dryly remarked, "So I asked them, 'Do you need anything else from me?' 'No,' they said. And so I left, having learned about their medicine things I had never known before."[35]

Usama does grudgingly acknowledge some useful facility with medicinal plants among the Christians, and he becomes sufficiently familiar with them to study their ways and habits firsthand. A crusader acquaintance on his way back from a pilgrimage to the Holy Land even offers to escort Usama's fourteen-year-old son to Europe so that the boy might learn proper "reason and chivalry" among the knights of Christendom and then return "like a truly rational man." Ever the gentleman, Usama quickly makes a polite excuse and deftly sidesteps the offer, but he reveals to his Muslim readers his true thoughts at the very notion: "And so there fell upon my ears words that would never come from a truly rational head! For even if my son were taken captive, his captivity would not be as long as any voyage he might take to the land of the Franks."[36]

He also notes, with obvious satisfaction, that those of the Ifranj who have lived the longest among the local Muslims are somewhat less objectionable than the boorish new arrivals. "Among the Franks there are some who have become acclimatized and frequent the company of Muslims. They are much better than those recently arrived from their lands, but they are the exception and should not be considered representative."[37] To bolster his case, Usama then tells a number of amusing tales of these bumptious newcomers, including one account of a knight who tries to forcibly "correct" the direction in which the local Muslims pray by turning them eastward and away from Mecca.

Such easy interaction between putative enemies reflects a central reality of twelfth-century life in the Levant, which was marked by periods of accommodation and cooperation, both personal and political, interspersed with bouts of enmity and outright conflict. Hamdan bin Abd al-Rahman, an Arab physician, served some of the early crusaders. He was rewarded with a village in the principality of Antioch after successfully treating one of the Christian lords. Hamdan was later made administrator of a local district on the crusaders' behalf, before entering the service of Imad al-Din Zengi, the Muslim ruler of nearby Aleppo. Hamdan, who died in 1159, recorded his own observations and exploits in *The Way of the Franks Who Went out to Syria in Those Years*, but no copy has ever been found.[38]

Usama ibn Munqidh had good reason to look down upon the Army of the Cross and to shrink at the notion of his son learning the "reason and chivalry" of the Franks, for he and his fellow Arabs were the beneficiaries of a glorious Muslim civilization created over the course of hundreds of years. By the mid-eighth century, the Abbasid caliphs had established themselves at the head of a huge empire. At its height, it stretched from the Atlantic to Afghanistan and created an enormous expanse of shared values, outlook, and opportunity. The Abbasids sought to legitimate their rule as rightful and worthy heirs to the classical traditions of Greece, Persia, India, and Mesopotamia, launching perhaps the most ambitious effort in history to gather and assimilate the world's learning. In southern Spain, their Arab rivals the Umayyads and their successors produced some of the greatest of the Arab philosophers and scientists, thinkers whose works would one day shake the foundations of Christian Europe. Known among the Arabs as al-Andalus, this region served as an important staging ground for ideas and technology that began to trickle into Western Europe as early as the tenth century.

None of that, of course, held any interest for Peter the Hermit, his legion of followers, or the Christian kings and knights who soon established the principalities of the Latin East in and around the Holy Land. The crusaders, abandoning Christ's theology of love for the pope's theology of war, slaughtered the local urban populations, mostly Muslims and Jews, in their zeal to "reclaim" Jerusalem for the one true faith. Eastern Christians, with their unfamiliar dress, language, and customs, often fared little better.

One Muslim traveler, venturing far from his native Spain, had found Jerusalem in the years shortly before the First Crusade to be an intellectual melting pot "teeming with scholars." His account details the competing schools of Islamic law and the famous intellectuals who gathered to debate around the central mosque: "We entered the Holy Land and reached the Aqsa mosque. The full moon of knowledge shone for me and I was illuminated by it for more than three years."[39] The city, he adds, provided an ideal meeting place for experts in all three of the great monotheistic faiths.

That all disappeared in the flash of a sword. The city's scholarly class was killed wholesale, along with much of the rest of the populace. Raymond of Aguilers, chaplain to Raymond of Saint-Gilles, who led the crusaders of southern France, records the carnage: "Piles of heads, hands, and feet were to be seen in the streets of the city. It was necessary to pick one's way over the bodies of men and horses. But these were small matters compared with what happened in the Temple of Solomon. What happened there? If I tell the truth, you would not believe it. Suffice to say that, in the Temple and Porch of Solomon, men rode in blood up to their knees and bridle reins."[40]

The extremes of violence that characterized the First Crusade—such as the cannibalism at Mara or the frenzied slaughter at the Temple of Solomon—reflected the potent Christian propaganda machine behind the campaign. At the time, the West knew little of Islam and its teachings, but church ideologues successfully sowed the seeds of holy war by painting a highly damaging portrait of the Muslims. The peoples of the Near East—Muslim, Jew, or "schismatic" Christian—were left to reap the whirlwind. Antipathy for the followers of Islam was particularly charged in those parts of Western Europe most distant from Muslim life. Attitudes in southern Italy, Spain, and Sicily—areas actually bordering on the Islamic world—were considerably more relaxed.[41] The less the Christians knew about the infidel, the more they hated him.

Charges against the Muslims of idolatry and reliance on violence and coercion were central to the crusader narrative. Another key element was the generalized claim that Jerusalem and the Holy Land were Christian, or more precisely Latin Christian, by right and always had been so. They had been seized and defiled by the Muslims—"seduced," in the language of some propagandists—and violence was necessary and even justified to right this great historical wrong. Similar language was applied to the Muslims in southern Spain. Here, church historians and others linked contemporary Christian kings to the earlier reign of the Visigoths before the coming of Islam. Only armed force could restore their rule; thus, the sacred notion of *Reconquista*, akin to the Crusades of the East, was born. Contempt was reserved for those kings who would not fight for the faith. The ninth-century *Chronicle of*

Alfonso III, for example, bitterly denounces one local Christian ruler, Silo of Asturias, who "had peace with the Ishmaelites."[42]

Looking eastward, the ever-enthusiastic Dominican theologian Humbert of Romans argued that in a proper Crusade there could be no innocent victims; all Muslims were guilty, for they destroyed both the body and the soul of pious Christians. Crusading, Humbert said, represented a just war, grounded in divine right and fought for faith, not spoils. He also dismissed the arguments of some traditionalists that Christianity had always opposed violence of any kind. In its early days, the church had been weak and thus had had to rely on miracles and humility. Now the military might of the Christian West allowed an armed response to its enemies.[43] To Humbert, it seems, Christ's teachings were just an exercise in realpolitik.

Clerical resentment at the use of real or imagined Christian holy sites as places of Muslim worship also ran deep.[44] The carnage at the Temple of Solomon, which at one point continued despite attempts by a senior crusader to protect the defenseless Muslims sheltering on its rooftop, should have come as no surprise. Witness the frank accounts of the contemporary Christian chroniclers, who display no real unease at the bloodshed and at times express their satisfaction that the brutal killing, such as that of the vanquished foe at the Temple of Solomon, was legitimate. "Indeed, it was a just and splendid judgment of God that this place should be filled with the blood of the unbelievers, since it had suffered so long from their blasphemies. The city was filled with corpses and blood," concluded Raymond of Aguilers.[45]

The epic *Song of Antioch* captures many of the prevailing themes of Crusades propaganda: the rightful recovery of the Holy Land, the godlessness of the Muslims, the home in heaven for the fallen martyrs, and the perfidy of the Jews. In one passage, Christ on the cross tells his fellow prisoners of the future coming of the crusaders: "'My friends,' he said. 'The people are not yet born who will avenge my death with their steel lances . . . They will regain my land and free my country.'" One of the prisoners, a robber crucified to the right of Jesus, says simply: "It would be good to see yourself avenged on these treacherous Jews who torment you."[46]

Not all Muslims were as indifferent to the arrival of the crusaders as the caliph and his court in distant Baghdad. Many Arabs had no doubt that the capture of Jerusalem and the creation of the crusader states along the Syrian coast were part of an ominous pattern of Christian expansionism that had to be resisted. From the Umayyad Mosque in Damascus, the legal scholar and preacher Ali ibn al-Sulami sounded the alarm. In his *Kitab al-Jihad*, or *The Book of Holy War*, published six years after the Muslims were first driven from Jerusalem, al-Sulami linked the coming of the crusaders to their earlier success against Muslim rule in Sicily. He saw the Christian campaign as a religious war against Islam.[47] And he blamed the crusaders' successes on infighting among the Muslims and their inability to adhere to their faith, particularly their abject failure to unite to defend the lands of Islam from nonbelievers. "This interruption [in waging defensive jihad] combined with the negligence of the Muslims toward the prescribed regulations [of Islam] . . . has inevitably meant that God has made Muslims rise up one against the other, has placed violent hostility and hatred among them, and has incited their enemies to seize their territories."[48]

Al-Sulami understood that the crusaders were intent on holding Jerusalem and would seek to expand their control of the region to secure the city and its prized Church of the Holy Sepulcher. But *The Book of Holy War* also rightly identified the enemy's vulnerabilities, in particular the crusaders' long supply lines back to Western Europe. And it predicted that a united Muslim *ummah*, or community of believers, could successfully drive the invaders into the sea. "One knows for sure their weakness, the small amount of cavalry and equipment they have at their disposal and the distance from which their reinforcements come . . . It is an opportunity which must be seized quickly."[49]

The Ifranj would soon discover just how prescient al-Sulami had been. The Army of God had failed to grasp that its remarkable military successes, however honestly won on the battlefield, were largely a reflection of the fractured, almost anarchic, state of affairs across Syria and Asia Minor. Within forty-five years, the Muslims began to roll back the Christian advances, a turn of events crowned by the triumphal entry into Jerusalem in 1187 of the political and military leader Saladin at the head of a unified force from Egypt and all of Syria.

Long supply lines and a unified Islam were not the only problems facing the Christian forces. Born in the West of iron and blood at the close of the eleventh century, the crusader movement immediately found itself deeply enmeshed in the life of the Muslim East in ways that would have horrified men like Peter the Hermit and Pope Urban II, who died just days before the news of Jerusalem's capture could reach his sickbed in Rome. As countless attackers had before it, the Army of the Cross discovered that the very act of invasion and conquest left its mark on the besiegers as well as the besieged. There would be numerous campaigns to come—even the enduring mystery of the so-called Children's Crusade of 1212, which, legend has it, ended in death by shipwreck or enslavement in Muslim lands—but the idea of crusade and crusading would never really be the same.

At first, such changes appeared relatively insignificant: Usama ibn Munqidh's bemused accounts of how the Muslims had quickly begun to civilize the Europeans; or the way the Christians slipped so easily into the local factional disputes, even siding at times with Muslim warlords and against their coreligionists. Other, more powerful factors soon came to the fore, including the spectacular growth of East-West trade. The church clearly recognized the danger that such trade posed to its anti-Muslim agenda, and papal orders and outraged church councils periodically sought to crack down on commerce with the infidel, particularly in such strategic goods as wood for shipbuilding, iron, arms, and even foodstuffs.[50]

Still, money from this new trade with the East began to pour into the merchant leagues of southern Europe. Genoa came to dominate commerce with North Africa and the Black Sea region, while Venice maintained a money-spinning stranglehold on trade with Egypt and Syria.[51] Along with shipments of oil, perfumes, textiles, and precious metals came new ideas, technologies, and systems of thought. Our modern Arabic numerals were popularized in the West thanks in large measure to trade documents and contracts drawn up between Muslim merchants and their Italian counterparts. Trade terms in numerous European languages still bear the mark of Arabic and Persian commerical usage: for example, check, tariff, traffic, arsenal, and the French douane, or "customs."[52] Long-haul seaborne commerce required navigational aids, such as sophisticated maps, charts, and instruments, all areas where the medieval Muslims excelled. One measure of the growing economic ties between East and West was the appearance in European royal treasuries, as far away as England, of considerable quantities of Muslim gold. The minting of gold coins, halted in ninth-century Europe for lack of bullion, resumed in the Italian city-states four centuries later, once supplies from the East were secured.[53]

The new rulers of the Latin East soon began to realize that their own fates were bound up with those of the Muslims, Christian Arabs, Jews, and others who populated the region; there would be no significant reinfusion of European Christians to help colonize the crusader states. The ever-adaptable Normans took on the best aspects of Arab life even as they expelled Muslim rulers from the eastern Mediterranean, creating sumptuous courts whose learning and culture began to rival those of the great caliphs. At the same time the symbolic value of Jerusalem as a place worthy of fighting, slaughtering, and dying for began to fade—if only gradually—in the face of these new economic, political, and cultural realities.

Changes in the behavior and tactics of the crusaders were also striking. Later campaigns, which continued off and on for centuries, were either largely defensive affairs designed to claim territory already retaken by the Muslims or else perverted by raw political ambition and outright greed, such as the sack of Christian Constantinople in 1204 at the instigation of the powerful merchants of Venice. One "Crusade" involved a negotiated and temporary transfer of authority over Jerusalem, a favor by Muslim sultan to Christian king—a circumstance few could have predicted at the time of Clermont. At other times, crusading armies were offered control of Jerusalem, once the object of their most fervent desires, in exchange for Muslim territory seized elsewhere; they declined only to leave the Near East empty-handed.

The steady success of Christian forces in Spain and the reemergence of Christian military power in the Mediterranean, especially the capture by the Normans of once-Muslim Sicily, had already brought the worlds of Islam and Christendom into close contact and direct competition. But the First Crusade opened a third pathway between East and West, one in which brute military struggle would slowly give way to a web of commercial, cultural, and intellectual bonds between two rival but ultimately inseparable worlds. By the time Adelard of Bath arrived in Antioch around 1114, Arab culture—if not Muslim military might—held sway over much of life in the so-called Latin East.

Chapter Two

THE EARTH IS LIKE A WHEEL

SEVEN YEARS BEFORE the earthquake that shook the moral foundations of crusader Antioch, Adelard surveyed the world around him and pronounced it rotten. His recent studies at the famed French cathedral school at Tours had provided him with the best education of his day. He enjoyed the support and patronage of the powerful bishop of Bath, the French court physician and scholar John de Villula. He practiced the art of hunting with falcons, a sign of his noble rank and the life of leisure it generally afforded. And he was an accomplished musician, who years later still fondly recalled the time he had been invited to play the *cithara*, a forerunner of the guitar, for the queen.

In short, Adelard of Bath was the model country gentleman. His father, Fastrad, was one of Bishop John's richest tenants and most senior aides, ensuring a life of privilege for his son. The family appears sporadically in official documents of church and state. The Pipe Rolls, or royal accounts, later list Adelard as the beneficiary of a pension from the revenues of Wiltshire, in southwest England. Still, young Adelard saw little of value in the contemporary world, and he despaired at the state of Western learning in particular. "When I examine the famous writings of the ancients—not all of them, but most—and compare their talents with the knowledge of the moderns, I judge the ancients eloquent, and call the moderns dumb," he proclaimed in the opening line of his coming-of-age essay and first known work, *On the Same and the Different*.[1]

Adelard's disdain for "the moderns" was understandable, for the West at the end of the eleventh century was a mess. Daily life staggered under the burden of rampant violence and social instability. Bands of mercenaries, answerable to neither king nor God, prowled the countryside, their commanders' word the only law of the land. Across Europe, primitive farming techniques could no longer keep pace with a growing population, while antiquated inheritance laws left many impoverished and desperate.[2] Violence—inflamed by the weakness of central political authority and uninhibited by the tenuous moral grip of the Catholic Church—was the currency of the day. As Pope Urban II had acknowledged at Clermont when he called for the First Crusade, religious leaders were helpless to halt the chaos across the continent. The best the church could do was to redirect its flock's baser nature against the infidels to the East.

Not even Adelard's remote corner of England was immune to the troubles. It was not long since the Norman Conquest of 1066, and political and social strife still plagued the land. The uneasy relationship—for centuries punctuated by bouts of armed conflict—between what today comprise the distinct nations of England and France was a regular feature of late medieval life. At the same time, political, cultural, and personal ties ran deep, and so it was not surprising that Adelard could pursue higher education in Tours and that many leading officials and courtiers, like Bishop John, hailed from the European mainland. In 1086, as a young child, Adelard had seen his native West Country town, including its once-proud abbey of black-robed monks, burned almost to the ground during an uprising against the heir to the throne, William the Red. The rebels had hoped to secure the rule of William's brother, Robert of Normandy, but their bid for power had ended in bloody failure and considerable destruction. Robert, eldest son of William the Conqueror, later died a royal prisoner.

Things were little better inside the elite cathedral schools. The chaos and disorder that had swept in with the Germanic invasions of the western Roman Empire, beginning in the fourth century A.D., had just about destroyed formal education and the perpetuation of classical knowledge. The Muslim conquests around the eastern Mediterranean three hundred years later sealed the West's isolation by choking off easy access to the Byzantine Christians based in far-off Constantinople, where some traces of the Greek intellectual tradition could still be found.[3] The wonders of classical learning were all but forgotten, or at best pushed to the extreme margins of European consciousness. Invaluable texts were lost through inattention, destroyed in war, or rendered unintelligible by the general ignorance of would-be scholars or simply by the lost ability to read Greek. The aristocracy of the Roman Empire read the Greek masters in the original, so there was no need at the time for Latin translations of the philosophy of Plato and Aristotle, the engineering wonders of Archimedes, or the geometry of Euclid. The wholesale disappearance of Greek as the language of learning meant centuries of knowledge virtually vanished from the collective mind of Latin-speaking Europe.

There were a few outposts—scattered monasteries in Ireland, northern England, Catalonia, and southern Italy—where the monks labored to keep the classical traditions alive. Yet the results were meager in comparison with the heights once scaled by the Greeks, or with the new and exciting work being carried out in the Arab world. At the West's leading center of mathematical studies, the cathedral school of Laon, the best minds of Adelard's day had no grasp of the use of zero. The masters at Laon taught the latest techniques employed by King Henry I, who ruled both England and Normandy in the early twelfth century, to manage his treasury. These included the use of a special tablecloth, marked out in rows and columns like a chessboard and based on the principles of the abacus, which had reached France from Arab Spain some years before. The cloth was known as the *scaccarium*, Latin for "chess-board," and was the origin of the English term for a national treasury, *exchequer*. Despite the importance of this royal mission, the standard of learning at Laon remained very low; one contemporary textbook reveals consistent errors in even the most basic calculations.[4]

More vexing than sloppy royal accounting was the inability to measure the hours of the day or keep the calendar. Even by the sleepy standards of medieval Christendom, time was a serious business, linked as it was with the pursuit of heavenly salvation. The Rule of St. Benedict, which governed thousands of monasteries from the sixth century onward, required eight sets of prayers at specific times every twenty-four hours. The practice was based on a reading of two verses in Psalm 119: "Seven times a day I praise thee" and "At midnight I rise to give thee thanks."[5] This was relatively simple during the day, when the changing position of the sun could provide a rough guide to the hour, but at night the monks of the Latin West were left literally in the darkness of their own ignorance.

Crude methods of timekeeping evolved to fulfill the demands of the rule. It was found, for example, that a twelve-inch wax candle of a certain diameter would last about four hours.[6] A handful of the more prosperous monasteries employed elementary water clocks, in which the regulated flow of water into a container measured the passage of a given unit of time. In an early example of practical astronomy, the sixth-century prelate Gregory of Tours offered a rule of thumb, possibly Babylonian in origin, that accounted for the changing length of the days by beginning at nine hours of daylight in December and adding one hour per month from December to June, to make fifteen hours. The process was then reversed from June back to December. Popular in its day for its simplicity and ease of use, the system is nonetheless undermined by a lack of scientific understanding: The ratio of fifteen to nine is better suited to the latitudes of the Mediterranean and the Near East than it is to the northern climes of Tours.[7] Gregory presented a similar method for keeping track of the changing phases of the moon through the course of the month, but he made no provisions for seasonal changes. And he identified some constellations in the northern sky—taking pains not to use their pagan names—that could be used on clear nights to help regulate the prayers.[8]

Other attempts at attacking the problem suffered well into the Middle Ages from flaws similar to those that marred Gregory's early efforts. A Saxon sundial at a church in Yorkshire dating to 1064, for example, divides the day into eight equal units, or "tides," but it fails to take into account the fact that Yorkshire's latitude requires that these tides vary in length.[9] Lacking any real understanding of the theory behind techniques borrowed from the southern Mediterranean of the Middle East, the Latins did not realize they had to adjust their approach to account for their own more northerly locales, such as Adelard's own town of Bath.

As late as the thirteenth century, monks in France relied on informal systems such as local observational markers that could be aligned with the constellations to correspond to certain prayer times. A text written on a piece of slate found at the Cistercian Villers Abbey, near Namur in Belgium, explains how to estimate the time by tracing the sun and stars as they appear at various windows.[10] Most common of all, perhaps, was the appointment of a senior and respected monk as the *significator horarum*, who would chant a set number of psalms to note the progress of the hours and then awaken his brethren for their vigils, to be held at the "eighth hour of darkness."[11] This had the obvious advantage of functioning even when the stars were obscured by the clouds. But the method was so imprecise that theologians were forced to concede that ordinary monks should not be held responsible for any resulting failure by the *significator* to start the required prayer on time.

Monastic timekeeping, however, was not only a matter for the soul. With no reliable way to measure the passing of the hours, Western man's imagination—and his very existence—remained hostage to the shifting cycles of night and day and the organic phases of planting and harvesting. Accurate timekeeping would one day free society from the dictates of sunrise and sunset and recast the day or the hour as an abstract notion distinct from daily existence. This would eventually foster a new way of looking at the universe as something that could be measured, calculated, and controlled, opening up the realms of science and technology. The regular ringing of the monastery bells, governed by the rhythms of the monks' devotional and practical duties, provided one of medieval daily life's very few sureties and marked the tentative beginnings of an organized social order.[12]

Like the counting of the hours, accurately setting the date for the movable feast of Easter—the holiest day in the Christian calendar and the reference point for the entire ecclesiastical year—proved beyond the abilities of even the most learned of monks. While politics, tradition, and regional and sectarian rivalries invariably intruded throughout the centuries, the essential problem in fixing Easter lay in its ties to the astronomical cycle of the solar year, which was out of step with the calendar of daily life. Majority Christian opinion puts Easter on the first Sunday following the first full moon after the spring equinox. This could be determined only by observation and advanced calculation. For a world alienated from the very idea of science by its own focus on the afterlife and cut off by choice and circumstance from the great intellectual traditions of the classical world, both accurate calculation and meticulous observation were in short supply. The result was endless wrangling over the very notions of time and date. Estimates of the spring equinox, for example, often varied by as much as two weeks.

Naturally enough, the early church fathers adopted the Roman system of dates that prevailed in their day. The so-called Julian calendar was created by the Greek astronomer Sosigenes of Alexandria and imposed with a few minor changes by order of Julius Caesar forty-six years before the birth of Christ. But there was a hitch: The calendar rests on a year that is roughly eleven minutes and fourteen seconds too long, a well-known flaw that would not have escaped Sosigenes and his fellow astronomers. The spring equinox fell on March 25 when the Julian calendar was first introduced, but it was slipping "backward" at the considerable rate of about one full day every 130 years, threatening to take Easter and the rest of the church calendar with it.

As the young Christian community grew and expanded its reach, it naturally sought uniformity in the celebration of its most holy day. "What could be more beautiful . . . than that this feast day, from which we receive hope of immortality, be observed by all according to one and the same order and certain rule?" Emperor Constantine asked in 325 from his place of honor at the Council of Nicea, which nonetheless failed to resolve the Easter controversy.[13] Still, church leaders were eager to head off disputes like the one that later erupted in England between Christians of the so-called Roman conversion and followers of the older Celtic tradition from Ireland.[14] This required either the command of a recognized central religious or political authority or an agreed-on set of principles—scriptural or astronomical—clearly spelling out the proper day to celebrate the Resurrection. Lacking all of these, Christendom instead came to rely on the *computus*, a system of practical astronomy that evolved slowly over the centuries to provide rough approximations of date and time. The calculations themselves were arithmetic, and so there was no need to master the geometric concepts, such as the circle and the sphere, so integral to the proper study of astronomy.

Even where explicit guidance from the ancients was on hand, the West proved beyond help. A Latin translation of a simplified, step-by-step guide by the great classical Greek astronomer Ptolemy for determining the positions of the sun and the moon survives in the form of a medieval manuscript dating from around 1000. This would have greatly improved the work of the "computists" in fixing Easter and related calculations. But apparently, even the rudimentary understanding of astronomical terms needed just to use Ptolemy's *Handy Tables*, much less to understand his full text, was well beyond the reach of contemporary scholars.[15] It was not until the late sixteenth century that the Christian West could mobilize enough scientific firepower to begin to gain control of time and grapple successfully with the problem of calendar reform. By then, the equinox had drifted backward about two weeks, to mid-March.

Given the magnitude of Europe's political, social, and spiritual woes, it was perhaps remarkable that anything at all remained of the arts and sciences by the time Adelard left Bath to pursue his advanced education in France, around 1100. Yet a handful of cathedral schools had managed by this time to assemble a course of study based on the so-called seven liberal arts. Borrowed from a late-Roman convention, the seven disciplines were commonly depicted as enticing young maidens. The basic course of grammar, rhetoric, and logic comprised the trivium; its elementary character is reflected today in the word *trivial.* The more advanced program was the quadrivium of arithmetic, geometry, music, and—Adelard's personal favorite—astronomy. The entire edifice rested on a shaky and uncertain foundation provided by the Latin encyclopedists, who centuries earlier had collated, synthesized, and simplified classical works of science and philosophy and then presented them for a relatively broad audience.

An unfinished collection by the Roman patrician Boethius, whose execution around 524 on trumped-up charges of treason cut short his lifework, preserved some crumbs of Aristotle's logical system, several treatises on music, and a few basics of practical geometry. Boethius had planned to translate into Latin all the writings of Plato and Aristotle, but his untimely death condemned this great legacy of natural science, metaphysics, and cosmology to limbo for more than six hundred years. The available teachings of Plato were reduced to one partial Latin translation and an accompanying commentary. This gave medieval Europe its only real glimpse of natural philosophy until the twelfth century.[16] Virtually nothing was known of metaphysics or cosmology. Surviving manuscripts of Pliny's *Natural History* captured other tidbits of classical works, as did a few other similar books that circulated haphazardly.

By far the most popular Western textbook was an encyclopedia of half-remembered knowledge and often far-fetched explanations of natural phenomena compiled in the seventh century by Isidore, bishop of Seville. In his *Etymologies,* Isidore laid out in twenty volumes every bit of knowledge he thought worth preserving in the face of what he feared was a rising tide of barbarism threatening his native Spain. This included, among other things, discussions of grammar and rhetoric, arithmetic and astronomy, zoology, agriculture, theology, and military science. The bishop was well read and industrious, but his actual understanding was a bit suspect. He was clearly no critical thinker, for he accepts the material of his various sources without question and—in keeping with the spirit of his times—is more interested in allegorical meaning than in any underlying truth.

Etymologies was a runaway success and a staple in medieval Christian libraries for centuries. Readers generally preferred it to the original sources, which it soon consigned to oblivion; ignored and unwanted, many were lost forever. Printed editions of Isidore's work appeared well into the Renaissance. His teachings were followed so slavishly that his assertion—based on the author's elementary mistranslation of classical sources—that the earth was flat and "resembles a wheel" long retained a hold on many in medieval Europe, even if a handful of scholars and learned monks knew otherwise. This popular notion contradicted the classical Greek and Arab conception of the universe—as a series of spheres and wheels moving in a mechanical dance of circular motion, with the earth at its center—and inhibited the West from participating in the huge enterprise of cosmology. It made no difference that the prevailing model, codified by Ptolemy in the second century A.D. and studied ever since, was wrong; the important thing was to take advantage of the enormous opportunity for fruitful scientific research that it nonetheless afforded.

The Venerable Bede, who died in 735 after a long life of study inside the walls of his monastery in northern England, was perhaps the most subtle and sophisticated thinker of this early intellectual cohort. Bede's *The Reckoning of Time* was an important early attempt at the Easter *computus*, the calculation of the hour, and solutions to related problems. From his careful reading of Pliny, he concluded that the earth was a sphere—a teaching hopelessly obscured by Isidore's far more popular claim to the contrary—and he had some understanding of the varying hours of daylight and the behavior of the tides. Bede's knowledge was rudimentary, but it was so far ahead of its day that his fame soon resonated across Christendom. Few had seen anything like him before. "God, the Orderer of natures, who raised the Sun from the East on the fourth day of Creation, in the Sixth Age of the world has made Bede rise from the West as a new Sun to illuminate the whole Earth," gushed Notker the Stammerer, a monk in far-off Switzerland.[17]

It fell to the French cathedral schools to slowly shape the early building blocks left behind by the encyclopedists and a handful of like-minded monks into a coherent, if still incomplete and deeply flawed, body of knowledge. At the behest of Charlemagne, Alcuin of York had created a basic curriculum for the first of these institutions in the late eighth century to provide Charlemagne's empire with competent, trained functionaries. Adelard's alma mater at Tours was the first such school, and it gradually emerged as something of a European intellectual center.[18] Other schools were founded at Chartres, Laon, and elsewhere. By Adelard's day, these cathedral schools had already been in existence for centuries. They attracted some of the best scholars from among the small educated religious class and drew ambitious young students from different parts of Europe. Bishop John himself had come from Tours, and he used his personal and church connections there to secure a coveted place at the

school for his protégé. The preference of the teachers at the cathedral schools
for the quadrivium, in particular for mathematics and astronomy, had a
profound influence on young Adelard's own outlook and interests.[19] These in
turn determined the ideas he would later adopt from among the teachings of
the Arabs and bring back to the West.

The early epicenter of Europe's medieval intellectual activity was the former
kingdom of Lotharingia. Once the heart of Charlemagne's empire, it comprised parts of western Germany, Belgium, the Netherlands, and France. Its
hub, Liège in present-day Belgium, was known as the "Athens of Lotharingia"
for its serious scholarship.[20] For decades, the kings of England had relied on a
steady supply of Lotharingian clerics to fill high royal and ecclesiastical posts.
Bishop John's predecessor had come from the region, as had Adelard's father,
Fastrad, and a number of other influential figures in eleventh-century English
intellectual and religious life. The schools and monasteries of Lotharingia had
emerged as the first tentative repositories of Arab science and technology,
including the Arabic number system; with no suitable educational institutions
of its own, the English crown was forced to rely on well-trained imports to
meet a growing demand.[21]

Among the earliest Western proponents of intellectual innovation, including that invaluable calculating device, the abacus, was Gerbert d'Aurillac, one
of the day's finest minds and the future Pope Sylvester II. Raised as an oblate,
or monk-in-training, in the monastery of St. Gerard, the precocious Gerbert
soon outgrew the limited learning available in his native France; there was
simply no one among the local monks sufficiently versed in mathematics or
astronomy to further his education. In 967, his superiors sent him for three
years of advanced studies at the monastery of Vich in Catalonia, then a distant
Christian frontier outpost abutting the scientific and cultural powerhouse of
Muslim Spain.

Catalonia enjoyed good trade relations with the Western Caliphate, based in
the imperial city of Cordoba. Muslim traders were a common sight in Catalonian
markets, and cultural trends, ideas, and inventions passed easily enough across
this border between Muslim East and Christian West. The Arabs' advanced
science of the stars, the game of chess, the earliest representation of what came to
be called Arabic numerals, and the Muslim astrolable—the most potent analog
computer until the modern era—were all awaiting "discovery" in Catalonia.[22]
Here, all seven of the liberal arts were available for study.

At a time when even the richest monasteries of France, Germany, and England might own just a few dozen volumes of mostly outdated learning, the Catalonian monks, particularly those of Santa Maria de Ripoll, enjoyed access to relatively large collections that included Arabic texts and their translations. These hinted at the secrets of ancient learning, as well as more recent Arab science, philosophy, and medicine. Young Gerbert visited the Ripoll monastery and may have brought back knowledge of basic Arab technology, such as the workings of the water clock, to his native France. Nonetheless, even at Ripoll, the standard of learning was woefully weak. The earliest Latin treatises on the astrolabe and related technologies were peppered with errors and half-digested Arabic terminology; the West was unable to produce its own coherent astrolabe texts until the mid-twelfth century.[23]

Gerbert returned home from Catalonia to take up a series of teaching posts. He immediately championed the very quadrivium—music, arithmetic, geometry, and astronomy—that he had been unable to pursue as a young monk in France. During his stay in Spain, he had acquired the translation of an Arabic book on the stars from the archdeacon of Barcelona and a separate work on mathematics and astronomy. Gerbert taught his students arithmetic by means of an unusual abacus consisting of individually numbered counters, one to nine; the concept of zero remained elusive. Soon, similar Latin abacus systems with the Hindu-Arabic characters—the figures we use today—in place of the prevailing Roman numerals, using crude transliterations from the original Arabic names for each figure, began to take root. The names for the figures were likely borrowed from the informal Arab practice of calculating on a dust board, a form of erasable easel. It would take another 150 years for proper Arabic numerals and the positional system of ones, tens, hundreds, and so on—fundamentally the same system we use today—to become the accepted means of calculation.[24]

Gerbert and his followers were fascinated by the course of the stars and the planets, and they insisted on the value of firsthand observation of the heavens—work that at the very least prepared the way for the coming of Arab astronomy. In a letter from the French city of Rheims to a fellow cleric around 978, Gerbert makes clear that he has broken free from the flat-earth teachings of Isidore of Seville. "In reply to your query about the sphere for demonstrating the celestial circles and constellations, my brother, it is made completely round, divided equally through the middle by the circumference, which has been divided into sixty parts."[25]

Medieval commentators hold that Gerbert was the first to introduce the West to the astrolabe as a way to address the troubling problems of monastic prayer time and the ecclesiastical calendar. This portable instrument could also measure the height of a tower or the depth of a well, determine geographic latitude, mark the direction of true north, and work out the position of the sun and the major stars. The origins of the device itself are obscure, but the design and theoretical approach were almost certainly Greek. Greek mathematicians and astronomers in Alexandria, Egypt, wrote numerous treatises on the basics of the astrolabe. A text by Ptolemy, now lost, detailed the underlying mathematical principles, also vital to mapmaking, but the more advanced planispheric astrolabe used by the Arabs was unknown in his day. Arab tradition, nonetheless, credits the great astronomer with the accidental invention of this powerful tool. Ibn Khallikan, writing in the thirteenth century, recounts one version: Ptolemy was out riding one day, a celestial globe in his hand; he dropped it, and his horse crushed it flat with his hooves, creating the planispheric astrolabe.[26]

Refined by the Arabs from these early Greek designs, the astrolabe was a virtual bronze book of the stars that projected the spherical universe onto a two-dimensional face. A treatise on the astrolabe, commonly ascribed to Gerbert or a member of his immediate circle, calls the device a great gift from God but also appears to warn against any broader usage: "[The astrolabe can be used] to find the true time of day, whether in summer or wintertime, with no ambiguous uncertainty in the reckoning. Yet this seems most suitable for celebrating the daily office of prayer and to be excessive knowledge for general use. How pleasing and seemly the whole proceeds, when with the greatest reverence at the proper hour under the rule of a just judge, who will not wish the slightest shadow of error, they harmoniously complete the service of the Lord."[27]

The astrolabe itself was beautiful to behold—elegant in form and powerful in function. The typical device was about the size of a salad plate, fashioned in polished, decorative bronze. Degrees of latitude, or perhaps the hours of the day, were commonly inscribed along the outer edge. A disk, painstakingly calibrated for the user's geographic location, sat atop the face of the astrolabe, with a rotating skeinlike cutout displaying the principal stars and the sun's annual path affixed to that and held in place with a wedge-shaped pin known as the horse. A pivoting pointer—the alidade, from the

Arabic *al-idada*—was mounted on the back to take readings while the astrolabe was held aloft, suspended at arm's length, by a ring at the top. In the daytime, the rays of the sun were lined up with two pinholes or notches in the alidade; at night, the user followed the same procedure but took aim at a known star. The position of the alidade against the astrolabe's scaled markings could then yield a wealth of corresponding celestial information. The perfection of the astrolabe reflected the genius of Arab science: it drew on classical sources but then went well beyond them to refine the device and to address the burning questions of the day in such fields as timekeeping, astronomy, astrology, and cartography.

As the early Latin scholars immediately recognized, however, descriptions of the workings and utility of the astrolabe cannot do it justice. In one of the earliest Latin references to the device, Radolphus, a teaching master at Liège, invites a colleague from Cologne to come and handle the astrolabe for himself, rather than rely on any written account or sketch that he might provide. "Otherwise, only to see the astrolabe will be of no more help than drawings for the . . . blind, or poultices for the gout-ridden," Radolphus informs his learned friend in a letter.[28]

Word of the astrolabe and its Arab provenance began to spread slowly throughout the West. Fulbert, a student of Gerbert and later the bishop of Chartres and the founder of its influential cathedral school, composed a short verse to help his pupils recall the Arabic names of eight of the most important stars in the constellations of the Western zodiac. The result is the earliest known use of Arabic words in a Latin text: "Aldeberan stands out in Taurus, Menke and Rigel in Gemini, and Frons and bright Cabalazet in Leo. Scorpio, you have Galbalgrab; and you Capricorn, Deneb. You, Batanalhaut [literally, *batan al-hut*, fish's gut], are alone enough for Pisces."[29] These same "stars of the hours" appear in one of the earliest European works on the astrolabe, dating from around 1000. Fulbert also prepared a glossary of Arabic and Latin names for parts of the astrolabe, opening the door to what would soon become a flood of Arabic terminology, concepts, and ideas in Western arts and sciences.[30] Today, our constellations and planets bear Latin names, but those of many of the major stars are Arabic in origin.

Gerbert's influence was particularly strong in Lotharingia, and he kept up a lively correspondence with a number of scholars in the region about the latest mathematical trends and ideas he had picked up in Spain. Loose ties between the local monasteries and those still active in Muslim Spain had already established pathways for the occasional exchange of ideas, and Germany and the Western Caliphate enjoyed periodic contact. A delegation sent to Cordoba in 954, headed by a well-traveled Lotharingian scholar, John of Gorze, is thought to have returned after a three-year stay with original manuscripts and a few early translations of Arabic manuscripts. The Spanish caliph Abd al-Rahman responded by dispatching a Mozarab, or Arabized Christian, as his representative to the Saxon court. From the schools and monasteries of Lotharingia, Arabic learning began to spread gradually into Germany, France, and England.[31]

Not everyone was so captivated by the arrival of these new ideas, with their seemingly magical powers and their suspicious association with the infidel Arabs. In a society where literacy and general education were rare, this same suspicion was easily directed at any type of nonreligious book learning. This trend would only be aggravated by the coming intellectual invasion from the Muslim world, with its foreign terms, mysterious symbols, and unimaginable innovations. Allegations of black magic were hurled at a number of the early Christian scholars who sought out Arabic learning, a phenomenon that would later see the deadly charge of heresy leveled against those who challenged church teachings in philosophy and the natural sciences.

William of Malmesbury, a monastic librarian and historian who died 140 years after Gerbert d'Aurillac, acknowledged the late pope's undoubted technical skills but nonetheless remained wary of his time in Spain: "There he learned what the singing and flight of birds portended, there he acquired the art of calling up spirits from hell."[32] William also dismissed Gerbert's mathematical ideas as "dangerous Saracen magic" and claimed that his election as pontiff, on the cusp of the millennium in 999, was due to a pact with the Devil. Another cleric noted sourly that, like Gerbert before him, the learned bishop of Hereford, Robert, had also wasted his time with such matters: "*Mathesis* [astrology] did not prolong his life, nor did the abacus which numbers years in a different way."[33] A thirteenth-century tradition calls Gerbert "the best necromancer in France, whom the demons of the air readily obeyed in all that he required, of them by day and night, because of the great sacrifices he offered them." These same demons, it was said, taught him to use the wondrous astrolabe in exchange for his soul.[34]

In Gerbert's day, these fears of Arab science had not yet crystallized into active clerical opposition, and they certainly did nothing to derail his brilliant career. After an appointment as personal tutor to the son of Otto, the Holy Roman emperor, he traveled to Rheims, where he taught logic and philosophy and later became the head of the cathedral school. Students from far-off corners of Europe flocked to his lectures. Yet just four years before his elevation to the papacy, Gerbert still evoked bitter opposition in some quarters for his worldly and unorthodox outlook. Philosophy, even what little was known of the classics, was still suspect. "The vicars of Peter and their disciples will not have for their teacher a Plato, a Virgil, or any other of that vile herd of philosophers," the papal legate protested to no avail.[35]

The Arab-based learning of Gerbert faced more than just the doubts of the clergy and the fears of the superstitious masses. It was also precariously prone to error, misunderstanding, and at times some comic confusion. Gerbert and his students may have represented the brightest lights of their generation, but they were wholly unable to absorb or even comprehend the full reach of Arabic science, with its profound grounding in Aristotelian metaphysics and Greek, Persian, and Hindu learning in general. The most basic concepts of geometry posed a problem. Two of Gerbert's leading pupils exchanged earnest letters around 1025 in an unsuccessful effort to discern just what the classical geometers might have meant by the interior angle of a triangle, a mystery they never resolved. Nor were they able to work out any geometric theorems. One reports his excitement at having acquired an astrolabe of his own. Stumped by such an elementary matter as the interior angle, they would have been completely unable to comprehend the geometric theory that lies behind the device.[36]

For this first generation touched ever so slightly by Arab learning, new devices like the astrolabe and the abacus, and new concepts like the Hindu-Arabic numeral system, remained just that—devices to be exploited rather than fully understood. These pioneers were far more concerned with practical use than with theoretical knowledge, more invested in the how than in the why. There was so far no serious attempt to master the underlying Arab knowledge of the heavens, developed over hundreds of years and captured so brilliantly in the polished face of the bronze astrolabe. Nor was there any real appreciation of the broader implications—for the church, for society, or for mankind in general—of this new learning from the East. They were content simply to try to determine the prayer times and make other basic measurements, much as the user of a modern pocket calculator or personal computer may produce accurate results without any real understanding of mathematics.

With much of Bath in ashes after the failed uprising against him, the victorious William the Red turned to Bishop John de Villula in 1088 to restore order and to reconstruct the town's famous monastery. Eager to secure the loyalties of so able a retainer, the new monarch sold the city to John for five hundred pounds of silver and allowed him to move his see from the unfortified town of Wells to the relative safety of Bath and its surviving stone walls. John's interest in Bath, however, extended well beyond simple political or military considerations. The town was closer to Worcester and the monasteries of the Severn basin, emerging centers of English learning that John found highly inviting.[37]

The ambitious cleric was also keen to take full advantage of the political turmoil all around. He seized the extensive holdings of Bath's Benedictine monastery for his personal property and launched a bold program of civic reconstruction. He attracted fellow French physicians and scholars to the revitalized town, built a medical center, complete with a royal bathhouse, around the famous mineral springs, and generally restored a measure of past glory to what had once been a bustling Roman spa. Construction began on a grand cathedral as well as a school. Under the learned bishop's patronage, the West Country soon found itself host to a small circle of scholar-monks aware of some of the newest ideas just beginning to reach Christendom from the Arab world.

An efficient administrator, Bishop John was generous to his lieutenants and their families. He took a strong interest in the upbringing of Adelard, whose family's position would have given him direct access to both the latest intellectual trends coming from France and the complex construction techniques used by the architects and stonemasons to build the great cathedral and other structures now taking shape under John's direction. The bishop also provided for Adelard's early schooling at the Benedictine monastery before securing his advanced education abroad.[38]

Adelard certainly justified Bishop John's confidence, and he threw himself into his studies in France despite his considerable doubts about the worthiness of "the moderns." At Tours, Adelard tells us in *On the Same and the Different*, he first learned of the constellations from a famous wise man. The experience sends him scurrying to a quiet locale beyond the city limits, where he can pause amid the smell of the flowers and the steadying rhythm of the flowing Loire River and reflect on the enormity of what he has just learned. There he has a mystical vision—one cast in imagery familiar to the readers of his day, who would have recognized the form from Boethius's popular *The Consolation of Philosophy*—that sets him on his intellectual journey.[39] Two women—one proffering wealth, fame, and power; the other, the mistress of the seven liberal arts—appear before him in a struggle for his heart and soul. Despite earthly temptation, Adelard declares himself a firm partisan of learning and knowledge, and he emerges from his dream more determined than ever to master his studies. "When I had thoroughly read one lesson, I desired the next with a greater passion, as if the one I had read would bring no benefit if what remained was lacking, hoping from this regime that I could keep in check my youth and console my old age."[40]

His decision appears confirmed during a trip home from Salerno, in southern Italy, an important early European center of science and medicine where he has gone in search of knowledge and understanding. On the road, Adelard finds himself locked in weighty discussion with "a certain Greek philosopher . . . who, more than anything else, could talk about the art of medicine and the nature of things."[41] The teacher challenges his new disciple with a difficult question: If a hole were opened all the way through the earth, would a stone tossed in fall out the other side? Adelard's answer—no, it would come to rest at the earth's center—appeases the wandering philosopher, who notes sagely that study of the liberal arts is never wasted. The same journey also took Adelard to Syracuse, on the formerly Muslim island of Sicily and once home to Archimedes. He would later praise the mathematical skills of his local host, Bishop William, and dedicate *On the Same and the Different* to him.

Adelard's first known work also introduces what was to become his favorite literary convention—an unnamed nephew who serves as intellectual straight man and foil for his own unorthodox views, a character Adelard revisits and refines with greater effect in later writings. Where the younger man stands for traditional Christian learning—rigid, unquestioning, ossified—Adelard increasingly presents himself as the champion of unbridled intellectual inquiry and reason. Where the nephew remains rooted in place, our hero is prepared to go to any length to find what he is seeking. Adelard uses this same literary device to put forward controversial views not so much as his own thinking but as responses to the ceaseless demands of his impatient kinsman.

On the Same and the Different, written when Adelard was in his early to mid-thirties, concludes with his defense against his nephew's allegations that his early intellectual wanderings in southern Europe were a waste of time. "Now, dearest nephew, I have sufficiently explained to you the cause of my winding journey to teachers of different regions, so that I might both lift from myself the burden of your unjust accusation, and urge the passion for the same studies on you, so that when the others display their riches in many ways, we may simply set forth knowledge. Good-bye and judge for yourself whether I have disputed rightly."[42]

Despite his uncommon taste for intellectual adventure, the Adelard who emerges from the pages of *On the Same and the Different* is very much a man of his times, albeit one well versed in the contemporary teachings of the leading schools of northern France and wholly at ease with the day's thorniest scientific and philosophical problems and questions. As a result, the book offers a compelling snapshot of the state of Western education at the beginning of the twelfth century, before encounters with Arab learning became more common. But even Adelard's unquestionable talent and seemingly limitless curiosity alone were not enough to break the bonds on the Christian imagination imposed by early church fathers.

For more than six hundred years, the authoritative teachings of St. Augustine had directed the Christian faithful to see only God's mystery in an unknowable world around them. Everyday life was imbued with allegorical meaning: The moon represented the church, for it reflected the divine light; the wind symbolized the Holy Spirit; and the number eleven stood for sin because it "transgressed" the number ten, which clearly represented the Commandments.[43] In fact, numbers in general were valued more for their scriptural meaning than as simple units of counting or calculation. Three clearly represented the Trinity, while four stood for the Creation; their sum, seven, revealed "perfection." This, in turn, explains the tendency of religious imagery—angels, seals, trumpets—to come in sevens.[44] When occasional tentative efforts were made to adopt the technological novelties starting to trickle in from the Arab world—the astrolabe, or the water clock that Caliph Harun al-Rashid of *The Thousand and One Nights* fame sent as a gift, along with an elephant, to Charlemagne in 801—the devices were either dismissed as curiosities, ignored outright, or condemned as black magic. As far as medieval Christians were concerned, God was the sole determining force in daily life; there was no reason to explore "the nature of things"—and thus no science.

St. Augustine of Hippo, born to a Christian mother and a pagan father, diagnosed the soul-damning "disease" of curiosity back in the fifth century. "Men proceed to investigate the phenomena of nature—the part of nature not beyond us—though the knowledge is of no value to them: for they wish to know simply for the sake of knowing."[45] Upon his conversion to Christianity in 387 while a professor of rhetoric at the imperial court in Milan, Augustine forswore both art and science: "Certainly the theaters no longer attract me, nor do I care to know the course of the stars."[46] Paul's Letter to the Galatians had already dismissed the tracking of time as too worldly for true believers: "Now that you have come to know God, or rather to be known by God, why do you turn back again to the weak and miserable elemental principles, to which you desire to be in bondage all over again? You observe days, months, seasons, and years" (Galatians 4:9–10). Many Christians had clung to Augustine's one-dimensional vision of life ever since. Earthly existence was but a shadow of Christ's eternal kingdom, and any attempt to delve into the mysteries of existence could only lead to error and sin.

Accounts of natural phenomena were presented as moralizing tales, fables pumped full of allegory for the betterment of the soul. One popular example can be found in the medieval bestiaries, collections of written texts and illustrations designed to edify humans rather than to describe nature. Stags, lions, and birds, even insects and rocks, were all proof of God's wisdom and mercy and, if properly studied, offered behavioral advice for the pious. "The Lord . . . created different creatures with different natures not only for the sustenance of men, but also for their instruction, so that through the same creatures we may contemplate not only what may be useful in the body, but also what may be useful in the soul," explains the English theologian Thomas of Chobham, in a guide to effective preaching.[47] The development of these works in the Middle Ages mirrors perfectly the way Christendom reworked what it retained of classical knowledge to meet its own spiritual needs.[48] In this moral taxonomy, the stag was loyal; the fox, a heretic; the bee, industrious; and the panther, sweet and beloved.[49] By discarding the recognizable elements of natural science, the authors of the bestiaries were imitating—perhaps unwittingly but just as surely—Augustine's determination to ignore the course of the stars.

Even where Augustine had some rare words of praise for the natural world—"All nature, in so far as it is nature, is good"—they were totally disregarded by his devoted readers.[50] In this way, the early medieval church benefited from the gloss of intellectual respectability provided by Augustine while still maintaining its general contempt for the philosophers. Augustine drew his own inspiration from Plato and, more important, from a school of thought developed in the third century A.D. by the Greek philosopher Plotinus and his successors. Since then, their ideas had predominated in all three leading centers of philosophy—Alexandria, Rome, and the Athenian Academy. Early Christian thinkers like Augustine helped introduce selective elements of these teachings into church doctrine. Crucially, this process saw the formulation of two powerful notions that would reign unchallenged for centuries: the unbridgeable distinction between the saintly kingdom of heaven and the "vile" existence of earthly life; and the inability of man to apprehend the universe through his rational faculties—that is, through experience, including the practice of science.

The sixth-century *Topographica Christiana*, written by the monk and former merchant sailor Cosmas Indicopleustes, presented the era's first real cosmological schema, one that reflected the general tenor of the day. The title of its first book leaves little to the imagination: "Against Those, Who While Wishing to Profess Christianity, Think and Imagine like the Pagans That the Heaven Is Spherical."[51] No less an authority than Isidore of Seville took the same stance, although somewhat less stridently: "The globe derives its name from the roundness of the circle, because it resembles a wheel; hence a small wheel is called a 'small disk.' Indeed, the Ocean that flows around it on all sides encompasses its furthest reaches in a circle," Isidore earnestly informed his countless readers.[52]

The good bishop's description—"It is divided into three parts, one is called Asia, the second Europe, the third Africa"[53]—was the basis for the long-running popularity of the so-called T-O maps of the world, in which the Mediterranean was depicted as a T, with Asia above it and Europe and Africa on either side of the stem; a great circle of water, the O, provided the map's outer boundaries. Holy Jerusalem, revered burial place of Christ, generally stood at the center. Those philosophers even willing to contemplate the existence of lands in the southern hemisphere, known since antiquity as the antipodes, saw little need to depict such an "absurd" region, where men—if there were any, that is—would have to walk upside down and endure life without the possibility of Christian redemption. Perhaps the only thing as absurd to us as the notion of an uninhabitable and unsanctified southern hemisphere, where trees would grow downward and the rain and snow fall upward, is the fact that the most serious thinkers of the age once debated it. Still, such controversies became a staple of medieval intellectual life, up there with the famous puzzlers of Thomas Aquinas and his fellow scholastics: How many angels *could* dance on the head of a pin? And what of the cannibal? How could he arise from the dead to face Judgment Day once he had consumed enough human parts that he was no longer himself but a composite of his victims, who would likewise be resurrected?[54]

The seeming unwillingness on the part of medieval Christendom to formulate or even imagine laws of nature gave rise to an obsessive fear of change and bouts of general hysteria amid the era's wars, famine, rampant disease, and periodic predictions that the end of the world was finally at hand.[55] The social chaos unleashed by the sudden appearance in Europe of the black death, in the mid-fourteenth century, offers a powerful case in point: Unfamiliar with any real notion of contagion, hygiene, or epidemiology in general, the Christian West was gripped by a frenzy of violence induced by the mass casualties of the plague. The French poet Guillaume de Machaut was so traumatized by his experience of the disease that he, like others of his day, refused to even utter the words "plague" or "black death" and instead took refuge in the more clinical, but then uncommon, euphemism of *epydimie*.[56] "Nor was there any physician or doctor who really knew the cause or origin, or what it was (nor was there any remedy), yet this malady was so great that it was called an epidemic," says Guillaume in his *Judgment of the King of Navarre*.[57] To the horror of many established churchmen, flagellant movements, seeking to regain God's favor through atonement and the bloody scourging of the body, flourished, and apocalyptic tales ran wild. The burning of Jews—accused of poisoning public drinking water, practicing witchcraft, and otherwise spreading the disease to destroy Christian Europe—was widespread in Germany, southern France, and Spain, while immigrant Catalans bore the brunt of similar public outrage and terror in Sicily.[58]

Many years before, on the final day of the year 999, Gerbert d'Aurillac, pioneer of abacus and astrolabe, found himself at the vortex of just such a storm. Now Pope Sylvester II, he was to officiate over midnight mass at St. Peter's in Rome on the eve of the millennium, a day some believers were certain would let slip the Beast of the Apocalypse. After all, the book of Revelation says, "And he cast him into the abyss, and closed and sealed it over him, that he should deceive the nations no more, until the thousand years should be finished. And after that he must be let loose for a little while" (20:3). Others yearned to be reunited with Christ and hurried to sell their possessions so they might travel to Jerusalem to witness the Last Judgment.[59] Sylvester and other senior churchmen did their best to counter these prophecies of doom, but the simple village priests, peasants, and townsfolk were wary of the learned pontiff, with his strange foreign ways and newfangled ideas. Sylvester's standing was further undermined by another prophecy, namely a coming alliance between a pope and the Antichrist.[60] That the end of days had not arrived as expected on New Year's morning was of little comfort; it was, many suspected, just a matter of time.

Adelard of Bath never succumbed to the apocalyptic fashion of his day. His mind was too subtle, his personality too confident, to take refuge in such talk. Yet *On the Same and the Different*, his first extant work, links him to some of the very philosophical traditions that lay behind the terror of life that dogged Christendom for so long. The title itself comes from Plato's creation story, *Timaeus*, which had survived in partial Latin translation and comprised an element of early Christian thought. Such Platonic notions were widely studied at the French cathedral schools, including Adelard's own in Tours.[61] For Plato and his later followers, the Divine One—commonly associated in the Christian mind with God—created the universe and surrounded it with a band of fixed stars. This is the circle of the Same, and it is, by definition, unchanging, uniform, and essentially perfect. Below it sits the circle of the Different, a band around the earth that represents change, diversity, and imperfection.[62]

In addition to the distinction between divine perfection and earthly change and corruption, Plato and his later interpreters also adopted the notion that these eternal forms or ideas exist only in the mind of "the Divine One," well apart from any material objects.[63] What we perceive as reality is only a pale reflection or shadow, knowable only through the senses. The church fathers and their medieval successors took comfort in what they saw as philosophical support for Christian doctrine, but this forced separation of Creator and Creation—of the god man worshipped and the universe he moved through each day—alienated believers from their surroundings in unpredictable ways, feeding religious manias, stirring apocalyptic visions, and inspiring severe penitential movements. This was, however, a natural outcome of the state of medieval Christian belief. So was the Middle Ages' deep-set conservatism, in which change was the mortal enemy of man and everyone had his or her place in the rigid social and cosmic order. When observed reality could no longer be ignored, a sort of dual personality emerged. For example, highly accurate navigational charts, for use by actual sailors who had to get safely from one place to another, coexisted for centuries with the idealized but practically useless T-O maps, with Jerusalem as the physical and spiritual center of the earth.[64]

In the centuries before the crusader era, the West had little interest in Islam, and there was certainly no real effort to paint Muslims as mortal enemies of Christianity. Generally identified in the early accounts as Saracens—that is, as the children of Abraham's wife, Sarah—the Muslims were just another "barbarian" annoyance to be tolerated and, with God's aid, defeated. The Venerable Bede's classic eighth-century *Ecclesiastical History of the English People* notes, "At which time a dreadful plague of Saracens ravaged France with miserable slaughter; but they not long after in that country received the punishment due to their wickedness," a reference to the Muslim defeat in 732 at Poitiers.[65] A chronicle of the Franks from 793 refers to Saracen raids on southern France as one of that year's two "terrible afflictions." The other is the revolt of the Saxons.[66] Both texts are notable for a general lack of religious animus directed at the Muslim enemy.

Even attacks on Rome and the sack of St. Peter's by Arab forces in 846 failed to generate the kind of aggressive anti-Muslim hysteria that began to take shape in the eleventh century. As late as 1010, feuding Arab and Berber armies in southern Spain each called on Christian allies for support.[67] Similar alliances of convenience followed, presaging the arrangements that would later characterize the Latin East after the early success of the First Crusade. The initial transformation of the Saracens from a simple affliction to a matter of spiritual life or death for all Christendom can be traced in some measure to the destruction of Jerusalem's Church of the Holy Sepulcher by the Muslims in

1009. This act, which recalled some of the dire prophecies associated with the end of days, appeared to reignite millennial fears after the near miss of the year 1000, and it linked the Muslims to the Apocalypse in the popular Christian imagination. It also unleashed a wave of pilgrimage to the Holy Land and identified the far-off Muslim caliph with the Antichrist.[68]

But events in the Near East were not the decisive factors in the early formulation of anti-Muslim propaganda. Like the division between thought and experience that characterized the age in general, the reality of the Muslims' beliefs, lives, and practices had nothing to do with their emerging image in the West. Instead, the view of the Saracen as hated Other was a function of Europe's own theological and political needs at the time—a phenomenon not unfamiliar today as the West wages its "war on terrorism." Under the direction of men like Gregory VII and Urban II, the eleventh century was dominated by the rise of centralized papal power at the expense of the fragmented and unstable political realm of kings and princes. The language of Christian holy war against the Muslim infidel was the perfect vehicle to consolidate church control.[69] Here are the roots of the mental contortions that still lie at the root of many of today's abiding views of Islam, presented as the reverse image of Western goodness: Where Christianity stands for love, Islam is a religion of cruelty; where Christ stands for truth, Muhammad and the Koran stand for deception; where Christians are chaste, Muslims are sexual deviants.[70] In other words, theology begat history; the views and behavior of Muslims, about which the West was almost wholly ignorant at the time, were beside the point.

Church ideology, even one powerful enough to mobilize tens of thousands for the hardships of holy war in far-off lands, was by no means the only force defining medieval Europe's early views of the Muslims and the Muslim world. There was also money to be made, whether wartime spoils for armed adventurers like the Norman conquerors of Muslim Sicily or profits from trade for the intrepid merchants of Pisa, Amalfi, and Venice. Among the more ambitious, opportunities for territorial conquest beckoned men like Baldwin, the future Count of Edessa, and Bohemond, Prince of Antioch.

Adelard, of course, had ambitions of his own. Well versed in the French cathedral tradition, the author of *On the Same and the Different* nonetheless displays a rather shallow level of learning. He gives no hint of the theoretical geometry that lies at the heart of astronomy, and his own observations rely on a primitive measuring stick, with no references to either the astrolabe or its simpler cousin, the quadrant. Likewise, his knowledge of philosophy, music, and mathematics is wholly conventional, heavily reliant on the sixth-century works of Boethius and the other texts prevalent in the cathedral schools.[71] Rededicating himself to his studies after his vision on the banks of the Loire, he declares that only complete devotion to his beloved philosophy can lead the way out of darkness. Already, his tentative explorations in southern Italy and Sicily had convinced him that he had to break free physically from the intellectual confinement of medieval Europe and explore firsthand the mysteries of the *studia Arabum*.

Entrusting his students to the cathedral school at Laon, the young Englishman set off alone in 1109 for the rumored intellectual wonders waiting in the Arab East. Adelard later recalls his farewell in *On the Same and the Different*, addressing the familiar figure of his unnamed kinsman and including a parting shot at the shortcomings of French learning: "You remember, dear nephew, that, seven years ago, when I dismissed you (still almost a boy) with my other students in French studies at Laon, we agreed amongst ourselves that I would investigate the studies of the Arabs according to my ability, but you would become no less proficient in the insecurity of French opinions."[72] Adelard's precise route to the East remains something of a puzzle, but there is no mystery about the rich intellectual tradition that had already been brewing there for centuries.

PART II
Al-Fajr/Dawn

Chapter Three

THE HOUSE OF WISDOM

ABU JAFAR AL-MANSUR was taking no chances with his new imperial capital, for this was to be a city like no other. The second Abbasid caliph of the Muslims turned for guidance to his trusted royal astrologers, the former Zoroastrian Nawbakht and Mashallah, a Jew turned Muslim from Basra and now "the leading person for the science of judgments of the stars."[1] The pair consulted the heavens and declared that July 30, 762, would certainly be the most auspicious day for work to begin. Still, al-Mansur hesitated. He ordered his architects to mark the layout of the walls of his proposed city—a perfect circle, in keeping with the geometric teachings of the caliph's beloved Euclid—on the ground, first in ashes and then again with cotton seeds soaked in naphtha. This was set ablaze to create a fiery outline of the so-called Round City, the geometric center of al-Mansur's future metropolis.[2] At last, the caliph was satisfied. "By God! . . . I shall live in it my entire life, and it shall become the home of my descendants; and without a doubt, it will become the most prosperous city in the world," declared al-Mansur, Arabic for "the victorious."[3] Abbasid coins and other official usage celebrated al-Mansur's capital as the Madinat al-Salam, or "the city of peace," but among the people it always retained the name of the old Persian settlement that had been on the same spot—Baghdad.

Twelve years before work began on the capital, al-Mansur's brother Saffah completed the overthrow of the Umayyad dynasty, which had risen to power in the Muslim world three decades after the death of the Prophet Muhammad in 632. In the revolutionary retribution that followed, Saffah—"shedder of blood"—sent his forces under the Abbasids' distinctive black banners to hunt down the remaining members of the House of the Umayyads. The only significant figure to escape alive was Prince Abd al-Rahman, who fled to North Africa before going on to establish the future Western Caliphate in southern Spain. But the victory of the rebels, who found it politically expedient to assert their direct lineage to the Prophet through his paternal uncle Abbas, was less a blood feud between an aging dynasty and an ambitious pretender than it was a wholesale cultural revolution throughout the Islamic lands.

Well before the Abbasid victory in 750, the armies of Islam had successfully retraced the path of Alexander the Great, one thousand years earlier, pushing across the Oxus River into Afghanistan and reaching India and western China. The conquest of Persia, to the east of the Umayyad capital, was complete by 651, and soon Muslim power was extending westward as well, through North Africa and into Spain. As a result of this rapid territorial expansion, Muslim Arabs no longer enjoyed a majority in the empire under their control. Now they had to contend with a daunting patchwork of ethnic and religious communities: large urban populations of Persians, both recent Muslim converts and traditional Zoroastrians; Aramaic speakers, Christians and Jews alike; Arab Christians of various stripes, including the many "dualist" sects that had broken with Eastern Orthodox Byzantium; and other groups.[4]

Many of the empire's newest Muslims, especially those in traditionally Persian lands, were openly skeptical of the Umayyad claims of political and religious legitimacy. The early Umayyad caliphs were descended from members of the Prophet Muhammad's inner circle but were not his blood relatives, something that did not always sit well with the Persian converts and other newcomers to the faith. They responded enthusiastically to rebel propaganda that asserted direct family links between the Abbasids and the Prophet and demanded "an acceptable ruler" from the family of Muhammad. With the final collapse of the old order at the hands of the Abbasids, the way was open to a range of newcomers—notably Persians, but also Sabeans, Jews, and many others—to assume an increasingly influential role in the intellectual and political affairs of the empire.

Territory seized from the Byzantines created an inviting haven for Syrian Jacobites, Nestorians, and other Christians, who in the seventh and eighth centuries began to flee Constantinople's enforced religious orthodoxy and increasing animosity toward ancient learning. Christian scholars were suddenly free to explore and develop classical teachings under the protection of the Muslims, who traditionally imposed a poll tax on those "People of the Book"—generally Jews and Christians but also Zoroastrians—who chose not to convert to Islam but otherwise left them alone. Important intellectual centers thrived across the region, from Edessa to the Iranian city of Jundishapur, from Harran, in present-day Turkey, to the Central Asian oasis town of Marv, offering the Abbasids a formidable body of indigenous linguistic skills, scientific talent, and cultural knowledge.[5]

Muslim conquest and empire building also restored ancient ties among historic centers of civilization across a huge landmass. This created an invaluable melting pot for intellectual traditions that had been forcibly kept apart for centuries by political divisions: Hellenistic learning that evolved in Greece and, later, Alexandria, on the one hand, and Sumerian, Persian, and Indian wisdom, on the other.[6] Muslims, Christians, Jews, Zoroastrians, the star-worshipping Sabeans, and assorted other pagans were all able to exchange ideas and teachings. Under Abd al-Rahman, the surviving Umayyad prince, and his successors, this same intellectual tradition put down deep roots in Muslim Spain. There, its guardians would one day hand over priceless gifts to the army of Latin scholars who, fired by the example of Adelard of Bath, set off on their own hunt for the *studia Arabum*.

Not all the consequences of Islam's great expansive push were as grand, perhaps, as the confluence of some of the world's great intellectual traditions, but they proved at least as vital. One such was the acquisition of the wondrous Chinese technology of paper, an enormous aid to the intellectual enterprise just beginning to take shape at the Abbasid court. Arab tradition tells us that a prisoner of war from the battle of Talas, where in 751 Muslim forces decisively defeated those of the Tang dynasty for control of Turkic western China, brought the art of papermaking to the Central Asian city of Samarkand. The Chinese prisoner taught his captors how to produce paper from linen and hemp. The story itself is most likely apocryphal, but its general account of the flow of paper technology from China and Central Asia to the Arabs still rings true.

The result was a relatively inexpensive, resilient, and convenient medium for recording information of all kinds—from tax rolls to love poems, from philosophical tracts to star tables. Samarkand soon became the leading Muslim center of papermaking. The art also flourished in Syria, Yemen, North Africa, and the Spanish city of Játiva, which specialized in the production of heavy, glazed sheets. The first mention of a paper factory in Baghdad dates to 795, and the Abbasid capital later boasted a fine stationers' bazaar, the Suq al-Warraqin, featuring hundreds of stalls with high-quality wares. In fact,

Baghdad paper was highly prized around the region, and some Byzantine Greek sources even refer to paper as *bagdatixon*, directly associating the product with the city on the Tigris.[7]

Christian Europe, meanwhile, relied on the painstaking task of reproducing its books and maps on animal skins that had been stretched, scraped clean, and then dried. The resulting parchment was unwieldy, difficult to work with and store, and expensive to make. Paper was none of these, and its ready availability and ease of use and transport accelerated the production and spread of manuscripts throughout the Abbasid Empire and beyond. This in turn allowed the rapid and efficient interchange of ideas and knowledge, prompting demand for further scholarly works, research, and writings. Papermaking also fostered a profound culture of the book among the Arabs. Knowledge and scholarship had always been prized by Muslim society. Now, book bazaars and specialty shops became a regular feature of urban life. Book production, bookbinding, and transcription services all flourished alongside writing, research, and translation. The work of individual calligraphers was prized by discerning buyers, while many of the best copyists also served as editors or authors in their own right. Books were costly to produce, and rare editions were coveted by both intellectuals and the rich and powerful. Price gouging and forgery were not unknown hazards for the unwary, while authors at times found themselves at the mercy of scribes holding out for more money before handing over their completed manuscripts.

Patronage among the elite for authors and their books soon led to the creation of great libraries, some of which were open to the public and featured reading rooms and copying materials. In Damascus, the Umayyads had created the first Arab library, collecting Greek and Christian works on alchemy, medicine, and other sciences. The Fatimid sultans of Egypt were also great collectors of books and patrons of affiliated academies to propagate their Shi'ite beliefs. By the late tenth century, the second Fatimid ruler, al-Aziz, maintained forty rooms filled with books, with the so-called ancient sciences represented in eighteen thousand volumes.[8] When Baghdad's al-Mustansiriya madrassa, or Islamic school, was founded in 1234, its initial endowment was said to have included eighty thousand books donated from the personal library of the caliph.[9] Even private collections were vast, often numbering in the tens of thousands of volumes. These were commonly left as charitable bequests on the death of the owner to mosques, shrines, or schools, where they could be properly looked after and made available to scholarly readers.[10]

Like many other aspects of Muslim public life, much of the Arab book industry revolved around the mosque. Lectures, debates, and discussions on a wide range of religious, scientific, and philosophical issues of the day were common at these houses of worship, which also served as centers of judicial proceedings. According to the fourteenth-century world traveler and writer Ibn Battuta, the Damascus booksellers' market was close to the great Umayyad Mosque; in addition to books, the merchants there sold all the tools of the literary trade, from inks to reed pens to fine paper. However, the book dealers of Baghdad were barred from setting up shop inside the austere walls of the Round City and instead took up residence in a prestigious district to the southwest.[11]

Caliph al-Mansur's decision to forsake Arab-dominated Damascus and base his new capital in Mesopotamia ratified fundamental changes at the heart of the Muslim world. Already, the tribal organization of traditional Arab society was giving way to a new, Islamic culture in which the individual and his family, not the wider clan, were the primary social and political actors. This opened the way for the rise of the recognizably modern city, in which unrelated, ethnically diverse citizens interact with one another under accepted codes of legal and personal conduct.[12] Al-Mansur's ringed city of Baghdad, with its two sets of walls, would represent a radical new beginning for the world of Islam.

Work was completed around 765, and the city's construction along Euclidean lines and at the direction of the most eminent astrologers seemed to promise a great future as an intellectual and scientific center. Even its basic construction techniques proclaimed the dawn of a new age. One of the project's overseers, a jurist and the founder of the oldest of the four schools of Sunni law, Abu Hanifa, abandoned the tiresome counting of the vast quantities of individual bricks needed to build the double ring of walls. Instead, he directed his workmen to use a measuring stick to compute the volume and thus calculate large batches in one easy step.[13]

In many ways the original Round City resembled an expanded version of a classic Persian citadel, built more for reliable defense than for comfort or luxury. At the center sat the caliph's palace, the royal mosque, and the government offices. There were no gardens, pools, or other sources of frivolous diversion. Later, a treasury and residences for al-Mansur's sons were added. Senior military officers, close aides, and loyal partisans received grants of scarce land inside the double rings.[14] The ninth-century historian Ahmad al-Yaqubi says that only the most trusted of the caliph's supporters, men who could be relied upon completely in case of "menacing events," were kept near at hand.[15] Others were given choice land outside the city walls—just in case.

The caliph's prediction that his new city would stand unrivaled proved no empty boast. Proximity to Indian Ocean trade routes, a vibrant multiethnic culture, and safe distance from the traditional military dangers posed by the Byzantine Greeks helped establish Baghdad for centuries as the world's most prosperous nexus of trade, commerce, and intellectual and scientific exchange.[16] Skilled craftsmen, merchants, and other worldly folk rushed in to meet the demands of the city elite. Baghdad then spread along the banks of the Tigris River, its rapid growth and unimaginable wealth fueled by the long reach of its economic muscle, military might, and imperial power. Syrian glassware, Indian dyes and spices, silks and other luxury goods from China and Persia, gold from Africa, and slaves from Central Asia all passed through its markets and enriched its traders.

Nothing survives today of early Abbasid Baghdad, but chronicles, archaeological evidence, and extant examples from the period elsewhere have provided enough hints of the sumptuous lifestyles and domestic surroundings of the rich and powerful. In a tradition that remains throughout much of the Middle East today, the buildings were generally nondescript on the outside, the pedestrian exteriors providing no real indiction of the riches couched within. Internal walls, however, were often covered in stucco that could be worked into rich patterns and designs, festooned with fine textiles and imported wood veneer, or decorated with gold leaf and the rich blue tones of lapis lazuli. Floors were fashioned from ceramic tiles or marble, or decorated with mosaics. Pitchers and goblets were made of glass, while utensils, at least in the case of the caliph, were shaped from gold or silver.[17]

Al-Yaqubi, writing about one hundred years after al-Mansur, offers a breathless description of life in the City of Peace the caliph left behind: "I mention Baghdad first of all because it is the heart of Iraq, and, with no equal on earth either in the Orient or the Occident, it is the most extensive city in area, in importance, in prosperity, in abundance of water, and in healthful climate . . ."[18] Warming to his subject, he meticulously enumerates the residents' many noble attributes: "No one is better educated than their scholars, better informed than their authorities in tradition, more solid in their syntax than their grammarians, more supple than their singers, more certain than their Koran readers, more expert than their physicians, more competent than their calligraphers, more clear than their logicians, more zealous than their ascetics, better jurists than their magistrates, more eloquent than their preachers . . ."

Al-Yaqubi is less impressed with the morals of some of the capital's more colorful residents, bemoaning that never were "voluptuaries" more dissolute.[19] And in fact tales of pleasure, drunken revels, and conspicuous consumption in general among the city's upper crust captured the attention of the literary class. Al-Shabushti's *The Book of Convents*, for example, provides a guided tour of Baghdad's best taverns, many based in local Christian religious establishments. Other writers cataloged the ornate modes of dress, ostentatious furnishings, and other points of style among the well-to-do, while erotic poetry flourished.

Ensconced behind the double brick walls and fortified gates of his new city on the western banks of the Tigris, the energetic al-Mansur set out to turn his disparate dominions into a scientific superpower and to secure the future of the Abbasids by associating their new state with the great classical traditions that had come before them. But first, he had to acknowledge the rising power and influence of the Persians, who played a large role in the success of the rebellion against the Umayyads. According to one account, the caliph publicly celebrated these ardent backers as "the mainstay of our dynasty."[20] Basing his capital in the Persian-speaking heartland, not far from the former imperial capitals of Ctesiphon and Babylon, was a good start. The caliph also invoked key elements of Zoroastrian imperial culture, including its elaborate protocol and heavy reliance on astrology. This affinity for Persian astrology was particularly important, for it suggested that the Abbasids were the ordained heirs to the great Iranian legacy and that their rise was sanctioned by the heavens.[21] And it helped tie astrology to the other emerging scientific disciplines, a tradition the West later found irresistible.

Finally, al-Mansur sought to link the triumphs of classical wisdom, especially those of the Greeks, to the achievements of the ancient Persians. According to the Abbasid ideologues, Alexander's defeat of Darius III and his conquest of Persia in the fourth century B.C. had seen the wholesale transfer of

Iranian learning westward, where it provided the kernel of later Greek advances.[22] Whatever its merits, this Abbasid tradition proved remarkably long-lived. Six hundred years later, the great Arab historian and sociologist Ibn Khaldun issued a similar verdict: "Among the Persians, intellectual sciences played a large and important role, since the Persian dynasties were powerful and ruled without interruption. The intellectual sciences are said to have come to the Greeks from the Persians, when Alexander killed Darius and gained control of the Achaemenid Empire. At that time, he appropriated the books and sciences of the Persians."[23]

Al-Mansur's young court was virtually surrounded by established centers of Christian, Persian, and pagan learning, but he had to go looking for one important element of what might be called Abbasid intellectual policy. At the caliph's invitation, an Indian scholarly delegation skilled in the movements of the stars arrived in Baghdad bearing Hindu scientific texts, an important jumping-off point for early Arab astronomy and mathematics. The Hindu sages understood how to solve equations based on the trigonometric sine function and had devised ingenious ways to predict eclipses. The caliph ordered an official translation of the Hindu material into Arabic, part of an increasingly organized effort to absorb Persian and Indian knowledge. This same approach, accompanied by much original research, would soon be applied with great effect to the third important strand of ancient learning, that of the Greeks.

The earlier Umayyads laid the groundwork for scientific inquiry, but much of their early focus was on questions of Islamic law and the practice of medicine, a field in which they, like their successors, relied heavily on Christian physicians from Syria and Persia. The Abbasid caliphs deliberately pushed back these boundaries to make more room for the study of both philosophy and the hard sciences. According to the Arab historian Said al-Andalusi, who died in 1070, much of the credit for this goes to the founder of Baghdad: "There was a surge in spirit and an awakening in intelligence. The first of this dynasty to cultivate science was the second caliph, Abu Jafar al-Mansur . . . He was—May Allah have mercy on him—in addition to his profound knowledge of logic and law very interested in philosophy and observational astronomy; he was fond of both and of the people who worked in these fields."[24] Another chronicler notes that the caliph directed numerous foreign translations into Arabic, including classic works of Hindu, Persian, and Greek scholars, and set the direction for future research. "Once in possession of these books, the public read and studied them avidly."[25]

To accommodate the vast scale of work needed to translate, copy, study, and store the swelling volume of Persian, Sanskrit, and Greek texts, al-Mansur established a royal library modeled after those of the great Persian kings. Working space, administrative support, and financial assistance were also required for the small army of scholars who would take up these tasks and then build on them in creative and original ways. This was the origin of what became known in Arabic as the Bayt al-Hikma, or the House of Wisdom—the collective institutional and imperial expression of early Abbasid intellectual ambition and official state policy. Over time, the House of Wisdom came to comprise a translation bureau, a library and book repository, and an academy of scholars and intellectuals from across the empire. Its overriding function, however, was the safeguarding of invaluable knowledge, a fact reflected in other terms applied at times by Arab historians to describe the project, such as the Treasury of the Books of Wisdom and simply the Treasury of Wisdom.[26] Experts affiliated with this imperial institution staffed the caliph's observatory as well and took part in scientific experiments at his behest. But the House of Wisdom also played an important role in the cultivation of Abbasid literary works.

Large sums of public funds were dedicated to the House of Wisdom and related projects of cultural and intellectual enrichment. Even diplomacy, and on occasion its cousin war, was harnessed to the drive for greater knowledge. Abbasid delegations to the rival Byzantine court often conveyed requests for copies of valuable Greek texts, successfully securing works by Plato, Aristotle, Hippocrates, Galen, and Euclid. A copy of Ptolemy's astronomical master-piece, soon famous among the Arabs, and later the Latins, as the *Almagest*, was said to be one of the conditions of peace between the two superpowers. The influential ninth-century scholar and translator Hunayn ibn Ishaq provides a taste of the length to which the Arab sages would go to obtain necessary material, in this case a missing medical manuscript: "I myself searched with great zeal in quest of this book over Mesopotamia, all of Syria, Palestine and Egypt, until I came to Alexandria. I found nothing, except about half of it, in Damascus."[27]

The caliphs and their official scholars were not the only ones behind this campaign. The effort became an integral feature of Abbasid society itself and was supported enthusiastically by the social and political elite, from high born princes to merchants, bankers, and military officers. Even the concubines of the caliphs were known on occasion to contract with scholars for specialized translations. A former highwayman and childhood friend of Caliph al-Mamun, the seventh Abbasid ruler, turned his own facility for astrology into vast political power and wealth; he later fathered three children, known as the Sons of Musa, all of whom did original research in astronomy, mathematics, and engineering and generously funded other scholars and translators.

Scholarship and other intellectual endeavors became an important means of social advancement, further breaking down what remained of the Arabs' traditional hierarchy.[28] They also fostered competition for patronage among scholars from different traditions, chiefly Arab and Persian, a phenomenon that ensured that high-quality scientific and literary work would be carried out for centuries.[29] The most skilled translators could earn huge sums for their work—one was reputed to have been paid the weight of each completed manuscript in gold—or rise to high office on the strength of their intellectual accomplishments. Without this institutional support, the considerable talents of the diverse scholars now under Abbasid rule would never have coalesced into a powerful intellectual movement.

Over the course of 150 years, the Arabs translated all available Greek books of science and philosophy. Arabic replaced Greek as the universal language of scientific inquiry. Higher education became increasingly organized in the early ninth century, and most major Muslim cities featured some type of university. One such institution, the al-Azhar mosque complex in Cairo, has been the seat of uninterrupted instruction for more than one thousand years. Scholars traveled great distances to study with the most celebrated masters, dotted throughout the empire. Travel, and the accompanying exposure to new experiences and new ways of thinking, was an important element of a scholar's education in a society that retained great reverence for the spoken word; other than face-to-face, how else could a learned man meet his colleagues and collect and debate their ideas?

The case of one scholar, recounted by the medieval Arab biographer Yaqut in his *Dictionary of Learned Men*, may have been a bit extreme, but it was by no means unheard of in its day. Born in Spain in 1147, this wandering intellectual later traveled to Cairo, then to Mecca, Medina, and Baghdad; from there, he set out for the cities of Persia and on to Afghanistan, before returning to Baghdad;

next came Aleppo, Damascus, and Mosul, followed by return visits to Mecca, Medina, and Cairo. His journeys took seventeen years and yielded a large number of scholarly books.[30] Another eminent intellectual noted that the greatest danger to scholars was the occasional "nuisance of corrupt and wicked highway robbers."[31] Just such an encounter ended the life of one of the Arab world's leading commentators on Aristotle, Abu Nasr al-Farabi, who was murdered by a criminal gang on the road outside Damascus around 950.

Still, the fruit of contemporary intellectual activity was centuries of uninterrupted, organized research and steady advances in mathematics, philosophy, astronomy, medicine, optics, and other pursuits, creating a remarkable body of work that can rightfully be called Arab science. The Muslims referred to this enterprise as *falsafa*—Arabic for the classical idea of "natural philosophy," a complete system of knowledge that encompassed both the physical sciences and metaphysics.

The rise of this new scientific and philosophical tradition generated demand for more, and better, translations from the Greek and other sources; it was not, as Western tradition often has it, the translations that gave rise to Arab science and philosophy.[32] A breakthrough in mathematics or optics, for example, would send Arab scholars back to the Greek literature, which was then translated, reworked, and frequently corrected or otherwise improved. Along the way, new scientific terminology also had to be invented, a task for which Arabic proved to be highly adept. Many of these words—*alcohol*, *alembic*, and *alchemy*, to take just a few examples from the beginning of the alphabet—are today a firm part of the Western lexicon. A tenth-century Arabic manuscript on arithmetic by the Persian mathematician al-Nawasi pays tribute to the precision of the language; the author says in his introduction that he first wrote the book in Persian but had to redo it in Arabic in order to convey his exact meaning. Syriac, the language of early Arab Christian scholars, likewise proved no match for the flexibility and nuance of Arabic. To the dismay of many leading churchmen, their parishioners generally used Arabic in their daily lives as well.[33]

Among the early achievements of the House of Wisdom was a translation of a rather uninspired work by Aristotle on the use of dialectics, chosen specifically to fortify Abbasid theologians against Muslim heretics and followers of the empire's competing faiths. The Arabized Christians, the Jews, and the Manichaeans of Persia, among other inhabitants of the Muslim empire, were all highly skilled at religious polemic, with many centuries of practice behind them. The neophyte Abbasids turned to Aristotle's *Topics* for help, and soon the notion of debate and formal disputation to address religious competition was well established. This in turn helped cement religious law as a central intellectual force within Islam, a step strengthened by the creation of the first religious schools designed specifically to teach such laws and the logical and rhetorical methods for determining and defending religious rulings.[34]

More important translations soon followed, as did incisive commentaries and original research that enriched ancient learning and made it accessible to the contemporary world. Aristotelian ideas and their seeming antagonism to traditional religious teachings soon became central to Arab thought. At first, Muslim thinkers, unlike their medieval Christian counterparts, found religious inspiration to pursue knowledge as a way to come closer to God. Tensions between the demands of faith and reason arose only later. As Christendom slumbered, the House of Wisdom emerged as the first great battleground for the conflict between the dictates of the new sciences and the medieval conception of the One God, which the Muslim Abbasids shared with the Christians and Jews. In the eyes of many theologians from all three faiths, any desire on man's part to understand and even control his environment seemed to clash with traditional notions of God's omnipotence. This paved the way for the same fateful struggle in Christian Europe centuries later.

As a young boy, al-Mamun memorized the Koran at the direction of his father, the legendary Caliph Harun al-Rashid, and then recited it word for word under the watchful eye of the court's leading religious scholar. Whenever the boy made a mistake, the caliph's biographers tell us, the theologian raised his bowed head ever so slightly and the error was immediately corrected.[35] Such memorization of long, complicated texts holds an honored place in traditional scholarship. Muslim authors of all kinds, not only theologians but scientists, poets, and philosophers as well, regularly recalled their original works from memory in public lectures, often delivered in the mosques. These were carefully written down by a star pupil, a favored disciple, or a professional scribe for final approval by the author before publication. Copyists then produced multiple authorized editions for the marketplace. This oral tradition was firmly established among the Muslims with the revelation of the Koran, which was repeated aloud among believers and only later fully transcribed and collated, after the Prophet Muhammad's death. Recitation from memory has retained a strong hold on the Arab imagination ever since.

Certainly, memorizing the Koran seemed to stimulate al-Mamun's intellectual faculties and his inquisitive nature. Unlike his older half brother and rival al-Amin, the future seventh caliph of the Abbasids was always a serious student, something his father had sought to ensure from the beginning. "Let no hour pass without giving him the benefit of some new piece of knowledge, but don't let him be bored or overwhelmed. Don't go too easy on him, and don't allow him to enjoy being idle," al-Rashid is reported to have ordered his son's tutor.[36] And al-Mamun, who reigned from 813 to 833, was later to be the driving force behind some of the greatest achievements of medieval Arab scholarship. Ibn al-Nadim's tenth-century compendium of Arab thinkers says the caliph's intellectual attributes defied enumeration. "We are too rich in famed traditions concerning him to go into detail when mentioning him," al-Nadim reports.[37] One Christian bishop praises al-Mamun's talents after entering a theological debate against Muslim scholars, with the caliph serving as arbiter: "When the renowned philosopher converses with al-Mamun, incapacity of speech dries up his tongue."[38]

A lifelong adept at science and philosophy, al-Mamun also took his astrology seriously, a view shaped by the cultural influences of the Persians in and around the court and soon augmented by translations of important Greek astrological texts. Among the Arabs, astrology long went hand in hand with the other sciences. One royal Baghdad astrologer dubbed it "the mistress of all sciences."[39] The astrologer had to study the nature of things and learn the changing states of animals, plants, and minerals according to the seasons. The expert practitioner of the art had to turn to complex trigonometric functions to capture the elusive movement of the planets. He needed to explore the mysteries of reflection and refraction to account for the projection of planetary rays that influenced events on the distant earth below. And he needed the utmost precision in instrumentation and timekeeping, preparing star tables accurate not just to minutes of degrees but to seconds and beyond.[40] In other words, the successful astrologer needed to possess the profile of the emerging modern scientist.

Throughout the Middle Ages, kings, princes, caliphs, and sultans—

Christians and Muslims alike—consistently sought the guidance of horoscopes and the astrologers who could tease these and other sophisticated readings from the complex motions of the celestial bodies. Few others could afford the full-time services of such rare and learned figures, or support the costly research and observations required for them to practice and refine their art. However, any insight into worldly events, such as a propitious time for war or a politically useful marriage, or simply on the fate of the dynasty, was seen as justifying the huge expense. Besides, many of the best astrologers doubled as valued physicians, personal counselors, or scientific advisers. This arrangement was also highly favorable to the early scientists, for the support of the local potentate offered a fair measure of protection against the more conservative theologians, distrustful of the scientists' activities and wary that these "philosophers" might be tempted to trespass on God's turf.

The integration of these two forces, astrology and classical science, proved a potent incentive for early Arab intellectual development. Some of Baghdad's greatest astrologers were also important translators and editors of major scientific works, and the best among them strove to make accurate astronomical measurements and calculations in support of their prognosticators' art. An early Abbasid text explicitly links the two, proclaiming that both God and the stars had commanded the Arabs to renew the state of the world's learning: "The people of every age and era acquire fresh experiences and have knowledge renewed for them in accordance with the decree of the stars and signs of the zodiac, a decree which is in charge of governing time by the command of God Almighty."[41]

Much of al-Mamun's patronage for the study of the stars was no doubt driven by a royal passion for astrology, but he also evinced a healthy curiosity about the natural world and a predilection for investigation and the scientific method. During a visit to Egypt in 832, the last full year of his life, the caliph sought unsuccessfully to learn the meaning of the ancient hieroglyphs but did manage to break into the Great Pyramid of Giza, only to find that the royal tomb had long since been emptied by robbers.[42] Four years earlier, the caliph launched a systematic program of astronomical studies at the first specialized observatories, established in Baghdad and Damascus, as well as the first large-scale expedition devoted to scientific experimentation.[43] These endeavors reveal how the Arab scientists approached and assimilated the classical texts—as starting points for their own research and studies, not as ends in themselves.

And such projects helped launch the careers of some of early Islam's greatest scientists and intellectuals.

Caliph al-Mamun took a deep interest in the work of the scholars at the House of Wisdom, going there regularly to discuss the latest research, royal funding, and related matters directly with his experts and advisers. He also emphasized greater study of mathematics and astronomy in the work already under way. But even with a phalanx of leading scholars at his disposal, he could not always get the answers he sought. "Al-Mamun wanted to know the size of the earth, so he made some investigations about this and found that Ptolemy had stated in one of his books that the circumference of the earth was so many thousand *stades*," recounts one of the caliph's finest astronomers, Habash al-Hasib. "Thereupon he asked the interpreters about the meaning of *stades* and they gave different interpretations."[44]

With his experts stumped, al-Mamun was determined to find out by measuring the length of one degree of the earth's Great Circle, mapping out an ambitious scientific experiment to solve the riddle. Extending an experiment by the ancient Greek mathematician Eratosthenes, the caliph dispatched two teams of astronomers, surveyors, and instrument makers to the desert plain of Sinjar, near Mosul, where they took initial readings of the sun's altitude before setting off in opposite directions, one group heading due north and the other due south. As they moved, they took care to note the distance they had traveled, inserting special markers into the ground along their path. When a second set of solar readings indicated they had traveled one degree along the meridian, they stopped and retraced their steps, double-checking the distance they had come.

The two independent results were then analyzed and compared, yielding a remarkably accurate final figure. Al-Mamun's researchers' calculation of the circumference of the earth was very close to what we know it to be today. Despite this success, one leading astronomer's account of the mission says that the caliph's teams could have saved themselves a lot of trouble by using one simple observation and some basic trigonometry. "There is another method for the determination of the circumference of the earth. It does not require walking in deserts," sniffs the accomplished mathematical astronomer al-Biruni in his *Determination of the Coordinates of Cities*.[45] Whatever the approach, medieval Arab readings of the position of the sun and the geographic coordinates of cities, determinations of time and date, and related findings

were all of similarly high caliber. The early Islamic observations were not
exceeded for accuracy until the time of Danish astronomer Tycho Brahe in the
sixteenth century.[46]

When things did go wrong, al-Mamun was quick to intervene. He once used
a wartime visit to Damascus to conduct a scientific fact-finding mission, after
data from earlier attempts to chart the sun and the moon across the heavens
from the Baghdad observatory proved grossly inaccurate. The caliph called on
his Syrian advisers to find a qualified astronomer who could improve upon the
Baghdad results. "Al-Mamun ordered him to make ready instruments of the
greatest possible perfection and to observe the heavenly bodies for a whole
year," says Habash al-Hasib. This wealth of astronomical material was then
collated, on al-Mamun's instructions, and published "for those desirous of
learning that science."[47] The chagrined Baghdad astronomers apparently
concluded that their best tack was to blame their tools; a brass instrument
used to take some of the faulty measurements, known as an armillary sphere,
was sold for scrap in the stationers' bazaar.[48]

The founder of Baghdad, al-Mansur, must have had high hopes when he first
sent an emissary to the holy city of Arin, then the Hindu center of astronomy
and mathematics, in search of Indian scholars.[49] A thirteenth-century Hebrew
commentary says the caliph had received word of the teachings of the Indian
sciences and, having satisfied himself that such matters were not contrary to
Islam, sent one of his Jewish subjects to entice the Indians to Baghdad to share
their wisdom.[50] But even the caliph could not have anticipated the profound
effects on Muslim intellectual life that would be produced by the sudden
infusion of a new and alien way of thinking about the physical world. By the
early eighth century, scattered outside influences had already begun to reach the
Arabs by way of early Indian and Iranian star tables. Such tables were known in
Arabic as *zij*, from the Persian word *zik*, or "guiding thread," with their orderly
rows and columns suggesting the warp and woof of traditional weaving. Soon
Arab astronomers, astrologers, doctors, and other men of science were
regularly consulting the *zij* to chart the movement of the heavens and even
to tell time and fix dates. The royal astrologers Mashallah and Nawbakht had
relied on one such Iranian example, the *zij al-Shah*, to fix the date for the
construction of Baghdad.[51]

Still, the visit of the Hindu delegation to the Abbasid court, around 771, marked a true turning point in Arab intellectual history. The Indian sages brought with them prized Sanskrit scientific texts, believed to be in part the work of the seventh-century scholar Brahmagupta and known as the *siddhanta*. According to a tenth-century account by the widely traveled geographer al-Masudi, the documents contained all Hindu knowledge of the spheres, the stars, mathematics, and other sciences.[52] Another account notes the heavy reliance in the *siddhanta* on the sine function—an invaluable contribution developed by the Hindus and later seized upon and refined further by the Arabs—as the basis for all its calculations.[53] By the ninth century, all six trigonometric functions—sine and cosine, tangent and cotangent, secant and cosecant—were known. Only the former was an import; the other five were Arab discoveries. This allowed the substitution of calculations in the place of geometric diagrams, paving the way for the full development of modern mathematical astronomy.[54]

Traditionally, Hindu scientific works were written in verse, for ease of memorization, and offered little if anything by way of explanation, procedures, or proofs. As a result, the early Arab scholars and translators were faced with two immediate challenges: to disentangle the scientific content from the stylized Sanskrit verse and then to discover for themselves the complex arithmetic and astronomical procedures implied in the text. Commentaries that could have shed much light on the latter operation were not part of the Indian largesse.[55] These problems proved both short-lived and ultimately beneficial to the Abbasid quest for knowledge. They forced the Arabs to grapple with the fundamental science of the *siddhanta* literature rather than rely on simple imitation, and they virtually ensured that Iranian and Greek scientific traditions would over time be brought to bear on the questions at hand. In these ways, the initial Arabic translation of the *siddhanta* helped launch a dynamic body of work that culminated in a synthesis of classical and contemporary learning.

No one did more to advance the latest trends and then explain and popularize the results than the mathematician and astronomer Muhammad ibn Musa al-Khwarizmi. Born around 783, al-Khwarizmi was able to take full advantage of the social mobility and intellectual meritocracy that characterized early Abbasid scholarly life in Baghdad. Little is known of his exact origins, although his name suggests that he or his family originally came from Khwarazm—Khiva in present-day Uzbekistan. Al-Khwarizmi's Muslim faith is made clear by the pious prefaces to some of his works, but his forebears may have been Zoroastrians. As a prominent researcher attached to al-Mamun's House of Wisdom, al-Khwarizmi went on to attain rare heights in such disciplines as astronomy, arithmetic, and algebra.

Given his expertise and interests, al-Khwarizmi may well have participated in the caliph's astronomical observations at Baghdad, or even the desert survey of the length of one degree. His work on the *siddhanta*, however, is more certain, for he produced around 825 an abridged version at al-Mamun's request, as well as two famous star tables, known as the *zij al-Sindhind*, which were used for centuries across the Muslim world and later in Christian Europe. Today, al-Khwarizmi's tables stand as the oldest extant example of the Islamic *zij*, although the surviving form has undergone significant modification in the intervening centuries. His work on the astrolabe, likewise the oldest extant Muslim example of its kind, resonated for centuries. "He was one of the masters of the science of the stars," Ibn al-Nadim recounts. "Both before and after [confirmation by] observation, people relied upon his first and second astronomical tables known as the *Sindhind*."[56]

The success and popularity of al-Khwarizmi's *zij* helped establish the star table as a fundamental element of the Arab scientific arsenal, a fact attested to by its widespread use, its remarkable longevity, and its almost continuous refinement. More than 225 such tables were compiled in the Muslim world between the eighth and the nineteenth centuries, although roughly half of these are lost and known only through references in commentaries or other scientific works.[57] Some were computed meticulously to reflect accurate data at a given location, while others were half-understood copies or sloppy redactions of earlier tables. The surviving versions of al-Khwarizmi's tables had their astronomical data transposed for use in Spain's Western Caliphate, where the work retained its popularity long after it had been surpassed by that of Muslim scientists in the East.

A correctly calibrated *zij* provided the user with all the tools needed to pinpoint the positions of the sun, the moon, and the five visible planets; to tell time day or night based on stellar or solar observations, which was especially useful for regulating Islam's five daily prayers; and to determine the possibility of sighting the crescent moon, which marks the start of the Muslim lunar month. The star tables were indispensable for casting a horoscope without time-consuming observations, perhaps their biggest selling point. The *zij* could also be supplemented by the use of astronomical instruments, mostly for solving complex problems in spherical geometry and timekeeping. One thousand years after its creation, the *zij al-Sindhind* of al-Khwarizmi was still in use in Egypt.[58]

The transmission of Hindu astronomy did not, of course, take place in a vacuum but was part of the wholesale Arab campaign to absorb, master, and build upon classical knowledge. The Indians' advanced art of reckoning— characterized by the decimal place system of nine numerals and a zero, virtually the system we use today—either accompanied the handover of the *siddhanta* or followed very quickly on its heels. It was certainly known within decades of the arrival of the Hindu astronomical science.[59] As he did with the *zij al-Sindhind*, al-Khwarizmi produced a successful treatise on the use of the new system, *The Book of Addition and Subtraction According to the Hindu Calculation*, the first known Arabic work on the subject.

"We have decided to explain Indian calculating techniques using the nine characters and to show how, because of their simplicity and conciseness, these characters are capable of expressing any number," al-Khwarizmi informs his readers. He then provides a detailed explanation of the positional principle of decimal notation, with reference to the Indian origin of the nine number symbols, as well as the use of the zero—"the tenth figure in the shape of a circle"—to prevent confusion over the position of the figures.[60]

Al-Khwarizmi's Arabic text has been lost, but it survives in twelfth-century Latin translation, the chief vehicle by which the so-called Arabic numerals were conveyed to the West. For Muslim readers, *The Book of Addition and Subtraction* explained fully a system that was already in some use by the early ninth century, and within a little more than one hundred years it had led to the discovery of decimal fractions. These were used to find the roots of numbers and later to calculate the value of pi—the ratio of the circumference of a circle to its radius—correctly to an impressive sixteen decimal places.[61]

Perhaps no work brings out the genius of al-Khwarizmi, particularly his ability to identify and master an emerging discipline or technology and then explain it fully and effectively, as much as his treatise on algebra. *The Book of Restoring and Balancing*—the second element of the Arabic title, *Kitab al-jabr wa'l-muqabala*, bequeathed the West the term *algebra*—was dedicated to his patron Caliph al-Mamun and wrapped in a shroud of religious and practical utility. "That fondness for science, by which God had distinguished Imam al-Mamun . . . has

encouraged me to compose a short work, . . . confining it to what is easiest and
most useful in arithmetic, such as men constantly require in cases of inheritance,
legacies, partition, law-suits, and trade, and in their dealings with one another, or
where the measuring of lands, the digging of canals, geometrical computation,
and other objects of various sorts and kinds are concerned."[62]

In one example, al-Khwarizmi guides the reader through the settlement of a
woman's estate after she dies and leaves a husband, a son, and three daughters.
Under the prevailing inheritance rules, a husband was entitled to one quarter of
the estate, and a son's share was twice that of a daughter—an improvement
over pre-Islamic Arab practice, in which women generally received nothing.[63]
As al-Khwarizmi shows, a relatively simple algebraic operation solves the
equation for any size estate. More complex problems, including the computation of the annual religious tax, or *zakat*, follow.

Here, then, was the beginning of the Arabs' study of algebra, a field in which
they excelled, as demonstrated by both the large number of scholarly
commentaries on al-Khwarizmi's work and their production of many original
algebra texts. Over the centuries, the pervasive influence of *The Book of Restoring
and Balancing* can be seen in the repeated, verbatim use of several of
al-Khwarizmi's most famous examples of quadratic equations. In his typical
fashion, al-Khwarizmi managed to combine Hindu and early Babylonian
influence in solving such equations by the means of algebra with the Greek
tradition of geometric proofs to validate the results.[64] By stressing the
relationship between analytic and geometric solutions to such problems
and introducing the decimal place system, al-Khwarizmi, for the first time
in mathematical history, established the art of analysis as a worthy discipline in
its own right and put it on an equal footing with the more glamorous
geometry. He also makes clear in later chapters that, his fine introductory
remarks to al-Mamun notwithstanding, he is interested in algebraic theory and
calculation for their own sake.[65]

Much of al-Khwarizmi's intellectual inspiration derived initially from
Indian science. The bulk of his astronomy relies on Hindu tradition and,
to a lesser extent, Persian teachings. The Indian city of Arin, for example, is
used in the *zij al-Sindhind* as the reference point for astronomical measurements,
much as the meridian at Greenwich, England, is used today. One version of the
zij calls Arin the "center of the sphere of the earth."[66] Methods for the
determination of the moon's motion and for measuring the true longitude of a

planet betray the work's strong Hindu roots.[67] Al-Khwarizmi devotes the beginning section of his text to conversions between the different calendar systems of the ancient and contemporary world—Arab, Christian, Egyptian, and Persian—and he takes June 16, 632, the beginning of the reign of the last Persian king before the Muslim conquest, as his starting point, or epoch.

Nonetheless, there are already scattered hints at the growing influence of Greek learning on the Arab sciences contained in the *zij al-Sindhind* and in his other works, particularly the algebra text. This is hardly surprising. Al-Khwarizmi's patron, al-Mamun, presided over the beginning of a turn among the majority of Arab scholars away from early Hindu and Iranian traditions in the hard sciences and toward those of Greece and Hellenistic Egypt. The centerpiece of this flurry of scientific activity under al-Mamun was the translation of Ptolemy's masterwork of classical Greek astronomy, the single most important book among medieval Arab scholars, after the Koran. Ptolemy was born around 100 A.D. and spent his working life in Alexandria, then the center of Greek learning and home to the world's greatest library, forerunner of Baghdad's own House of Wisdom.

There he produced invaluable works on geography and astrology, among other topics, but none was as vital as the book known among the Greeks as the *Megale Syntaxis*, or "the great composition," but later recognized universally by the Arabic corruption of its name, the *Almagest*. Ptolemy's text presents an elaborate and all-encompassing theory of the movement of the fixed stars, the sun, the moon, and the five visible planets—Mercury, Venus, Mars, Jupiter, and Saturn—one that would hold up until the mid-sixteenth century. In terms of Greek science, Ptolemy so dominated the field of astronomy that the works of his most important predecessors virtually disappeared.[68] In the West, which would learn of Ptolemy much later through its encounter with Muslim science, he became a mythic, almost mystical, figure often confused with those heirs to Alexander the Great, the Ptolemaic kings of Egypt; medieval images commonly featured the famous astronomer with a crown on his head.

But for the Arabs, the *Almagest* provided a priceless road map for research and study, so much so that it was subject to periodic retranslation, revision, and commentary by the leading scholars of the House of Wisdom throughout the ninth century and beyond. Al-Mamun's innovative program of astronomical observations at Baghdad and Damascus, for example, was designed to test the results of the *Almagest* and compare them with its own. The star tables that resulted from these experiments eventually superseded those grounded in Hindu science, notably al-Khwarizmi's *zij al-Sindhind*. The caliph's geodetic survey on the hot, dusty plain of Sinjar likewise was motivated by questions culled from a careful reading of the *Almagest*. These and other experiments yielded results that often improved significantly on the data provided by Ptolemy—who was notorious for making relatively few observations of his own and instead relying on the earlier observational work of others. Yet there was no immediate sign that such shortcomings in the master's work dismayed or shocked the Arabs or prompted doubts about the reliability of the general theories presented in the *Almagest*.[69] That would come later, after Arab science and philosophy had matured over the course of several centuries.

The royal endorsement of Greek learning may have had almost as much to do with contemporary politics and diplomacy as with intellectual taste or scholarly analysis. The death in 809 of al-Mamun's father, al-Rashid, sparked a civil war among the Abbasids, and al-Mamun was able to secure power only after a long period of bloody struggle with the forces of his half brother al-Amin. Badly weakened by this war of succession and his own prolonged absence from the capital, al-Mamun took up residence in the Round City determined to centralize political and religious authority in his own hands.

This ruthless consolidation of power was accompanied by a new aggressive tone in the caliph's foreign policy, one that recast the traditional geopolitical rivalry with the adjacent Byzantine Empire in the stark terms of religious struggle. Even here, state intellectual policy came to the fore: In the new Abbasid view, not only were the Eastern Orthodox Byzantines infidels, but they were also guilty of rejecting classical Greek learning after the coming of Christianity. The religious superiority of Islam was augmented by the fact that the Muslims had had the good sense to recognize the genius of ancient Greece. To oppose the Byzantines was to be in favor of Greek learning, and vice versa.[70] Earlier Byzantine harassment of the Nestorian, Syrian, and other eastern Christian scholars, many now taking refuge among the Muslims, appeared to bear out this new propaganda. Al-Mamun was also a supporter of a radical rationalist reading of Islam, a position that appeared to mesh easily with renewed interest in Greek philosophical studies.

Yaqub ibn Ishaq al-Kindi, celebrated as the Philosopher of the Arabs, soon took up the anti-Byzantine refrain. He posited a mythical past in which the ancient forerunners of the Greeks and the Arabs were represented as siblings. It was only natural, al-Kindi suggested, that the Arabs inherit and build upon the earlier work of their brothers, the pre-Christian Greeks, a view that became increasingly entrenched in the Muslim world.[71] One century later, the geographer al-Masudi made the link between the arrival of Christianity and the decline of learning explicit: "During the time of the ancient Greeks, and for a little while during the . . . [Roman] empire, the philosophical sciences kept growing and developing, and scholars and philosophers were respected and honored. They developed their theories on natural science—on the body, the intellect, the soul—and on the quadrivium . . . The sciences continued to be in great demand and intensely cultivated until the religion of Christianity appeared among the Byzantines; then they effaced the signs of philosophy, eliminated its traces, destroyed its paths, and they changed and corrupted what the ancient Greeks had set forth in clear expositions."[72]

The policy of fostering scientific and philosophical activity, research, and innovation addressed the vital political, religious, and diplomatic interests of the early Abbasid state. But one industrious chronicler of medieval Arab intellectual history preferred another explanation, ascribing al-Mamun's passion for the work of the House of Wisdom to a mystical dream. According to Ibn al-Nadim, the sleeping caliph spotted a bald, light-skinned Aristotle sitting on his bed. Overcoming his initial shock at finding himself face-to-face with the great philosopher, al-Mamun asked him to define "that which is good." Aristotle replied that reason and revelation—that is, science and religion— were both good and in the public interest, a response the caliph took as confirmation that scientific scholarship was a religious duty. "The dream," Ibn al-Nadim concludes, "was one of the most definite reasons for the output of books."[73]

Chapter Four

MAPPING THE WORLD

AL-MAMUN'S GREAT Abbasid Empire owed much of its enormous vitality to the spiritual and intellectual energies unleashed two hundred years earlier in a remote corner of the Arabian Peninsula. There, in 610, a former caravan driver and small-time merchant began to receive revelations from God during periodic retreats in the nearby mountains. After receiving his initial revelations, Muhammad was troubled and at first told no one, except his beloved wife Khadija. But he was soon commanded by God to make his message public: "O you enveloped in your cloak, arise and warn (Koran, 74:1–2)."[1]

Muhammad's message of social justice, the need for good works, and the oneness of God attracted some members of Mecca's elite, such as Khadija, herself a wealthy business owner. And it resonated with members of the lesser Arab tribes and the urban poor in his native city of Mecca. But it also drew the anger of many among Mecca's powerful merchant class, grown fat on their command of valuable trade routes and their monopoly over lucrative religious tourism to the city's cube-shaped Kaaba shrine, then a center of traditional idol worship.

In recent decades, the rise of these same wealthy tribes had largely displaced the old order in and around Mecca, reducing the standing and power of Muhammad's own clan, the Banu Hashim, and others like it. In keeping with the Arab tradition of collective clan responsibility, Mecca's oligarchs pressured the Banu Hashim elders to rein in Muhammad before he could destabilize the entire economic and social order. His opponents imposed a boycott against anyone who supported the firebrand preacher. Muhammad found himself the subject of taunts, insults, even an assassination attempt. Loudmouthed cynics demanded that he produce a miracle in support of his revelations. In the face of such pressure, recruitment of new followers tailed off sharply. With the death of his uncle Abu Talib,

Ottoman miniature of astronomers at work with an astrolabe and other instruments in the Galata observatory, Istanbul. (Istanbul University Library, Istanbul/The Bridgeman Art Library)

Aristotle teaching astronomy. The Arab scientific tradition was greatly influenced by the work of the classical Greek scholars, whose "natural philosophy" represented a complete system of knowledge that encompassed both the physical sciences and metaphysics. (Topkapi Palace Museum, Istanbul/ The Bridgeman Art Library)

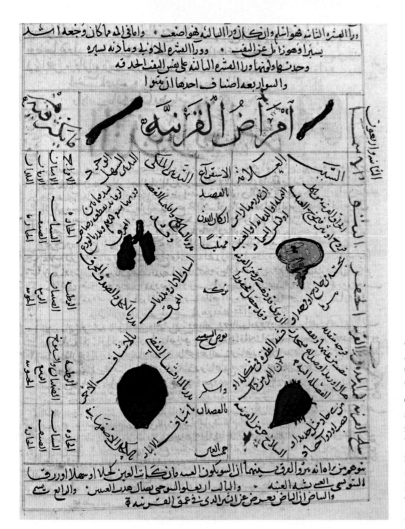

A page from Avicenna's great *Canon of Medicine*, written in the eleventh century. It served as the leading medical text in the West for more than five hundred years. (National Museum, Damascus/ The Bridgeman Art Library)

God creating medicine and bestowing the healing arts on the doctors. From the Latin translation of the Avicenna's *Canon of Medicine*, carried out in Spain by Gerard of Cremona. Gerard was said to have rendered more than seventy Arabic texts into Latin. (Bibliothèque Nationale, Paris/Archives Charmet/The Bridgeman Art Library)

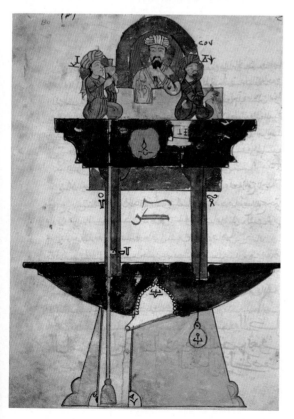

A clepsydra, or water clock, designed by the greatest of the medieval engineers, Ibn al-Razzaz al-Jazari, who flourished in the twelfth century. His technical writings were so accurate that they have been used in modern times to re-create some of his unique machines. (Topkapi Palace Museum, Istanbul/Giraudon/The Bridgeman Art Library)

A European copy of al-Idrisi's Map of the World, originally created at the commission of the Christian ruler of Sicily, Roger II in the mid-twelfth century. (Bibliothèque Nationale, Paris/The Bridgeman Art Library)

A traditional T-O map representing Christian sacred geography, with stylized depictions of the three known continents, Asia, Europe, and Africa. Typically, Jerusalem was placed at the center of a flat earth. (British Library/ The Bridgeman Art Library)

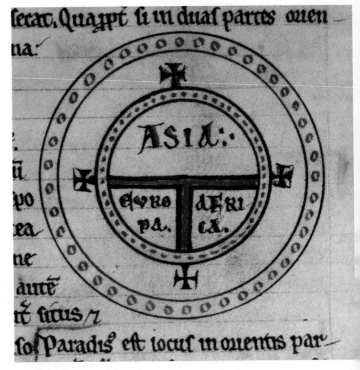

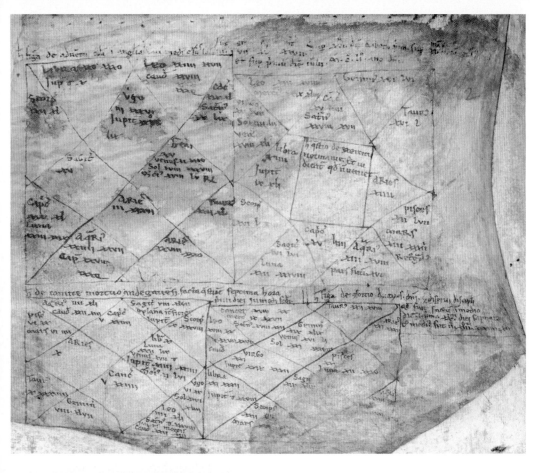

English horoscopes dated to 1151 and thought to be the work of Adelard of Bath, who would have been about seventy years old at the time. The well-traveled scholar and leading Arabist of his day apparently died not long afterwards. (British Library/The Bridgeman Art Library)

Scientists at the Maragha observatory, built in 1259 in what is northwest Iran today. The extraordinary team of astronomers, mathematicians, and engineers assembled at Maragha helped lay the foundation for the revolutionary heliocentric theory of Copernicus. (British Library/The Bridgeman Art Library)

Claudius Ptolemy's *Almagest*—the name comes from the Arabic translation of his work—was the leading astronomy textbook from the second century A.D. until its final overthrow by the Copernicus Revolution fourteen hundred years later. He was a mythical figure for medieval Christendom, which often confused him with the Ptolemies who ruled Egypt after the death of Alexander the Great and portrayed the scientist wearing a crown. (Private Collection/Archives Charmet/The Bridgeman Art Library)

A medieval depiction of geometry, from a thirteenth-century collection of philosophy, science, and poetry. (Bibliothèque Sainte-Genevieve, Paris/The Bridgeman Art Library)

A Muslim and a Christian playing a duet on the lute, from thirteenth-century Spain. This work was dedicated to Alfonso the Wise, the Christian ruler of Castile, Leon, and Galicia. (Monasterio de El Escorial, El Escorial, Spain/The Bridgeman Art Library)

The constellation of the dolphin, from the *Liber Introductorius* of Michael Scot. Michael was the influential translator of Averroes, and a scientist and mathematician in his own right. He was widely suspected of sorcery. (British Library/The Bridgeman Art Library)

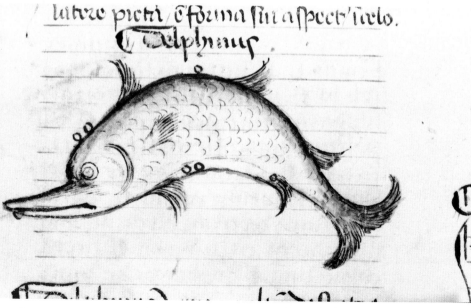

A diagram by the mathematician al-Biruni, one of the most accomplished scholars of the medieval world. He was the first to determine accurate geographic locales with the techniques of spherical trigonometry. (Copyright © British Library Board. All rights reserved/Or. 5593, f.6v)

Muhammad lost the protection of the leading voice among the Banu Hashim. Life in Mecca was no longer tenable.

The result was the emigration, called the *hijra*, in 622 of Muhammad and a small band of followers north to the oasis town of Medina, an event that would prove so momentous that it was later taken as the starting point for the Islamic calendar and thus for all of Muslim history. Muhammad had cut a deal with Medina's fractious Arab tribes, mostly pagans but also several important Jewish clans: He would arbitrate their interminable disputes in exchange for protection for himself and his supporters against the merchants of Mecca. Once Muhammad was secure in this new base, his relationship to the young community of believers around him and the content of his preaching began to change dramatically.

Revelations from the Meccan era, recorded among the 114 chapters of the Koran, are largely in the age-old Near Eastern tradition of spiritual warning. They were revealed to Muhammad over the course of more than two decades and consist of brief messages, generally in rhymed prose, calling on humanity to mend its ways and please the one true God before Judgment Day. For their part, the Holy Book's Medina sections, longer and more detailed, generally reflect more quotidian concerns. They also provide specific guidelines for ordering the political, social, and economic affairs of Muhammad's growing number of followers.[2] Only now is he portrayed as the messenger of God, the last of the line of divine prophets that includes Abraham, Moses, and Jesus.[3]

There is every indication that Muhammad had high hopes that his preaching would find favor among Medina's Jews, less powerful than they once were but still important players in the political and economic life of the town. After all, Muhammad must have reckoned, his central message of strict monotheism augmented that which had already been spelled out to the Jews by their prophet, Moses; surely the influential tribes of Medina would recognize that and once again conform their behavior, which had drifted badly over the years, to the word of God.[4] The period immediately surrounding the *hijra* saw a number of attempts by Muhammad to woo Jewish support. These included recognition of the Jewish Sabbath, fasting on the traditional Day of Atonement, general alignment with Jewish dietary laws, and the practice of intermarriage. Some have found suggestions in the Koran that Muhammad may have at one point considered a sort of federation linked by shared religious precepts.[5] "Say: O People of the Scripture! Come to an agreement between us

and you: that we shall worship none but God . . . and that we shall ascribe no
partner unto Him, and that none of us shall take others for lords beside God"
(3:64).

Perhaps the most public expression of Muhammad's early policy toward the
Jews was the decision shortly after his arrival in Medina to adopt the Jewish
notion of reciting daily prayers in a specific direction, known in Arabic as the
qibla. Facing Jerusalem during prayer was an established tradition among the
Jews. The Bible recalls that King Solomon built the First Temple in Jerusalem
and then declared that the Jews would henceforth "pray to the Lord in the
direction of the city which You have chosen, and in the direction of the House
which I built in Your name" (I Kings, 8:44). Solomon's promise became
incorporated into Jewish law, and early synagogues were generally constructed
in accordance with this dictate.

Any hopes Muhammad may have had for mass support among the Jews of
Medina proved unfounded. It soon became clear that the leading Jewish tribes
were not prepared to accept his teachings. Nor would they recognize him as a
true prophet. In response, the Muslim leader began to step up political pressure
on the Jews, while the later revelations collected in the Koran sharpened the
intellectual and theological challenge to Judaism. In particular, the Jews were
reproached for worshipping the golden calf, a throwback to impermissible idol
worship, and for developing a legal code outside the strict confines of biblical
teachings. As Islam first began to emerge as a faith in its own right, it adopted a
month of fasting, as distinct from the single day set aside by the Jews. To
distinguish his message from earlier revelations, Muhammad began to stress his
spiritual ties to Abraham, who preceded the Jewish and Christian prophets.
Abraham, the Muslims now taught, founded the sanctuary at Mecca, the
Kaaba, and prayed for a prophet from the ranks of the city dwellers there.[6]
Sealing his break with the Jews, Muhammad abandoned their traditional
Jerusalem-facing *qibla* for that of the Kaaba. According to some early Muslims,
he did so while leading communal prayers by turning abruptly toward Mecca,
at a place known ever since as the Mosque of the Two Qiblas.[7]

The notion of sacred geography, measured less by the cartographer's
coordinates than by spiritual need or scriptural reading, has long flourished
in the human imagination. Its contours are shaped by religious experience
grafted to common understandings of time and space, rather than by the
physical features of the earth or the shifting political boundaries of city, state,

or nation. The pilgrimage site, the scene of miracles, or the setting of another holy event—all may define the topography of the sacred map. Perhaps nowhere has this idea proved more compelling than in the Near East, birthplace of the three major monotheistic faiths. Here, geographies sacred and profane intersect in the ritual of prayer and in competing claims on holy space, as believers seek to align themselves physically with the divine.

Among the Muslims, the precise direction of prayer took on great religious, cultural, and political importance. As a result, Islam has historically gone to considerable lengths to define and determine the *qibla* and to honor the sacred geography centered on the *qibla*'s terminus at the ancient Kaaba— timeless symbol of God's power and presence. In addition to the daily devotions, accurate knowledge of the *qibla* is required for the ritual slaughter of animals for food, the burial of the dead, and the call to prayer. The location of Mecca is, of course, also crucial for the hajj, the once-in-a- lifetime pilgrimage, which is a religious obligation for any able-bodied Muslim who can afford the trip. Over time, a huge theological and scholarly enterprise grew up around the observation of Islam's sacred geography in general and the *qibla* in particular.

Today, many tend to see religion as the enemy of scientific progress. Yet early Islam openly encouraged and nurtured intellectual inquiry of all kinds. Muhammad once said of the pursuit of knowledge, "Seek for science, even in China." Another of the many sayings attributed to the Prophet, carefully collected, collated, and studied down through the centuries and known as the hadith, celebrates scholars as the true "heirs to the prophets." The hajj, meanwhile, ensured the annual gathering of Muslims from all over, creating a global marketplace of ideas, innovation, learning, and cultural exchange.

Arab scientists and philosophers readily found divine support for science in the revealed word of God. A number of verses in the Koran refer to the order inherent in God's universe and to man's capacity to recognize and exploit this order for his own needs, such as keeping time: "He [God] it is who appointed the sun a splendor and the moon a light, and measured for her stages, that you might know the number of the years, and the reckoning [of time] . . . He details the revelations for people who have knowledge" (10:6). Elsewhere, the Holy Book advocates the use of elements of God's creation for orientation amid the featureless deserts and navigation across the vast oceans: "He has appointed the night for stillness, and the sun and the moon for reckoning . . .

And He it is Who has set for you the stars that you may guide your course by them amid the darkness of the land and the sea" (6:97–98).

At the same time, many of Islam's rituals and obligations as laid out by the Prophet demanded a relatively sophisticated understanding of the natural world. Believers could not simply follow the advice of the Christian philosopher St. Augustine and allow piety to close their eyes "to the course of the stars." Rather, Muslims must know the proper times of the five daily prayers, the direction of Mecca, and the start of the lunar fasting month of Ramadan. "Knowing the prayer times is a prescribed duty for discerning Muslims. This is summarized in the Koran, my friend, and was explained by [the Prophet Muhammad] . . . There is no virtue in a person who is neglectful of the prayer times, and he has no knowledge of Him who is to be worshipped," writes the medieval astronomer Ibn Yunis.[8]

Such problems of religious practice were addressed with relative ease by the early believers, grouped in a few communities in and around the Arabian Peninsula. For the most part, the ways of Muslim folk astronomy—based on visual cues and lacking the scientific astronomers' theoretical basis—were sufficient. This was particularly the case in the regulation of the prescribed daily devotions, often denoted by the changing shadows cast by a special stick, called a gnomon, inserted into the ground or built into a sundial. The present-day definition of the prayer times dates back to the eighth century, with each to be completed within a certain period as marked by astronomical signs. The daytime devotions are defined by the length of the shadows, while those at night are tied to observable celestial events. The first prayer is said after sunset, the traditional start of the Muslim day, and must be completed before nightfall. The second is recited after nightfall, while the third is completed shortly before sunrise. The fourth, commonly known in the West as the noon prayer, actually begins when the sun has already begun its decline from the meridian, directly overhead. The final, afternoon prayer is also marked by the progression of the shadow and must be finished before the sun goes down, marking the end of one day and the beginning of the next.[9]

Early Muslim scholars immediately grasped the importance of grounding their research in the faith, and many devoted the opening passages of treatises, commentaries, and other highly technical works to asserting the importance of their science to the daily concerns of the pious. This same concentration on practical issues may have left them vulnerable at times to conservative backlash.

Once such problems were solved to the satisfaction of the believers, Muslim science would need to find new justifications for further study.[10] But for now, faith and reason made for provocative bedfellows.

The rapid spread of Islam across much of the known world that followed in the years after Muhammad's death began to put the accurate determination of time, date, and direction out of reach of basic folk astronomy. By the time of the Abbasid Empire, the Muslim seafarer off the Chinese coast, the Arab merchant in faraway Spain, the pious believer in remote Central Asia—all required information that was increasingly hard to communicate from a distant central authority. The desire to observe religious obligations uniformly across the great expanse of Muslim territory mirrored the unanswered plea from Emperor Constantine four centuries earlier for all of Christendom to agree on a single recognized date to celebrate Easter. It also neatly complemented the intellectual ferment induced by the policies of the Abbasid court. Under the patronage of the early caliphs, the demands of religion and the imperatives of science were free to interact for centuries in ways unimaginable in medieval Europe. They also created ample scope for early work on fundamental scientific principles. Invaluable spin-offs included breakthroughs in geography, instrumentation, optics, and navigation.

At first the muezzin, the town crier to daily prayer, was selected for his upstanding character and strong voice with which to summon the faithful from the top of the minaret. Over time, knowledge of the heavens was added to the list of requirements. "Only an honorable, reliable, and trustworthy man who is acquainted with the times of prayer may pronounce the call to prayer from the minaret . . . The muezzin must know the [twenty-eight] lunar mansions and the shapes of the star groups in them, so that he may be able to tell time at night," advises the Egyptian commentator Ibn al-Ukhuwwa.[11] In urban areas, the rise of the mosque-based timekeeper, a sort of holy astronomer, gradually displaced the older folk customs. These professional scientists regulated local prayer times, but they also built astronomical instruments, wrote treatises on spherical astronomy, and taught students. Their work included the production and publication of meticulous almanacs—from the Arabic *al-manakh*—that listed the prayer times for each day of the year in such distant locales as China and Morocco. In medieval Cairo, a leading center of such activity, some two hundred pages of special tables were available for keeping time by the sun and other celestial markers.

Perhaps nowhere was the interaction of faith and science more important than in the question of the *qibla*, seen in the careful arrangements in all mosques to orient the believer. The earliest Muslims of Central Asia and Spain simply directed their prayers to the south, in imitation of the Prophet Muhammad when he was in Medina, 270 miles to the north of the holy city and the Kaaba. As the Arabs' understanding of their universe became more sophisticated, they naturally demanded greater accuracy in conforming their practice to the sacred geography of Islam. "The Kaaba with respect to the inhabitants of the world is like the center of a circle with respect to the circle. All regions face the Kaaba, surrounding it as a circle surrounds the center, and each region faces a particular part of the Kaaba," writes the twelfth-century religious jurist Zayn al-Din al-Dimyati.[12] But where, exactly, was Mecca?

One common approach invoked pre-Islamic Arabian directional systems of the four winds—the word *qibla* itself may derive from the traditional name of the prevailing easterly wind, *qabul*[13]—while others relied on the positions of prominent stars, the direction of the winter sunrise, or other easily observed phenomena. Another popular schema identified the four corners of the Kaaba with each of Mecca's traditional regional trading partners: Syria, Iraq, Yemen, and "the West." Thus, sacred geography easily complemented established practical systems used for centuries by the Arabs' desert caravans and ocean-going merchant fleets as they followed traditional trade routes. Over time, finer distinctions were made by associating more narrow geographic zones with specific architectural features of the shrine, such as a waterspout or a doorway.[14] A thirteenth-century Yemeni text, exquisitely titled *The Sun, the Moon, and the Movements of the Fixed Stars Made Easy as a Gift to the Desirous and a Luxury for the Seeker*, spells out a system of twelve geographic sectors centered on the Kaaba. Other versions featured as many as seventy-two divisions.[15]

Such informal systems found favor with the Muslim jurists, who generally agreed that they met the requirements of the faith. But at times, confusion and conflict over the correct *qibla* prevailed. In one far-off land, for example, bewildered believers were faced with four different choices: One school of thought favored due west, in the direction of the traditional pilgrimage road to Mecca; another advocated the older, southern tradition of the Prophet at Medina; a third honored the *qibla* of the region's earliest mosques; while a fourth preferred to leave the matter up to the astronomers.[16] The use by the Muslims of earlier religious structures—such as synagogues or churches, with existing *qiblas* of their own—further complicated the picture. A mosque in the Negev Desert has been found with two different *qiblas*, one facing east toward Jerusalem and a later one, south toward the Kaaba.[17] To this day, the prayer niches of many mosques fail to point the correct way to Mecca. This is particularly a problem in distant Indonesia, where lengths of string or other markers are commonly used to correct the *qibla*.[18]

Understandably, such a state of affairs failed to satisfy the new breed of medieval Arab scientists, well versed in trigonometry, spherical geometry, and astronomy. One of the greatest Arab treatises on mathematical geography was a work by al-Biruni, written in the eleventh century, on finding the direction of Mecca from a city in Afghanistan.[19] *The Determination of the Coordinates of Cities* was the first in the history of the field to determine accurate geographic locales with the techniques of spherical trigonometry. His exacting approach was designed to replace the difficult and less reliable method then in widespread use for determining differences in longitude: the simultaneous observation of a lunar eclipse from two distinct points. Al-Biruni's dedication to his science was so absolute, we are told, that "his hand scarcely ever left the scroll, nor his eyes ceased observing and his heart pondering except on the two . . . [Persian holidays], Nowruz and Mihragan."[20] While his work contains some minor errors, it was not surpassed in any meaningful way until the nineteenth and even twentieth centuries.[21] For the likes of al-Khwarizmi, al-Biruni, and their empirically minded colleagues, the huge expanse of the Arab empire also fueled the arts of mapmaking and navigation, drove the development of portable scientific instruments such as the astrolabe, and created scope for major advances in many other disciplines that would later prove essential to Western science.

Astronomy and related disciplines were not the only beneficiaries of Islam's flush of enthusiasm for learning. Magic, experimentation, and science all came together in the form of *al-kimia*, the cornerstone of modern chemistry. Controversy over whether it was acceptable in theological terms to depict man and animals in art led to the heavy use of precise, stylized decoration for public structures, ceramics, and textiles that captured the Muslims' highly developed understanding of geometry. A mathematical study in 2007 found that medieval Muslim architects had worked out complex mosaic patterns using just five different shapes of tiles that could in theory form patterns that were infinitely large yet never repeated. One example from a fifteenth-century Muslim shrine in the Iranian city of Isfahan displays geometric patterns whose underlying mathematics was only understood in the West five hundred years later.[22]

Koranic injunction on the need to heal the sick, meanwhile, spurred enormous gains in medicine and the creation of advanced hospitals, complete with such innovations as specialized wards, regular doctors' rounds, free health care for indigent patients, and humane treatment of the insane. Grounding their work in Greek learning initially passed along by Nestorian Christians fleeing Byzantine religious persecution, the Arabs went on to develop new medicines and new methods for preparing the active ingredients of these drugs. They made important discoveries in the field of vision and optics and advances in surgery. Revealing an early and growing recognition of germs and other disease pathways, the authorities chose to base Baghdad's main hospital at a site where tests had shown that raw meat putrefied most slowly.

Major medical schools were established in Damascus, Baghdad, Cordoba, and Cairo. The Persian physician and philosopher Avicenna's eleventh-century *Canon of Medicine* served as the leading medical text in the West for more than five hundred years, while the medical school at Salerno, in southern Italy, was a primary conduit conveying Muslim medical learning to Western Europe. Adelard of Bath visited Salerno during his grand tour, but there is no record that he ever delved into the healing arts. Unlike the medieval Christian West, which tended to view illness and disease as divine punishment, the Arab physicians looked for imbalances or other physical causes that could be treated as part of their religious mission.

Islam also places a premium on personal hygiene, a fact underscored by the ritual washing of the hands, feet, and face before each of the five daily prayers. Many medieval mosques and other public buildings featured sophisticated water-delivery systems, a field in which early Arab engineers excelled. Among the innovations they pioneered were elaborate feedback mechanisms and automatic controls to regulate machinery without human intervention. Other developments included the twin-cylinder pump with true suction and the crankshaft, for the efficient transmission of power. The latter did not begin to appear in European machines until the fourteenth century.[23] A treatise from 1206 by the greatest of the medieval engineers, Ibn al-Razzaz al-Jazari, discusses water clocks and candle clocks, wine dispensers, sophisticated fountains, and musical automatons—most famously, a programmable drum machine consisting of four figures in a boat—as well as advanced systems for raising water from wells, cisterns, and the like. His descriptions are so accurate that they have been used in modern times to re-create some of his unique machines.[24]

As the symbolic heir to the Prophet, Caliph al-Mamun was responsible—at least in theory—for the religious well-being of the vast community of believers. At the same time, he was the head of an enormous empire, with all the attendant political, economic, military, and administrative complexities. For help with both realms, the spiritual and the temporal, the caliph turned to the scholars at the House of Wisdom. Inquisitive by nature and well disposed toward science by upbringing, he called on these experts to determine the precise locations of Baghdad and Mecca in order to define the correct, religiously mandated qibla. Such information would also aid the hajj pilgrims, who were interested in the distance to Mecca, as well as the shortest route to the Kaaba, and assist in proper observation of the sacred lunar calendar. The latter was particularly tricky. Religious practice dated the start of the month to the first sighting of the new moon, requiring the astronomer to know the lunar orbit as well as the corresponding positions of the sun and the earth in order to predict "crescent visibility." Like any self-respecting potentate, the Abbasid caliph also wanted an accurate portrayal of the length and breadth of the world now at his feet.

For the astronomers and other scientists from the House of Wisdom, all of these matters could be reduced to fundamental problems of spherical geometry. With the help of the ancients, they had mastered the system of geographic coordinates—that is, the use of imaginary circles of longitude and latitude girding the earth to provide each point with a unique, identifiable location. Unlike medieval Christendom, Islam offered no resistance to the classical notion of the earth as a globe; from the start, Arab scholars readily applied the mathematics of the sphere to questions of geography. From Ptolemy, author of the *Almagest* and the almost equally influential *Geography*, these scientists learned of the problem of projection, the representation of the round surface of the earth on a flat, two-dimensional map. Al-Mamun's geodetic survey in the desert plains of Sinjar had already yielded the length of one degree in Arabic units of measurement, while the Muslims' corrections and additions to

Ptolemy's table of coordinates for eight thousand cities and other locales provided new, more accurate data for astronomers and geographers alike.

Taken together, the information and techniques developed by al-Mamun's experts and others like them—basically a matter of geometry and trigonometry applied to the sphere of the earth—could determine the *qibla* with remarkable accuracy from the local north-south meridian along the Great Circle of the earth's globe. The tradition of sacred geography defined the *qibla* as a "commonsense" straight line between the believer and Mecca, but the mathematicians and astronomers of the House of Wisdom knew that the spherical shape of the earth meant that the true *qibla* was in reality a curved line at a specific angle from the point of prayer, known to this day by the term *azimuth*, from the Arabic *al-sumut*. This difference between the two approaches to the problem of the *qibla* became more pronounced as the distance from Mecca increased, and it was a measure of the influence of the mathematical astronomers that theirs was generally adopted as the consensus among believers. Such a system of Great Circle measurement lies at the foundation of modern-day calculations of geographic distance and direction.[25] It also formed the basis for one of al-Mamun's greatest scientific triumphs, the construction of a world map, with an accompanying description of the earth's people, places, and wonders and an updated table of geographic coordinates to aid future research.

Such efforts were not unknown in the early Muslim world. Al-Masudi tells us that two hundred years before al-Mamun's day, the early Muslim authorities sought information on the expanding realm of Islam. "The custodians of the tradition say that when by Allah's will the Muslims conquered the lands of Iraq, Syria, Egypt and other countries, [Caliph] Umar ibn al-Khattab wrote to one of the learned men of the age: 'We are nomads, and Allah made us conquer these lands, and we want to settle in them and dwell there. Describe therefore to us the towns, their air, their position, how people are affected by the land and the air.'" According to al-Masudi, the sage responded with descriptions of Syria, Egypt, Iraq, and parts of Persia but deliberately omitted any word of India, China, or the West. "You do not need any description of them, for they are very far and out of the way, countries of unbelievers and tyrants."[26]

Al-Mamun and his researchers could also rely on some more technically proficient works, including early military maps and surveys and detailed accounts of the Muslim empire's elaborate system of post roads, complete with records of routes, distances, and travel times. Stone markers showing the distance from Baghdad have been found as far away as Palestine and Georgia, in Caucasia.[27] The postmaster and head of intelligence in northwest Persia later compiled a famous survey of such data into *The Book of Roads and Kingdoms*. Merchants, sailors, spies, and postal authorities across the empire were ideal sources of information for the caliphs and their administrators back in the Abbasid capital. *The Book of Roads and Kingdoms* also includes major sea routes to Persia, Bahrain, Oman, and Yemen and beyond to Cambodia, the Malay Peninsula, and finally the harbor at Canton, China.[28] Similar works in this vein later added a wealth of economic data, useful for trade, tax collection, and related imperial matters.

Still, al-Mamun had far greater ambition for his world map and its account of human geography. He assembled a team of several dozen scholars. The scope of the project, says al-Masudi, included nothing less than "the universe with its spheres and stars, the land and the sea, inhabited and uninhabited parts, the populated areas of the peoples, cities and similar aspects."[29] A later account, by Abu Abdallah al-Zuhri, reports that along with prominent geographic features, the royal geographers of early ninth-century Baghdad included "what famous and marvelous things are to be found in individual parts of the earth and what historical monuments and edifices are to be found in the individual countries."[30] Among these "famous and marvelous things" was a geographically accurate description of the Great Wall of China.

In addition to such curiosities, the Mamun map and survey depicted 530 important cities and towns, five seas, 290 rivers, and 200 mountains, nothing their estimated size and any deposits of metals or precious stones. These features were apportioned among the seven so-called *climata*, the traditional Greek division of the known world into equal parallel zones extending northward from the equator. This system had been introduced to the Arabs by Ptolemy, but the scholars of al-Mamun made some refinements, including the introduction of two new, barely inhabited zones just below the equator to conform to more up-to-date information at their disposal. They also revised the length of the Mediterranean, reducing Ptolemy's measurement of sixty-two degrees of longitude to fifty-two degrees; this was later trimmed again in the early eleventh century by Arab geographers to forty-two degrees, very near to its modern value.[31] Most important of all, the caliph's scholars corrected Ptolemy's traditional representation of the Indian Ocean as a landlocked sea and, for the first time, made it clear that a global body of water surrounds the inhabitable world[32]—a significant breakthrough in the history of cartography that prefigured by six hundred years the coming of Europe's so-called Age of Discovery, beginning in the mid-fifteenth century.

The sustained effort of such a large team of geographers, mathematicians, and other scientists would have been impossible without the personal interest and support of al-Mamun, whose death in 833 coincided with the completion of the project. Individual Muslim scholars then developed and refined the disciplines of geography and cartography over the succeeding centuries. Such an evolution was in keeping with the Arabs' fundamental view of scholarship, that it was a dynamic process in which succeeding generations built on the work of their forerunners and all were united in a single grand enterprise. In the case of geography, the next phase was dominated by detailed descriptions of peoples, cultures, and the environment.

This increasingly popular endeavor saw sophisticated travel writers and ethnographers gradually replace the mathematical astronomers behind the Mamun map and similar research. Such works were in the same tradition as Usama ibn Munqidh's *Book of Contemplation*, that entertaining and edifying account of the Christian newcomers to the Middle East. In addition to its literary appeal, this new human geography also met the growing demands of central state administrators for better information on the lands and peoples under their dominion. Notably, it exhibited the Arabs' genius for exploring in great detail the foreign practices, beliefs, and lifestyles of the cultures they encountered across the empire and beyond. This genre, writes one of its leading practitioners, Muhammad ibn Ahmad al-Muqaddasi, "pleases the king as well as the beggar."[33]

This quip must not be allowed to obscure the seriousness of purpose behind al-Muqaddasi's classic text, *The Best Divisions for Knowledge of the Regions*, completed in 985 and based on two decades of travel and exploration across the Muslim world. His work is particularly notable for its insistence on the primacy of material that he has collected personally; such an approach, al-Muqaddasi notes with a touch of self-pity, at times subjected him to severe privation and "cost lots of money." It is only when he is physically unable to reach an area that interests him that he is forced to rely reluctantly on the reports of others, but only "men of intelligence, whom I knew to be neither careless nor confused."[34] Throughout, al-Muqaddasi deliberately invokes the legal tradition of the Muslim jurists, with their strict hierarchy of religious sources. In this system, the Koran is the supreme authority, followed by the sayings of the Prophet, the hadith. Next comes the consensus of the theologians, and finally the art of legal reasoning by analogy. However, al-Muqaddasi dismisses the use of analogies as completely unsuitable for the geographer's art.[35]

Such precision in identifying the source of information and the insistence, wherever possible, on personal observation and experience is a hallmark of medieval Arab science. It is also the invaluable legacy of Islam's religious traditions, in which enormous efforts were devoted to preserving and assessing critically the chain of transmission for any recorded saying of Muhammad. Thus, each such statement is accompanied by a scholarly pedigree that spells out whether it is "strong" (that is, reasonably certain to reflect the Prophet's words and intent) or "weak" (of dubious provenance and thus of little value for jurists and theologians). Al-Muqaddasi, too, puts an explicit premium on direct experience over hearsay: "This book of ours, then, falls into three parts: first, what I myself have witnessed; second, what I have heard from persons worthy of confidence; and third, what I have found in books devoted to this subject . . . No royal library remained without my persistent examination of it, no literary works of any sect that I have not scrutinized, no people with whose opinions I have not acquainted myself; there is no group of ascetics with which I did not mingle, no preachers anywhere whose convocations I have not attended. In this way, I attained to the soundness of knowledge I strove for in this science."[36]

Some time around 1138, the Arab scholar and fallen aristocrat al-Sharif al-Idrisi received one of the most remarkable invitations in the history of science. A widely traveled poet, pharmacologist, and botanist—his technical works give the names of plants in Arabic, Persian, Latin, Greek, Berber, and Sanskrit—al-Idrisi was offered a once-in-a-lifetime commission to oversee the production of a new world map, to be etched into a three-hundred-pound silver disk by royal engravers, and to write an accompanying text of descriptive geography.[37] Only this time, the patron was neither caliph nor sultan, but the upstart Christian king of once-Muslim Sicily, Roger II.

Roger's Norman forebears arrived in Sicily, mostly as mercenaries in the service of local Christian and Muslim warlords, in the early eleventh century and decided to stay. They gradually increased their hold on the island and

made significant inroads on the southern Italian mainland, then mostly
inhabited by Greeks under Byzantine rule. When Roger reached the age of
maturity, in 1112, he resolved to make the former Arab administrative center
of Palermo his permanent capital. In a colorful description of the city three
decades after Roger's death, the travel writer Ibn Jubayr sets aside his bitterness
at the Christian conquest just long enough to praise Palermo's charms: "It is an
ancient and elegant city, magnificent and gracious, and seductive to look upon.
Proudly set between its open spaces and plains filled with gardens, with broad
roads and avenues, built in the Cordoba style, entirely from cut stone . . . The
king, to whom it is his world, has embellished it to perfection and taken it as
the capital of his Frankish kingdom—may God destroy it."[38]

Ibn Jubayr, whose accidental visit was the result of a shipwreck on his way
back to Muslim Spain after completing the hajj, found a city and a kingdom at
the very meeting point of East and West. At a time when many of his
contemporaries, including some close family members, were inflamed with the
ideology of holy war, Roger II deliberately settled into his predominantly
Muslim city, then home to more than three hundred mosques. He adopted
Islam's established approach to religious minorities, assessing a special poll tax
on the Muslims and Jews but generally leaving them to manage their own
affairs. He promulgated new laws that expressly recognized existing religious
customs and traditions, organized the state bureaucracy along Arab lines, and
promoted Muslim retainers to some of the state's most powerful positions.[39]
Roger even entrusted important military units to his Arab subjects. The
majority of the king's foot soldiers and many of his horse archers were
Muslims, a fact that scandalized the visiting archbishop of Canterbury.[40] Arabs
also comprised the bulk of the royal corps of engineers, responsible for the
construction of fortifications, one of Roger's keen interests, and for building
and operating his fearsome mangonels and others engines of war.[41]

Roger also patronized the island's Arab artists, artisans, and craftsmen. A
royal cloak created for the king around 1133 of the finest silk, now in a
museum in Vienna, bears a distinctive Islamic design and an inscription in
Arabic: "[This mantle] belongs to the articles worked in the royal treasury, in
which fortune and honor, prosperity and perfection, merit, and distinction
have their home."[42] Sicilian architecture under the Normans, including
churches and chapels, features a compelling amalgam of mostly Arab and
Eastern Christian design. Muslim poets were active at court, and the work of

six survives in a twelfth-century Arabic compendium kept short by its editor so as not to offend religious sensibilities with its praise of the "infidel Normans."[43] The only extant depiction of Roger, a mosaic in the Church of la Martorana in Palermo, shows the king with full black beard and mustache and dressed in Byzantine imperial robes with stylized Arabic Kufic script in the background.[44] No wonder one prominent Arab chronicler reports that rumors swirled among the people that their king was really a secret Muslim, a reputation no doubt enhanced by Roger's frequent clashes with the popes and his refusal to endorse the Crusades.

Still, it is not clear how eager al-Idrisi was to settle in a Christian kingdom, albeit one as highly Arabized as Roger's Sicily, and the circumstances surrounding his commission remain vague. The Arab chroniclers generally pay him scant attention in later life, perhaps a sign of disapproval over his association with the infidel king.[45] At one point, Roger resorted to thinly veiled scare tactics, reminding the scholar that as a member of the former ruling Idrisid family he was at risk from the dynasty's political enemies in Spain and North Africa. "You belong to the house of the caliphs," Roger writes. "If you live among the Muslims, their rulers will contrive to kill you, but if you stay with me, you will be safe."[46] Alternatively, Roger may just have been showing off his considerable knowledge of Muslim history and internal politics in order to win al-Idrisi's confidence.

In any case, al-Idrisi accepted the king's summons and soon settled in Palermo, where the pair began a fifteen-year collaboration that would produce one of the masterpieces of medieval geography. The great silver planisphere was stolen and melted down not long after its completion, but distinctive lapis hand-copied editions of al-Idrisi's Map of the World survive, as do some partial sets of associated regional maps, ten for each of the seven traditional world climates. "So the total number of these sectional maps is seventy," al-Idrisi tells us, "not counting the two extreme limits in two directions, one being the southern limit of human habitation caused by the excessive heat and lack of water and the other the northern limit of human habitation caused by excessive cold."[47]

Al-Idrisi and his team of researchers and scholars depicted the inhabited world as occupying one full hemisphere, or 180 degrees, stretching from Korea in the East to the Canary Islands in the West—the last confirmed lands before the inky black waters of the Atlantic, feared among the Arabs as the Sea of

Darkness. Ten degrees on each side were allotted for the so-called Encircling Ocean that surrounds the earth's landmass. Al-Idrisi drew on a wide range of sources, including the classics of Muslim geography and cartography, for knowledge of Africa and Asia. For information closer to home, he relied on his own career as a traveling scholar after his classical education in Cordoba, supplemented by the accounts of European travelers, merchants, diplomats, and members of Roger's large navy.[48] Al-Idrisi's great geographic compendium, dated January 1154, is extant as well. By order of the king, the work was given the fanciful title *Amusements for Those Who Long to Traverse the Horizon;* understandably, the Arabs commonly referred to it simply as *Kitab Rujar,* or *The Book of Roger.*

Al-Idrisi's *Book of Roger* offered the medieval West the most comprehensive descriptions to date of the peoples, lands, and cultures of the seven climates. This was particularly the case for Africa, a region that generations of Arab sailors, traders, and adventurers knew well. Al-Idrisi provides detailed and generally accurate depictions of the gold trade of Ghana and the salt industry in the far west of the continent. He also describes the complex geography of the Upper Nile.[49] Further to the east, *The Book of Roger* informs its readers of the practice of cannibalism on the island of Borneo, the intelligence of elephants, the caste system of India, and the Buddhist beliefs of the kings of far-off China.[50] Gone is the traditional attention to details useful for efficient taxation, administration, trade, or conquest that characterized many earlier Arab works of descriptive geography. In their place is a full-fledged attempt to piece together the latest knowledge to create a coherent, comprehensive whole.[51]

Al-Idrisi's Map of the World was also important for the future of Western cartography and navigation, for it drew on the scientific traditions of Caliph al-Mamun and the researchers at the House of Wisdom and helped introduce them to a whole new audience. Western imitations of Arab maps began to appear by the late thirteenth century, including a work of cosmology by the Italian philosopher Brunetto Latini. The great German Scholastic Albertus Magnus also produced a basic world map around this time; it depicts Baghdad and the southern Iraqi city of Basra but not Paris and could only have been based on Muslim sources.[52]

By their nature, maps are fragile and subject to the rigors of hard use. This is even more the case with navigational handbooks and coastal charts. In the days before printing, they were also difficult and costly to reproduce. So it is little wonder that not much has survived in the way of a "paper trail" directly linking specific advances in European maps and navigational charts to the earlier achievements of the Arab geographers and mariners. Still, a convincing picture of significant Muslim influence emerges from the scattered comments of Western sources as well as from an examination of the evolutionary course of early European cartography, particularly in the absence of contemporary European exposure to the distant Islamic world.

One such clue lies in the marked improvement throughout the fourteenth century of European depictions of the Indian subcontinent, the Red Sea, the Persian Gulf, and Siberia, long known among Arab merchants as *balad al-Sibir*. These representations attained levels of precision unthinkable without reliable models to copy. European works also displayed accurate depictions of southern Asia and the eastern coast of Africa long before Western travelers had made their way to such remote regions.[53] The Muslim understanding of Africa and the Indian Ocean was particularly important for the future of European exploration, for in overturning classical notions that the latter was landlocked, it showed that circumnavigation of southern Africa was not impossible.

Another clue that early Christian cartographers were almost wholly reliant on foreign sources can be found in the curious history of mapping the Caspian Sea, actually the world's largest lake. Fourteenth-century European maps, following the Muslim tradition, correctly captured the Caspian's primary north-south orientation. By the early sixteenth century, however, Western geographers under the influence of recent Latin translations of much older works of Ptolemy had suddenly undone years of research by the Arabs and reverted to the classical representation of the Caspian as an oval running east to west. It would take another two centuries to repair the damage, eight hundred years after the Arabs had successfully charted the Caspian.[54]

More important for the West than any specific borrowings from the Muslim geographers, however, was the general Arab intellectual legacy, conveyed in full by *The Book of Roger*, and its understanding of the world as a place that could be mapped, charted, and explored in a systematic and scientific fashion. World maps in the tradition of al-Mamun and al-Idrisi directly challenged the graphic representation of Christendom's sacred geography, the flat-earth T-O maps with their stylized three continents, Europe,

Asia, and Africa. At the same time, the Arab works of human geography presented the world as a place of marvels, diverse cultures, and varied peoples to be noted, cataloged, and studied, not shunned in favor of exclusive contemplation of eternal life in heaven.

This Arab intellectual conception of the world was accompanied at times by some vital practical assistance. The Portuguese explorer Vasco da Gama, who had already completed his celebrated voyage around Africa's southernmost point, the Cape of Good Hope, in 1497, was then guided to India by a Muslim map and, perhaps, even a Muslim pilot. According to a contemporary Portuguese account, da Gama and his officers were given a glimpse of a detailed map of the entire Indian coastline, "equipped with numerous meridians and parallels in the manner of the Moors."[55] Arab sources, acknowledging the calamity of allowing European powers to penetrate the Indian Ocean and its vital trade routes, all agree that the Muslim pilot must have been drunk at the time to commit such treachery against his fellow believers. Portuguese naval forces later captured invaluable maps of the eastern Spice Islands. These were rushed back to Lisbon for translation and incorporation into the Europeans' increasingly accurate charts and atlases.

Christopher Columbus also benefited from the work of the Arabs, particularly a Latin translation in the mid-twelfth century of the Sabean Tables, which summarized the latest techniques of Arab mathematical geography. In addition, Columbus and other explorers of his generation were influenced by recent Christian interpretations of classical Arab and Hindu notions of a symmetrical earth, a worldview that supported Columbus's strategy of going east by sailing west. They may also have been encouraged by their mistaken reading of the Arabic sources, particularly accounts of the Abbasid determination of the length of one degree, which led them to believe the earth was 20 percent smaller than it really is.[56] Finally, there are suggestions that Muslim seafarers—Arab, Malian, and Chinese—all made early voyages into the distant reaches of the Sea of Darkness, possibly extending as far as the New World.

King Roger II was one of the first of a new breed of Europeans beginning to emerge from firsthand experience of the Arabs, not as enemies in holy war but as undisputed masters of science, philosophy, and high culture. He read Arabic and was widely familiar with the works of the leading Muslim scholars.

Coins minted by Roger in 1138 are the earliest known in Europe to use the new Arabic numeral system popularized by al-Khwarizmi.[57] His court physicians were all Arabs and, says the twelfth-century historian Ibn al-Athir, he relied on them more than on any Christian monk or priest at the palace.[58] A Christian chronicler says the king above all else esteemed "honest and wise men, whether from his own land or born elsewhere, laymen or clerics."[59] So it was only natural that Roger would entrust his scientific lifework to a Muslim scholar.

Al-Idrisi himself tells us that Roger's Map of the World project was rooted not in ignorance on the part of the king but rather in a deep dissatisfaction with the works of the earlier Arab geographers, including *The Book of Roads and Kingdoms* and the accounts of al-Masudi. Roger had pored over these and many other texts in search of an understanding of "other lands, [and] their division into the seven climate zones upon which the scholars agree." But, says al-Idrisi, the king did not find the information he sought in any scholarly work. "In fact, he found them to be rather simpleminded."[60]

Roger responded as would have al-Muqaddasi or any other self-respecting medieval Arab scholar: He collected more data and then sifted through the results in search of general trends and confirmed facts. Al-Idrisi recounts the king's approach with his researchers: "They studied together, but did not find much extra knowledge from [other scholars] over what he found in the aforementioned work [of the Muslim geographers], and when he had convened with them on this subject he sent out into all his lands and ordered yet other scholars who may have been traveling around to come and asked them about their opinions both singly and collectively. But there was no agreement among them. However, where they agreed he accepted the information, but where they differed, he rejected it."[61]

According to al-Idrisi, this continued for fifteen years, until at last Roger was satisfied. He ordered the preliminary outlines of his Map of the World to be traced onto a special drawing board in accordance with the "opinion and consensus of the scholars." Once the draft map's "true description and pleasing form" was confirmed, the artisans began the laborious process of copying this prototype onto the large silver disk, in effect its final publication. Al-Idrisi says all that remained was the preparation of the hand-drawn sectional maps and the completion of his supporting text containing "the descriptions of the provinces and the appearance of their peoples, their dress and their adornments and the practicable roads and their mileage and *farsangs* [a traditional unit of measurement] and all the wonders of their lands as witnessed by travelers and mentioned by roaming writers and confirmed by narrators. Thus after each map we have entered everything we have thought necessary and suitable in its proper place in the book, as much as our knowledge and our ability will allow."[62]

By any standard, *The Book of Roger* was a monumental achievement, more than anything for the sheer scope of the project and its success in assembling the views of so many learned sources across so many fields of knowledge. It also helped enshrine the Arab scientific method that reached back to the work of the early Islamic jurists and theologians. Most of all, it showcased the glories of Arab geography, a field in which the Muslim scholars greatly surpassed their Greek, Persian, and Hindu predecessors. This collaboration between the Muslim scholar and his charismatic Christian patron brought the Arab tradition to the very crossroads of the known world. As a Mediterranean power, Roger's kingdom of Sicily and southern Italy maintained vital trade, diplomatic, and military relations with all the important states of East and West. From there, *The Book of Roger*, with its potent mix of ancient and modern traditions, was well placed to shape emerging Christian conceptions of the outside world.

The Book of Roger enjoyed a long shelf life. Al-Idrisi's work took special root in North Africa, where a family of Tunisian cartographers specialized in sophisticated navigational charts that incorporated many of his findings. Traces of his maps can also be found in Europe's emerging tradition of portolan charts, navigational aids and coastal maps of considerable detail and accuracy. An abridged Arabic version of al-Idrisi's masterpiece was printed in the West in 1592, one of the earliest secular Muslim works produced by Rome's academic Medici Press and a sign of the book's enduring importance. A Latin translation appeared in Paris twenty-seven years later, but the original text was credited only to an anonymous "Nubian geographer."

In one of those odd footnotes to literary history, Edgar Allan Poe invokes this same Nubian geographer and the Sea of Darkness in his tale of nature's overwhelming power and fury, "A Descent into the Maelstrom," dated 1841.[63] At the outset, Poe's narrator recalls peering warily down from the heights of a craggy Norwegian cliff: "I looked dizzily, and beheld a wide expanse of ocean, whose waters wore so inky a hue as to bring at once to my mind the Nubian geographer's account of the *Mare Tenebrarum* [the Sea of Darkness]." A French scholarly translation of *The Book of Roger* was produced in 1840 with an eye to improving contemporary Western knowledge of the world, particularly that of Africa, which was just emerging as a prize quarry in Europe's great colonial expansion.[64]

Roger II died at age fifty-eight in early 1154, shortly after al-Idrisi's text was completed. One spiteful churchman, no doubt reflecting popular gossip that this Arabized king kept a harem, tells us: "He himself surrendered to fate, overcome by early old age, both worn down by his immense efforts and more devoted to sexual activity than the body's good health requires."[65] The more sympathetic archbishop of Salerno, Romuald, on the other hand, recalled a man "large of stature, corpulent, leonine of face, somewhat hoarse of voice; wise, far-seeing, careful, subtle of mind, great in counsel, preferring to use his intelligence rather than force."[66] Whatever Roger's personality, it is clear that the king's commitment to the pursuit of knowledge, not to mention his patronage of al-Idrisi and his own deep involvement with *The Book of Roger* and the great Map of the World, comprise a legacy worthy of the tradition of the early Abbasid caliphs, such as al-Mansur and al-Mamun. This new hunger for the latest in Arab learning, still on the margins of European intellectual life, also fueled the pilgrimage to the East of Roger II's intrepid contemporary, Adelard of Bath.

PART III

Al-Zuhr/Midday

Chapter Five

THE FIRST MAN OF SCIENCE

No one knows where Adelard learned Arabic—perhaps in Syracuse, on the once-Muslim island of Sicily, perhaps only later in Antioch itself. Before setting out for the East, he had asserted the common medieval notion that completely mastering the subject of grammar would ultimately give the reader access to any text in any tongue. He also noted the advantages of studying individual languages, suggesting he was well prepared to succeed at such an undertaking himself.[1] Adelard tells us that he spent approximately seven years in and around the crusader lands able to communicate effectively with local scholars, something that would have required considerable facility with Arabic. Along the way, he mentions various Arab mentors who guided him in his research, and he worries aloud whether he may have attended so many lectures that they have blunted his memory. Among his teachers was a master of anatomy, an "old man of Tarsus," in southern Asia Minor, not far from Antioch. His instructor, an adept at advanced Arab medicine, taught him sophisticated dissection techniques, including how to immerse a cadaver in running water to gently wear away the soft flesh and expose the body's intricate networks of blood vessels and nerves.

The path Adelard traced to Antioch is almost as obscure as the course of his language studies. He provides only a handful of clues about his wanderings in search of the *studia Arabum*, leaving much to be reconstructed from scattered hints in his books and translations and a few obscure references from fellow scholars. In 1109, Adelard deposited his nephew and other students then in his charge at Laon, where he left them to the "insecurity of French opinions." Almost immediately the trail goes cold, until he resurfaces five years later in the principality of Antioch, huddled on the "trembling bridge" at Mamistra during the earthquake. Given his earlier visit to the archbishop of Syracuse, memorialized in *On the Same and the Different*, it seems likely that he returned to Sicily and used it as his jumping-off point to the East. The island was linked to Antioch by close family ties between their respective Norman rulers, making communications, travel, and trade relatively easy.

At the time, Antioch was just beginning to emerge as an important center for the translation of Arabic texts into Latin, particularly in the field of medicine, where Muslim science was second to none. Traders from the Italian city-state of Pisa, who had earlier helped ferry the crusaders to the Holy Land in exchange for booty and territory, now wielded enormous influence in Antioch. They controlled their own quarter in the very center of the city and the whole of the nearby port of Latakia. As a result of these and other commercial and political links around the eastern Mediterranean, Pisa found itself to be a vital hub in the spread of Arab wisdom. Arabic texts seized by conquering Christian armies around the region swelled the book bazaars, transforming the city into something of an entrepôt of Muslim science. Antioch's Pisan quarter bordered on the monastery of St. Paul, a Benedictine institution that surely would have welcomed Adelard, whose father, Fastrad, and mentor, Bishop John, were both prominent members of the same order back in Bath.

Like Adelard, the Italian translator and scholar Stephen of Pisa—sometimes known as Stephen the Philosopher—soon made his way to Antioch to learn from the Muslims. There he translated a prominent medical encyclopedia, *The Royal Book*, by Ali ibn al-Abbas al-Majusi, known in the West as Haly Abbas. This work, dating from the tenth century and comprising ten chapters on medical theory and another ten chapters on clinical practice, was already widely used across the Muslim world. Stephen's Latin version quickly became a European standard as well. Stephen begins chapter eight, on medical practice, with a personal note: ". . . The translation from Arabic into Latin of Stephen the disciple of philosophy. He wrote the copy himself and completed it in the year from the passion of our Lord 1127, on Saturday, November the third, at Antioch. Thanks be to God, the beginning and end of things."[2]

To accompany the text, Stephen fashioned his own glossary of Arabic and Greek medical terms, with some Latin equivalents—a work so valuable that it was meticulously copied and recopied by hand in the West for hundreds of years and even printed centuries later, during the Renaissance. Stephen himself was apparently less impressed with his own handiwork; he was not a physician and instead considered himself a "disciple of philosophy." Next time, he promises, he will translate something from among "all the secrets of phi-losophy that lie hidden in the Arabic tongue."[3] Medicine, he notes, is but the lowest rung of the philosopher's art, but one has to begin with the needs of the body before addressing the improvement of the soul.[4]

While Stephen at first concentrated on matters of the lowly human body, Adelard reached for the heavens. As a young student in France, he had confidently predicted that the knowledge available in the Arab East could help cure the ills of the West—a decidedly unorthodox view in the era of the anti-Muslim Crusades. But not even Adelard could have anticipated what he would find in the *studia Arabum*. Among his trophies were the geometric system of Euclid; an elaborate Arab table of the movements of the stars; techniques for using that powerful computer, the astrolabe; several major works of Arab astrology; and a book of alchemy revealing ways to dye leather, tint glass, and produce green pigment—Adelard's favorite color. The man from Bath plunged headfirst into the world of astronomy, philosophy, and magic.

In all, about a dozen surviving works can be traced directly to the restless Englishman. The scope of his interests is breathtaking, from the royal art of falconry to applied chemistry, from geometry to mathematical astronomy and cosmology—the text often written in the accessible style of the natural-born teacher and raconteur. Adelard's works also offer a useful window onto the state of Western borrowings from the Arabs, for his original works can be neatly broken down into those completed before his intellectual encounter with the East and those that followed it.

Upon his return to Bath, Adelard found himself besieged by friends and family, all eager to learn of his seven years abroad. "Among those paying their calls was a certain nephew of mine, who, in investigating the causes of things, was tying them in knots rather than unraveling them. He urged me to put forward some new item of the studies of the Arabs," Adelard recounts.[5] The result is *Questions on Natural Science*, a series of queries and responses on what the classical authors call natural philosophy. The Western-educated nephew does the asking, and the learned Adelard, this time speaking for the Arabs, responds. "This is how the causes of things work," the well-traveled scholar declares at the outset, in what might serve as the motto for his long career as a scientist and scholar. "So let us start from the lowest objects and end with the highest."[6]

*　　*　　*

Among the first Arabic texts to capture Adelard's imagination was a classic work on *tilasm*, or the art of "talismans"—elaborate charms thought to invoke celestial influence—horoscopes, and astrological images by Thabit ibn Qurra, one of the leading lights of medieval science. Thabit ibn Qurra was a member of the star-worshipping Sabean sect, whose religious practices engendered a close affinity for astronomy, astrology, and mathematics. The Sabeans were also well grounded in Greek philosophy. According to Arab tradition, Thabit was a former money changer in the bazaars of Harran, with an impressive facility for languages. He caught the eye of a prominent Baghdad aristocrat and scholar, who arranged for him to study and work at the House of Wisdom. While the Sabeans were viewed with suspicion by many Muslims, the sect's advanced Greek learning and invaluable skills afforded them a considerable measure of influence and status during the early Abbasid years.

The talented Thabit flourished in the learned environs of Baghdad, and he went on to serve as royal astrologer in the late ninth century. One of the empire's great scholars and linguists, Thabit revised and corrected Arabic versions of the *Almagest* and other Greek classics and produced original works on number theory, calculus, and mechanics. He also wrote several texts on the philosophical and religious views of his fellow Sabeans and was regarded among the Arab scholars as an expert on talismans.[7] In the preface to his own translation of Thabit's text on magic, the twelfth-century Latin scholar John of Seville suggests that Adelard, the only other Westerner to have seen the original Arabic work, procured a copy while in Antioch: "This book, then, I, with the help of God's spirit, obtained from my Master—a book which no Latin other than a certain Antiochene, who once obtained a part of it, ever had." That "certain Antiochene" is none other than Adelard of Bath, who earlier published an abridged version of the same text.[8]

Where others feared the influence of Saracen sorcery, Adelard celebrated the notion that man might aspire to understand and even conquer nature. He also directly linked the practice of magic to other scientific endeavors, noting that the study of talismans first requires the mastery of astronomy and astrology. "Whoever is skilled in geometry and philosophy but without experience of the science of the stars is useless; for the science of the stars is, of all the arts, both the most excellent in its subject matter and the most useful because of the effects of talismans," Adelard tells us in his own version of Thabit ibn Qurra's work.[9] The text, known as *The Book of Talismans*, includes incantations for driving away mice and techniques for rekindling love between husband and wife. There is even a talisman for ridding a town of scorpions. First, an image of a scorpion is fashioned from metal while Scorpio is in the ascendant. Next, the name of this constellation and other astronomical details are inscribed on the talisman. Finally, it is buried in the place to be protected—or better yet, in all four corners of the place—while one recites, "This is the burial of it and of its species, that it may not come to that one and to that place."[10]

Adelard leavened his translation with a liberal use of Arabic phrases, giving it a mysterious appeal in a Latin world starved for both novelty and basic information. In the prescription for a wife seeking to regain her husband's affections, he spells out the required incantation: "O fount of honor, joy and light of the world! Mix together the loves of these two people, o spirits, using your knowledge of mixing, and being helped toward this end by the greatest power and the might of *al-malik al-quddus wa al-hayah al-da 'ima*," an Arabic phrase that Adelard translates as "the king, the holy and eternal life."[11] This noble appeal to God or his intercessors, not to demons, is in keeping with Islamic tradition and sets it apart from the notion of black magic in Christian Europe.[12] At one point, Adelard gives us a rare hint as to what might have compelled a young man from the English West Country to push deep into uncharted intellectual territory, alone in a strange and distant land. The practitioner of magic, he writes, must remain focused on the task at hand, and he should always act with confidence. For "lack of hope is the mother of hesitation, and hesitation is the mother of ineffectiveness."[13]

Under the influence of Thabit ibn Qurra and other such thinkers, Adelard developed a lifelong fascination with the occult as part and parcel of his science. As far as many of the Muslim scholars were concerned, astrology and magic fit right in with astronomy, medicine, chemistry, and weather forecasting, a convention that Adelard did much to popularize among early Western scientists. Arab doctors, for example, routinely consulted the stars to identify the best time to draw blood or conduct surgery, matching parts of a patient's body with an astrological map of the heavens. This system was first propagated by ancient Greek medical practice: Aries was associated with the head, and one continued down the body and around the signs of the zodiac to Pisces, which corresponded to the feet.[14] The University of Bologna, one of the medieval West's great centers of medical training, had a special master dedicated to teaching future doctors how to assess the influence of the stars on the human body.[15]

Adelard, it seems, also dabbled in alchemy, an important incubator of early experimental science and the forerunner to modern chemistry. Although its origins lay in the philosophical investigation into the nature of substance and reality, much of medieval alchemy came more and more to comprise specific techniques for manipulating materials with solvents and reactive agents or creating metal alloys and dyes, all basic processes that would one day find a home in the chemist's laboratory. Today, the word *alchemy* mostly conjures up the secretive, even mystical, pursuit of ways to create gold from lesser metals. One surviving medieval reference ascribes to Adelard a lost twelfth-century manuscript of alchemical recipes and techniques, known as *A Little Key to Drawing*. An extant version—without attribution to Adelard or anyone else— features a series of instructions for refining gold and silver, working in precious metals, tinting glass, and coloring leather, many dating back to the alchemical traditions of Hellenistic Egypt. In all, it presents 382 chapters, or recipes, about one third of which appear to be relatively recent additions.[16] One salient feature of *A Little Key to Drawing* is its complete lack of reliance on Latin sources for the central material—there is, for example, no hint of the canonical works of Vitruvius in its architectural sections—making it one of the earliest examples of technology transfer to the Christian West.[17]

A number of clues suggest that Adelard may have augmented the older core text based on his own research and personal interests. These hints include a reliance on Arabic terminology similar to that found in his translation of Thabit, *The Book of Talismans*; the introduction into the Latin text of two English words in a section on techniques for producing green pigment, a color Adelard adopted as his trademark; a pair of recipes for making candy from sugarcane, a plant unknown at the time in northern Europe but familiar to one who had traveled as widely as he had done; and, finally, some passages that mirror text from Adelard's known writings, including his earliest work, *On the Same and the Different*.[18]

The alchemical manuscript's innocuous title may have been selected to obscure its true contents from casual curiosity, for *A Little Key to Drawing* is a gold mine of medieval technology, containing the industrial secrets of contemporary artisans making glass, leather, and other products, as well as the fundamental techniques and methods of early Western science.[19] Among its treasures is a recipe, written in code, for the distillation of alcohol—a key ingredient in many alchemical procedures. Such works reveal a great deal about the underlying state of knowledge passed along by the Arab masters of the day, for the art of Muslim alchemy was dedicated, in part, to the search for pure "essences" through distillation, crystallization, reduction, and other fundamental chemical processes. Arab authorities on the subject taught that mixing particular distillates together could create a rarefied substance, the elixir, capable of curing disease, purifying lesser materials, and even prolonging life. This was later known in Europe as the fifth essence—the source, literally, of our word *quintessence*—and was a complement to the classical Greek schema of the four basic elements: air, water, earth, and fire.

The great ninth-century Arab alchemist Jabir ibn Hayyan taught that each of the earth's metals consisted of different mixtures of sulfur and mercury, allowing for the possibility that they could be "transmuted" if one broke them down into these two intermediate elements and then rearranged the proportions and relative purities. This provided a theoretical basis for many of the alchemists' early scientific investigations, a search that proved equally popular in the East and the West—not least for the expectation that one could ultimately produce gold from more common, base metals.[20] Jabir, known in Latin as Gaber, to whom countless European alchemical texts were later spuriously ascribed, was closely associated with Shi'ite and mystical Sufi teachings, and his alchemical practice mirrored those sects' spiritual quest to penetrate natural phenomena and reach the inner, revealed meaning. Here, then, was the philosophical basis for the now-discredited art of alchemy, and any change in material substance in the laboratory was, for Gaber and his like-minded colleagues, symbolic of a transformation of the soul.[21]

In the hands of some later Arab alchemists, this vital symbolic component was gradually stripped away, easing the transition from the spiritual discipline of alchemy to the practical science of chemistry. The works of such scientists covered the classification of mineral substances, basic processes and techniques, and discussions of apparatuses and other equipment—all easily assimilated into an emerging Western scientific language.[22] The arrival in the Latin world of Arab alchemy stimulated centuries of research into chemical properties and experimental procedures, very much as the geocentric worldview contained in Arabic studies of the *Almagest* helped push back the boundaries of mathematical astronomy. The thirteenth-century English scientist and philosopher Roger

Bacon, who shared Adelard's enthusiasm for magic, saw great promise in what he termed a practical approach to the discipline: "But there is another alchemy, operative and practical, which teaches how to make the noble metals and colors and many other things better and more by art than they are made in nature. And science of this kind is greater than all those proceeding because it produces greater utilities."[23]

The politics of alchemy also played an important role in the rise of Western science, for requirements of state at times afforded its early practitioners invaluable protection against the condemnation of religion. In this way, it mirrored the development of astrology, which also had its many religious critics in both the East and the West. The princes of Europe were eager to bolster their flagging coffers by employing, in the words of one English monarch, "men learned in natural philosophy" to increase the royal holdings of gold coins through the practice of alchemy.[24] In reality, the best the alchemists managed to do was devalue the crown's currency through the stealthy introduction of impurities that swelled the number of coins but diluted their actual gold content. This technique was not unlike a modern paper-money economy's simply printing new currency to cover its mounting expenditures. The forces of the church, who stood to lose power and influence at the hands of secular kingdoms so "enriched," denounced the practitioners of these arts as charlatans. The popes and their allies also invoked church teachings to warn against interference by man in God's natural order. "They promise that which they do not produce," complained Pope John XII, in a papal bull of 1317.[25]

The earliest mention of *A Little Key to Drawing* is contained in a ninth-century library catalog from the Benedictine monastery on Reichenau, in Germany, but the lost manuscript to which it refers would have been older still.[26] Clearly, European artisans had mastered and preserved some important industrial techniques throughout the turmoil of the early Middle Ages. This, however, did not blunt the enormous impact of the arrival of Arab alchemy and early chemistry beginning in the twelfth century, introduced by the likes of Adelard. Within a few short decades, his fellow Englishman Robert of Ketton produced the first full Latin text on the Arab art, *The Book of the Composition of Alchemy*. "Since what Alchemiya is, and what its composition is, your Latin world does not yet know, I will explain in the present book," Robert promises his readers in the preface.[27]

Soon a flood of translated Arab alchemical works began to pervade the West, threatening to overturn Christendom's traditional relationship between man and nature and prompting vigorous philosophical and theological debate about the use and abuse of technology.[28] Spurred on by the arrival of these Arab teachings, the Latin alchemists were among the earliest pioneers in the West's discovery of the natural world, while their theories of nature, such as that on the composition of matter, would contribute to the scientific revolution of the sixteenth and seventeenth centuries.[29]

Long before Adelard arrived in Antioch, ignorance, disorder, and self-imposed religious isolationism had cut the West off from centuries of scientific and philosophical advances. The natural world was largely unquestioned and unexplored, and early attempts to penetrate its mysteries often aroused suspicions of sorcery or the mischief of demons. With little or no grasp of physical laws that might explain the spread of deadly disease, for example, or illuminate the arts of navigation or telling time, medieval Christendom tended to see the universe as a dark and frightful place. Superstition ruled the day. In short, there was no method, only a sort of mania or madness—as witnessed by the widespread claim of apocalyptic visionaries on the popular imagination and extravagant explanations of natural phenomena. All that began to change with Adelard's discovery of one of the greatest scientific works in history, the mathematical system of Euclidean geometry.

The thirteen books of Euclid, known as *Elements*, include six chapters on basic geometry, three on number theory, and a single section on "incommensurables"—what are known today as irrational numbers. The side and the diagonal of a square represent the most familiar example of incommensurable numbers. There is no single unit that can measure both lines; thus, their relationship cannot be written as a fraction or ratio. It has been suggested that the problem of incommensurables forced the Greek philosophers to discard the notion that the universe could be described fully in terms of positive whole numbers and to concentrate instead on developing geometry as a more accurate and useful representation of physical reality.[30] The final three chapters of *Elements* are devoted to solid geometry.

Euclid's own life and origins are obscure and subject to much speculation, although it is known that he founded a school in Alexandria, where he flourished around 300 B.C. His masterwork represents a collection and reworking of much of Greek mathematics to date, presented in a compelling, logical format. Euclid begins by introducing the basic building blocks of geometry and then spells out a problem to be solved. Next, a proposed solution is presented. Finally, the *proof* reasons from the earlier propositions, or axioms, to establish the truth of the construction, and the *conclusion* confirms that the problem has been solved satisfactorily within the agreed rules of the game. Each successful demonstration forms part of the basis for later, more sophisticated problems.

Taken together, the thirteen books of *Elements* offer a comprehensive logical system and an introduction to deductive reasoning, essential to the development of the scientific method and rational philosophical inquiry. Yet medieval Europe knew almost nothing of Euclid's science, except some poorly understood fragments preserved by Boethius and a few of the other Latin encyclopedists. Isidore of Seville, for example, devoted a total of just four pages of his *Etymologies* to the subjects of geometry, arithmetic, music, and astronomy combined.[31] Such scraps afforded Christian scholars no glimpse of the intellectual riches contained in Euclid's *Elements*.

Euclid fared far better at the hands of the Arabs, who recognized his importance and made the mastery of *Elements*, along with the *Almagest*, the techniques of Hindu astronomy, and the natural philosophy of Aristotle, a cornerstone of their intellectual enterprise. It is worth noting that Arab scholars also identified the most serious shortcoming of the Euclidean system, the fifth postulate, which advances the notion that parallel lines can never intersect even as they extend to infinity. The essence of the problem lies with asserting the behavior of such lines outside human experience, and Euclid himself seems to have expressed some doubts about this aspect of his own work. All attempts to date to establish this rule as absolute have failed. However, the medieval Arab mathematicians repeatedly attacked the problem over the centuries in new and creative ways—work that eventually found its way to the West, where it later influenced a number of leading mathematicians.[32]

Caliph al-Mansur invoked Euclid's teachings in the geometric design of his Round City, and his successors ensured that *Elements* was one of the first major Greek texts translated into Arabic. The works of two Abbasid scholars on *Elements* have survived to this day. The first scholar, al-Hajjaj, completed a full translation and an abridgment, the latter at the direct request of Caliph al-Mamun. A second, later version, one that more effectively tracks the Greek original, was edited and revised by Thabit ibn Qurra, the researcher at the caliph's House of Wisdom whose *Book of Talismans* Adelard translated.[33]

The Arabs also produced dozens of commentaries on *Elements* and translated other important works by Euclid. Almost immediately, the Muslim approach to both science and philosophy began to reflect the Greek mathematician's fundamental insistence on demonstrable proofs. This approach soon extended to questions of theology and religion, prompting the aristocratic scholar al-Kindi to seek out the teachings of Greek philosophers on metaphysics in order to subject matters of faith to this same form of rigorous analysis. Toward this end, al-Kindi commissioned Arabic translations of Greek philosophical texts that would one day pose a major challenge to the theologians of both the East and the West, including Aristotle's works on cosmology and the soul.[34]

For medieval Europe, the discovery of the complete Euclid was a sensation. The three earliest Latin versions, based on the translation of al-Hajjaj three centuries earlier, have historically been attributed to Adelard.[35] Editions by other scholars soon followed. Notations in a number of surviving manuscripts and the testimony of later medieval intellectuals establish Adelard's close links to the earliest texts. Roger Bacon quotes from the third of these treatises—actually a commentary on Euclid rather than a translation—and refers to it approvingly as the "special edition of Adelard of Bath."[36] And there is no reason to doubt Adelard's own account when he tells us in a later work that he already translated *Elements* some years before.[37]

No one has yet succeeded in unraveling the mystery of exactly which texts bear the master's own hand. Still, Adelard's fingerprints are all over the successful introduction of Euclidean geometry to the Latin world, as early as 1126. Whatever their exact provenance, these first manuscripts reveal much about the ways in which Adelard and the early Latin scholars who followed in his path assimilated and gradually mastered Arabic scientific texts. The oldest editions bear all the hallmarks of an early, tentative encounter with the *studia Arabum*. The translation of technical terms is often inconsistent and relies heavily on imprecise or erroneous Latin terms; at other times, failing to find any Latin equivalent, the author simply transliterates from the original Arabic. Such linguistic poverty was soon to plague the translations of Muslim philosophy as well; one early version of a major work of Arab metaphysics is forced to fall back on a single Latin word, *esse*, to represent thirty-four distinct Arabic expressions for being and related notions.[38]

According to a modern linguistic analysis, the earliest translation relies on more than seventy direct transliterations from the Arabic in order to present basic geometric concepts for which medieval Latin had no ready terminology. These include *diameter, tangent,* and *ratio.* However, a slightly later version has reduced its reliance on Arabic to fewer than two dozen transliterations and has replaced all of the terms above with suitable Latin equivalents. This suggests that Adelard—or perhaps a colleague or one of his pupils—had since made considerable strides in mastering the material at hand and identifying or producing Latin variants.[39] Some of the extant Euclid manuscripts also include marginal notations discussing Arabic vocabulary or explaining points of grammar, a technique that Adelard himself used in other works—in one, he highlights the foreign words in special red ink—and one that was carried on by his students.[40]

Virtually all surviving examples of the second of the three early Latin Euclids explicitly identify the work as that of Adelard. This version proved a "bestseller" for five centuries and formed one of the centerpieces of the West's emerging new sciences. At least fifty-six manuscripts have survived, a relatively large figure that attests to the work's general appeal and widespread use.[41] It served as the basis for what later became the definitive scholarly text of the day and was cited widely in commentaries throughout the thirteenth and four-teenth centuries. In the realm of theory, Euclid gave the Latins their first explicit model of scientific thinking and exposed them to the classical approach to logical deduction.[42] In practical terms, his geometry was crucial to the development of medieval astronomy, for it allowed the measurement of far-off celestial bodies in terms of angles and degrees and helped explain and predict their movements through the heavens.

These first Latin translations, which sought to interpret Euclid for a Western audience, set the stage for the rigorous Arabic program of study that culminated in mathematical astronomy and applied astrology.[43] They also had a profound effect on the overall development of early European scientific and philosophical thinking. Robert Grosseteste—literally "the big-headed," prompting one contemporary to call him "Robert of the big head but subtle intellect"[44]—recognized the fundamental importance of the new geometry. "The utility of a consideration of lines, angles and figures is the very greatest, since it is impossible that natural philosophy be known without them. They obtain absolutely in the whole universe and in its parts," writes Robert, an early chancellor at Oxford, who died in 1253. Without lines, angles, and figures, he notes, it would be impossible to know the true nature of things.[45]

Roger Bacon, Robert's younger colleague, repeatedly invokes Adelard's special edition of Euclid as an authority for the idea, just beginning to take root in the West, of the uses of proof in both logic and the theory of knowledge, or epistemology. Roger draws explicitly on Adelard for his own groundbreaking work on theories of vision and on the broader question of the role of experimentation in science. "An axiom, as Adelard of Bath says in his edition, is interpreted as a dignity, for it explicates the definitions of things. And this is especially true when the axiom is taken strictly, although in a wide sense all principles are called axioms, as Adelard of Bath's epilogue at the end of the book supposes," Roger writes in his *Geometrica Speculativa*.

He then goes on to link Adelard directly to Aristotle's own work on experience and experimentation, before adding, "A postulate is, as Adelard of Bath says, that which being conceded nothing inconvenient follows from the hypothesis." The union of these three elements—geometry; the system of axioms, postulates, and proofs explained by Adelard; and direct experience— formed the basis for much productive Western research and scholarship, including the development at Oxford of calculus and formal analysis.[46] The new art of geometry was also central to medieval philosophical investigation into light, color, and vision.

Euclid's *Elements* was soon featured in the classrooms of the cathedral schools, most notably at Chartres, a leading center of education ever since the French monk and future pope Gerbert d'Aurillac returned from Spain with Arab-inspired learning to popularize mathematics and the other subjects of the quadrivium. This early affinity for Euclid at one of France's greatest cathedrals proved of enormous practical and aesthetic value after a fire in 1145 forced the wholesale redesign and reconstruction of the massive structure. The extensive effort paid homage to Euclid, literally and figuratively: Decorative statuary dedicated to the seven liberal arts now included the Greek mathematician, while the architecture of the rebuilt cathedral demonstrated a new sophistication in the principles of geometry and proportion.[47] The result is one of Christendom's greatest architectural achievements.

Already, European building and architecture had begun to show a marked technical improvement, as had the art of draftsmanship. This sudden upturn, as well as the appearance of specific skills and techniques not present earlier, dates to the direct transfer of practical technology from the master builders and masons of the East. In at least two well-known cases, Arab artisans arrived in the West and shared their knowledge. One, a Muslim known as Lalys, was captured in the Crusades and brought to England, where he eventually became court architect to King Henry I.[48] In another instance, the Syrian chronicler Usama ibn Munqidh tells us, a stonemason who once worked for his family moved to the Christian lands and took his valuable skills with him. The Crusades also exposed Western craftsmen among the pilgrims and warriors to the latest Arab building techniques, while other tradesmen arrived in the West from Muslim Spain in the wake of the Christian military victories.

Among the innovations derived from the Arabs was the introduction of the pointed arch, an integral feature of the new Gothic style of cathedral.[49] Related technology allowed the remarkable vaulting that opened up these massive new cathedrals to the air—not unlike that of the modern greenhouse—and led to the construction of huge windows in what had in the past been massive unbroken walls. The reliance on the pointed arch in place of the semicircle between support pillars also gave the builders and architects greater flexibility, as they could now vary the distance between pillars without compromising or distorting the design.[50]

Along with their high level of skill with technical drawings, the rules of proportion, and specific masonry techniques, the Muslim artisans offered a keen awareness of general geometric principles then unknown to the West. As a result, the traditionally irregular angles, crooked walls, and off-kilter doors and windows that made up much of twelfth-century European church architecture began to give way steadily to far greater precision in design and construction.[51] The geometry of the Arabs, as popularized by Adelard, was soon adopted by the European master builders, the masons, as central to their craft. That "worthy clerk Euclid" became their guiding light. "Ye shall understand that among all the crafts of the world of man's craft masonry hath the most notability and most part of the science of geometry," proclaims a fourteenth-century guild document.[52]

These innovative geometric techniques almost certainly formed the central core of the "secret" knowledge of the future Freemasons, around which so much legend still swirls. A notebook originally belonging to the twelfth-century French architect Villard de Honnecourt includes this typical reference to the practical uses of geometry: "It is thanks to geometry that the height of a building or the width of a river can be measured." Villard's compendium of geometric methods includes how to halve the area of a square, a necessary skill in the construction of pinnacles and other architectural features characteristic of the period.[53]

Here, too, the Arab provenance of these new methods proved of great value, for the Muslim intellectual tradition was more than ready to use science to address practical questions. The masons and other artisans at work in the thirteenth century on the cathedral at Wells, not far from Adelard's native town of Bath, were already using Arabic numerals to mark and identify components of the project, while their clients, the learned clerics, clung to the less supple Roman numerals in their account books for another four hundred years.[54]

The sweeping importance of the restored Euclid was neatly complemented by Adelard's other great revolutionary work, the translation of al-Khwarizmi's star tables, the *zij al-Sindhind*. Adelard's *zij* almost overwhelmed the West, for the tradition of the tabular handbooks reflected centuries of Muslim scientific advances and rested on mathematical assumptions that far exceeded anything Christendom had ever seen. An entirely new body of study, as well as a wholly new vocabulary, had to be developed in order for the West to comprehend the full scope and import of the *zij*. This process of assimilation occupied Latin scholars for hundreds of years, and it was not until the sixteenth century, with the arrival of Copernicus, that the West could field an equal to the classical Arab astronomers.[55] Even the great Polish scientist could not have completed his groundbreaking work without the crucial aid of his Arab forerunners.

Although the particular *zij* that Adelard transmitted to his fellow Latins around 1126 was obsolete by contemporary Arab standards, its own colorful history reveals the depth and breadth of science as fostered at the House of Wisdom and taken up elsewhere in the Muslim world. And it was more than enough to spur a flurry of activity among the West's new scientists. The work itself consists of 116 tables, relying initially on Hindu teachings to catalog the movements of the sun, the moon, and the five visible planets. The tables are accompanied by thirty-seven brief chapters of explanation. Despite some basic errors in the translation of the Arabic text, the figures and tables are represented accurately, suggesting that Adelard understood the complex calculations, if not all of the linguistic niceties.[56] He also continued his earlier practice, seen in the translation of Euclid and elsewhere, of sprinkling the text with Arabic words and phrases, highlighting important foreign terms, and providing useful explanations and other notations in the margins.

A basic *zij* table, like the common astrolabe, is valid only for the specific locale for which it was designed. This was the source of considerable error and frustration among the early Western astronomers and mathematicians, for they first had to master the implications of the *zij* and then experiment with ways to update and adjust it properly before it could be of any real practical use. This same phenomenon allows modern researchers to work out, often quite precisely, where and when a specific *zij* was written or revised. In the case of the *zij al-Sindhind*, this record extends across thirteen hundred years of astronomical history, from the time of the Hindu scholars who provided the basis for the tables to our own.[57]

Al-Khwarizmi used his base in the Abbasid capital, Baghdad, as the reference point for some of his calculations, and he relied on the Persian solar calendar common to his ancestral town, Khwarazm, on the Aral Sea. However, the Arabic version on which Adelard based his translation had been reworked significantly in the intervening three centuries. These tables reflect the meridian at Cordoba, in Muslim Spain, while the dates have been refashioned to fit the standard lunar calendar in use across the Islamic world. These revisions were the work of the eleventh-century Spanish mathematician Abul Qasim Maslama bin Ahmad, commonly called al-Majriti—meaning a native of Madrid—who added calendar conversions and various trigonometric and eclipse tables, as well as information designed for astrological calculations.[58] The Spanish flavor of the *zij* raises the possibility that Adelard visited this former Muslim land, or perhaps nearby North Africa, during his seven-year grand tour. However, Adelard left behind no mention of such a trip, and it seems more likely that al-Majriti's version fell into his hands elsewhere.

In the late tenth century, the Umayyad caliph of Cordoba, al-Hakam II al-Mustansir, set out to challenge the intellectual supremacy of the rival Abbasids in Baghdad. The caliph assembled a huge collection of learned texts and attracted leading scholars to his kingdom of al-Andalus. Central to this effort was the work of al-Majriti and his followers, experts in astronomy, mathematics, astrology, and the theory of the astrolabe.[59] "Abulqasim Maslama bin Ahmad, known by the name al-Majriti, . . . was the chief mathematician in al-Andalus during his time and better than all the

astronomers who came before him. He was extremely interested in astronomical observations and very fond of studying and understanding the book of
Ptolemy known as the *Almagest*. He wrote a good book . . . [on] the
mathematics of business transactions,'" records the medieval chronicler Said
al-Andalusi. "He also worked on the *zij* of Muhammad bin Musa al-
Khwarizmi and changed the dates from the Persian to the Hijra [Islamic]
calendar . . . but he followed al-Khwarizmi even when he was in error without
indicating the areas where such errors were committed."[60]

Al-Majriti's reworking of the *zij al-Sindhind* must have proved irresistible to
Adelard, for it combined the Arab mathematical astronomy with the study of
astrology and the technology of the astrolabe—all subjects near to the
Englishman's heart. Before setting foot in the Muslim world, Adelard wrote
in *On the Same and the Different* of his passion for astronomy, above all the other
"maidens" of the seven liberal arts: "This maiden whom you see standing
before you with splendor . . . sketches the shape of the world, as contained in
her teaching, the number and size of the circles, the distance of the orbs, the
course of the planets, the positions of the signs of the zodiac; she paints in the
parallels and colures, she divides the zodiac into twelve parts with thoughtful
reason, she is aware of the size of the stars, the opposite positions of the two
poles, the axis stretching between them."[61]

The same early work also hints at Adelard's coming love for the Arab
science of astrology—that is, for the study of the celestial bodies for clues to
events here on earth. "If anyone could make her [astronomy] his own, he would
be confident in declaring not only the present condition of lower things, but
also their past or future conditions. For, those higher and divine animate beings
are the principles and causes of the lower natures."[62] When Adelard first wrote
those words, he was still a long way from mastery of the tools and techniques
of astronomy. Now, fifteen or twenty years later, his Arab star tables,
illuminated by Euclid's *Elements*, could begin to fill in the significant gaps
in his understanding and knowledge.

Even before Adelard introduced the *zij* tables and offered a glimpse of the
Arab mathematical astronomy that lay behind them, scattered pockets of
scientific activity dotted the Western intellectual landscape. The scholar-
monks of Catalonia, which bordered on the Muslim lands, had partly
assimilated the astrolabe texts of al-Majriti and his colleagues. Gerbert
d'Aurillac had successfully popularized elements of the quadrivium at the

French cathedral schools. And Adelard's hometown and the nearby monasteries of the Severn basin played host to a lively circle of mathematicians and astronomers, mostly Lotharingians and all trying to make sense of the early teachings trickling in from the Muslim world. There was even a failed attempt to introduce the *zij al-Sindhind* to Latin readers, a development that may ultimately have compelled Adelard to produce his own, successful translation of al-Khwarizmi.[63] It is no wonder that in 1138 the annalist John of Worcester took great pride in the fact that he had helped copy the treasured star tables at the Worcester Cathedral priory, seventy-five miles north of Bath: "I set down here the first month of the Arabic year and the day and hour with which it began so that the work which in Arabic is called 'Ezich' and which the learned Elkaurexmus [al-Khwarizmi] wrote most carefully on the course of the seven planets, and laid out in tables, is not consigned to oblivion."[64]

At first the explicit conjunction of astronomy and astrology that characterized many of the first Arabic texts to appear in Latin attracted little notice in the West. However, the use of astrology to forecast coming events soon caught the attention of Christian orthodoxy, for the relationship between the heavenly bodies and events here on earth had much in common with both magic, the realm of the sorcerer, and theology, the realm of the priest. The Muslim world had already begun to experience a backlash, with some of the luminaries of Arab thought lining up to challenge astrology and its prediction of the future as un-Islamic. Likewise, the Christian theologian John of Salisbury denounced the work of the "*mathematici*," or astrologers, as antithetical to morality and incompatible with both man's free will and God's unquestioned omnipotence. "He—the astrologer—decks out the years with a kaleidoscope of things to come, as though he were painting a fresco; and he winds a rope of future events through the flying wheel of time . . . [But] . . . the will of God is the first cause of all things, and *mathesis* is the way of damnation," John thunders in his *Policraticus*.[65] As in the Arab world, the Latin astrologers largely carried on with their art unimpeded.

Such difficult, technical works as Euclid's *Elements* and the *zij* of al-Khwarizmi reflect the mature scholarship of Adelard, after years of immersion in Arab learning. The surviving examples of the geometry text and the star tables were completed after his return to England and may have been intended for use as textbooks or study guides by Adelard's students and other budding scholars.

But Adelard also left behind his accessible and highly readable essay *Questions on Natural Science*, in which he sets out to encapsulate the spirit of learning and inquiry he found in the East—framing the text as a response to his pushy nephew's demand for some "new ideas" from the *studia Arabum*.

The topics begin with the vegetable and animal kingdoms and proceed to the moon and stars overhead, before bumping up against the delicate question of God's very existence. Chapter 7 addresses the question of "why some brute animals chew the cud, but others do not." Chapter 19 explains "why the nose is placed above the mouth," while chapter 58 answers what has since become a classic question of elementary physics: why water does not flow out from a narrow vessel with holes at the top and bottom if the upper opening is covered with the thumb. Likewise, Adelard understands the concept of the conservation of matter: "And in my judgment certainly, nothing at all dies in this sensible world, nor is it smaller today than when it was created. For if any part is released from one conjunction, it does not perish but passes over to another association."[66] Adelard then goes on to explain the mysteries of lightning and thunder, the moon's apparent lack of light, and whether the stars are animate and, if they are, what they might eat—"the moistures of the earth and the waters, thinned by the very long distance they travel when they are drawn up to the higher regions."[67]

Finally, the nephew touches on the problematic question of God's existence: "From you, then, I want to hear, using reason alone and keeping away from the flattery of authority, whether he exists or not, and what he is, and what he does."[68] Already, Adelard has exhibited a certain wariness about advancing views that might be unwelcome to Western ears. He often hides behind the opinions of "the Arabs" to express what may well have been his own views on man, nature, and the universe. "No one should think I am doing this out of my own head but that I am giving the views of the studies of the Arabs . . . For I know what those who profess the truth suffer at the hands of the vulgar crows. Therefore, I shall defend the cause of the Arabs, not my own."[69]

Faced with his nephew's persistence, Adelard stalls for time, pointing out that he is more accustomed to dispelling what is false than to proving what is true. Then he suggests that any such discussion of God would exceed all others in the "subtlety of its intellectual content and the difficulty of its expression."[70] Wisely, he notes that the hour is late and it is time for bed, promising to take up the matter of the "beginning of the beginnings" at a later date. Somehow, that day never comes.

The preservation over the centuries of many of Adelard's works bespeaks their popularity and importance in their day. Still, the absolute numbers are small, in keeping with both the low level of "book culture" at the time and the many practical obstacles to the dissemination and storage of information. The simple survival of a medieval text is no mean feat, for each one had to be laboriously copied by hand onto stiff sheets of parchment, which in the West was generally done over many months by professional scribes in monasteries scattered across the Latin-speaking world. For every one that has come down to us today, there must have been many others that were lost; were damaged by fire, vermin, or other hazards; or simply fell into disfavor and were no longer given priority within the limited confines of the medieval monastic scriptoria.

Early copies of Adelard's *Questions on Natural Science* were made both in his native England and on the European continent. Thirteen examples from the twelfth century are extant, a number of which were produced in small, portable editions for ease of use and study. Ten others survive from the thirteenth century, but just three from the fourteenth and two from the fifteenth, suggesting a decline in popularity as other texts came to the fore. However, the work later enjoyed a brief revival, especially in Adelard's native England. Editions were also produced in Hebrew and quite possibly in French, while large sections were translated into Italian.[71] Dozens of the early Latin Euclid texts have been found, as have nine copies—but only two complete ones—of Adelard's translation of the star tables of al-Khwarizmi.[72]

Adelard's greatest achievement, however, lay less with his individual manuscripts than with his intuitive grasp of the broad significance of Arab teachings just beginning to penetrate Christian consciousness. This strand runs through *Questions on Natural Science*, which features such phrases as "my Arab masters" and "the cause of the Arabs." Unlike the handful of intellectual explorers who came before him, Adelard was not content simply to borrow the outer trappings of new ideas and technologies. Instead, he sought to reinvent himself and the very idea of the West in accordance with Arab learning. At its core was the proposition that experimentation, rational thought, and personal experience trumped convention and blind acceptance of traditional authority. Adelard seemed to realize that in order to absorb and exploit these great discoveries, he had to do more than simply master Arabic; he had to jettison almost everything he thought he knew and adopt a whole new way of looking at the world around him.[73] "If you wish to hear anything more from me, give and receive reason. For I am not the kind of man for whom the painting of the skin can satisfy. Every letter is a prostitute, open now to these affections, now to those," he lectures his nephew.[74]

As for the crusaders who preceded Adelard to Syria, the overwhelming majority were too blinded by ignorance and sectarian hatred, or by their own moral smugness, to recognize the accomplishments of the advanced civilization they now faced in battle. This tendency is reminiscent of the present day, when the West looks eastward and sees only barbarism. Adelard's outlook proved a remarkable exception to the mood of his own times—which held that Islam was an evil faith with nothing to offer Christendom but the role of sacred enemy—and he came back to England very much a new man. Everything that was once familiar in his native land now appeared part of an alien and distasteful world.

Upon the insistence of friends and family, with whom he had just reunited, Adelard surveyed the state of English society. "I found," he writes in *Questions on Natural Science*, shortly after his return home, "the princes barbarous, the bishops bibulous, judges bribable, patrons unreliable, clients sycophants, promisers liars, friends envious, and almost everybody full of ambition."[75] Ever the teacher, Adelard resolves that knowledge offers the best antidote to the "moral depravity" on display in his homeland. "I undertook the following treatise, which I know will be useful to its auditors, but whether it is pleasant, I do not know. For the present generation suffers from this ingrained fault, that it thinks that nothing should be accepted which is discovered by the 'moderns.'"[76]

During his wanderings, Adelard tells us, he adopted his trademark flowing green cloak and began to sport a prominent signet ring, set with an obscure astrological symbol, in the same rich green, "less extensive but more efficacious" in its emerald hue. Adelard's new intellectual outlook is no less startling. Gone is the young country gentleman who once dedicated earnest prose to the goddess of philosophy, in pale imitation of the bygone classical age; in his place stands the relentless seeker of knowledge and scientific truth. The new Adelard, now a citizen of the world, challenges the intellectual corruption, complacency, and rigidity that has dogged the West for centuries. Unlike the student from the cathedral schools who once branded the moderns "dumb," the reborn Adelard is an ardent proponent of contemporary scholarship—only now his world is shaped by the new and dynamic Arab learning from the East.

Such knowledge, he says, can liberate the Western world from the burden of orthodoxy and give man permission to make his own way through the universe: "For I have learned one thing from my Arab masters, with reason as guide, but you another: you follow a halter, being enthralled by the picture of authority. For what else can authority be called other than a halter? As brute animals are led wherever one pleases by a halter, but do not know where or why they are led, and only follow the rope by which they are held, so the authority of written words leads not a few of you into danger, since you are enthralled and bound by brutish credulity."[77]

Man should take refuge in God, he declares, only when his intellect proves incapable of understanding the world around him. Such a declaration connects Adelard of Bath directly to his spiritual and intellectual heir, the pioneering astronomer Galileo, whose public showdown with religious orthodoxy five centuries later would seal the end of the beginning of the Western scientific revolution. This wanderer in the flowing green robes issues the first explicit assertion in the Christian Middle Ages that the existence of God must not prevent man from exploring the laws of nature. "I will detract nothing from God, for whatever is, is from Him . . . We must listen to the very limits of human knowledge and only when this utterly breaks down should we refer things to God."[78]

Chapter Six

"WHAT IS SAID OF THE SPHERE . . ."

ONE PALE DAWN, twenty-two years before the Antioch earthquake, a scholar-monk not far from Adelard's West Country home quietly made scientific history. Pointing an astrolabe—one of the very few then in use in Europe—at an eclipse of the moon on October 18, 1092, Walcher, the prior of the monastery in Great Malvern, carried out the first known Western experiment to improve astronomical predictions. A year before, while traveling in Italy, the clergyman had witnessed a lunar eclipse but found he had no way to record the events overhead, other than to guess the approximate time. A brother monk who said he had witnessed the very same celestial phenomenon to the west in England gave a strikingly different estimate of the time.[1] Walcher or his colleague was almost certainly in error, for any time difference between the two locales would have been perceptible but slim.[2] Still, this was the same phenomenon once exploited by the early Abbasid astronomers to establish the difference in geographic coordinates between cities and other important places.

Confusion over the reported sightings stirred Walcher into action: "I still had no certainty about the time of the eclipse and I was distressed about this, because I was planning to draw up a lunar table and had no starting point." He vowed not to be caught unprepared again. One year later, Walcher got his chance when an eclipse again darkened the nighttime sky, this time fifteen degrees above the western horizon. "I at once seized my astrolabe." He used the device to note the position of the eclipse and to determine the time of day.[3]

Walcher was a leading figure in a small circle of local clerics with personal and intellectual roots back in Lotharingia, source of many of eleventh-century England's most learned courtiers and churchmen. At the time, there was simply no secular education of note available, a circumstance that began to change, slowly at first and then picking up steam, with the Norman Conquest of 1066.

The invaders brought the books and teaching masters of the European continent to England for the first time, although it would take until around 1130 before a serious scholastic community became established at Oxford.[4] The late bishop of Bath and Wells, Giso, whose successor was Adelard's own mentor, John de Villula, had been another member of this loose intellectual movement.[5] So, too, was Robert, bishop of Hereford—like Walcher a native of Lotharingia and a keen astronomer and mathematician. At the time his friend and colleague was in Italy, Robert consulted the stars in preparation for a proposed journey to the dedication of Lincoln Cathedral; his reading of the stars correctly predicted that the ceremony would not take place as scheduled, allowing him to avoid a difficult and unnecessary journey.[6]

For a time, Prior Walcher worked closely with a converted Spanish Jew, Petrus Alfonsi, who arrived in the English Midlands with a basic knowledge of Arabic astronomy and mathematics. The pair collaborated on a failed attempt to present al-Khwarizmi's *zij* to a Western audience, a project Adelard completed successfully.[7] Petrus, born and educated in the Arabic cultural world of al-Andalus, was an effective polemicist. His diatribes against both the Jews, his former coreligionists, and the Muslims endeared him to many in positions of power. Little remembered today, the man known by Chaucer as Piers Alphonse was also the author of *The Priestly Tales*. This volume had a long-lasting influence on the development of Western literature, for it introduced European readers to the Arabic literary form of the framed tale—a story within a story—further popularized by the later translation of *The Thousand and One Nights*. Chaucer adopted Petrus's novel approach in his own *Canterbury Tales*, as did Boccaccio in *The Decameron*.[8] Petrus's reports on the ways of the Muslims, including the spurious assertion that idol worship continued at the Kaaba in flagrant violation of Muhammad's demand for absolute monotheism, helped shape some of the earliest anti-Muslim attitudes among the Christians.[9]

Many of these West Country monks were scholars at heart, and in their enthusiasm for the new learning they openly embraced such innovations as the astrolabe, the abacus, and the rudiments of the Arabic number system. Walcher's determination to establish the correct time for his observation of the eclipse was typical of the new thinking—rational, precise, and grounded in experience—that slowly began to accompany these novelties. A basic text on the astrolabe, partially drawn from a very early Latin translation from Spain of the work of al-Khwarizmi, has been tentatively ascribed to Walcher or a member of his circle.[10] At his death in 1125, the mathematician-cum-cleric was remembered as a "philosopher, astronomer, geometer and abacist."[11]

Ignoring traditional religious questions that had preoccupied his predecessors, such as the annual dating of Easter, Walcher instead used his observational data to create a pair of new lunar tables. His new approach was in contravention of the teachings of the church fathers—and the authority of no less than the Venerable Bede.[12] Walcher also adopted the modern system, already well established among the Arabs, of recording astronomical data in degrees, minutes, and seconds. This replaced the clumsy and less precise Roman fractions then in common use across Europe.[13] Walcher's tables were far more accurate than those that came before, which were based not on direct observation but on the traditional medieval *computus*. Nonetheless, they proved grossly inadequate. Walcher soon found that his prediction of a full moon for New Year's Eve, 1107, for example, was off by as much as sixteen hours.[14]

Despite their new empirical basis, Walcher's tables still suffered from the medieval convention of assigning an equal number of days to each of the twelve months. This made for tidy calculations, but it seriously undercounted the days of the year. An almost contemporaneous revision of the calendar in Persia by the savant Omar Khayyam—known in the East not for the poetry of *The Rubaiyat* but for his supremely elegant mathematics—calculated the length of the solar year to eleven decimal points. Lacking a theoretical understanding of the movement of the planets, Walcher and his colleagues were unable to exploit their newfound precision in scientific measurement. They needed help from the Arab astronomers.[15]

Adelard's translation of the *zij al-Sindhind* provided one piece of the puzzle, giving the West its first real look at the inner workings of the Arabs' mathematical astronomy. The geometry of Euclid supplied another, for it allowed the vast magnitudes involved in measuring the celestial bodies to be captured and expressed in terms of "angular distance" relative to the earth or to one another. It also allowed the accurate calculation and mapping of terrestrial and celestial positions, either on a sphere or "projected" onto a two-dimensional map or chart, or onto the faceplate of the astrolabe. With the publication of his original treatise *On the Use of the Astrolabe*, probably around 1149 or 1150, Adelard further revolutionized the way Western man understood the universe around him.[16] He also made explicit the link between the new technology and the comprehensive Arab scientific edifice that stood behind it. From timekeeping to navigation, the secrets of the physical world could now be fully explored.

To Adelard, the astrolabe was more than just an instrument to aim at the sun or a prominent star and then use to take measurements or tell time; it was a polished bronze symbol for a fresh way to view the world, informed by classical philosophy and the innovations of the Arab scholars of the House of Wisdom. Armed with such a device, man could measure and begin to decipher the regular movements of the stars and the planets. He could explore the laws of nature and gain new insights into how things work. The universe was no longer an ineffable divine masterpiece; it was transformed into a giant laboratory, as well as an object of research to be studied and analyzed like any other. Attributes such as time and distance were no longer vague abstractions but took on real numerical values, opening the door to the rise of empirical science and the creation of organized, modern societies.

On the Use of the Astrolabe presented the Latin world, for the first time, with the beginnings of a coherent and comprehensive cosmology. Adelard laid to rest Isidore of Seville's misguided teaching that the earth was flat and "shaped like a wheel" and other expressions of Western sacred geography. At the center of this new worldview sat the sphere—the "perfect solid" of the ancient Greeks and the only one that can rotate on its axis in absolute symmetry, always displacing the same space—and its two-dimensional representation, the circle. "Concerning the universe . . . and its different parts I will write in Latin what I have learned from the Arabs. You can take it for granted that the universe is not square, or rectangular, but a sphere. What is said of the sphere can be said of the universe," Adelard informs the future King Henry II.[17] Adelard dedicates the work to Henry, whom he may have earlier served as personal tutor.

Working in the tradition of al-Khwarizmi and other Arab scholars, who frequently introduce their scientific works as responses to entreaties that they share their learning with friends, students, or patrons, Adelard opens his astrolabe text with just such an appeal. Prince Henry, he tells us, turned to him for "the opinions of the Arabs about the sphere and circles and motions of the stars." By this time a respected scholar and England's foremost Arabist, Adelard forgoes the ritual humility of his Muslim mentors to lecture the teenage Henry on the vital importance of a scientific understanding of the natural world. "You say that whoever dwells in a house is not worthy of its shelter if he is ignorant of its material and makeup, quantity and quality, position and peculiarity. Thus if one who was born and raised in the palace of the world should forebear after the age of discretion to know the reason for so marvelous a beauty, he is unworthy of it and, were it possible, ought to be cast out."[18]

Adelard first presents the basic tenets and concepts of spherical and theoretical astronomy, as well as key points of geography. He uses a globe as a model of the sphere of the earth, before introducing the computational powers of the astrolabe, the subject of the rest of the book.[19] Available Latin sources offered some of the same material, but the powerful influence of at least two Arab scholars stands out. The first, of course, is al-Khwarizmi, whose *zij al-Sindhind* Adelard translated earlier. The author of *On the Use of the Astrolabe* assumes the reader is familiar with the *zij*, as well as with his own Latin version of Euclid, and the treatise relies heavily on the Arab star tables to complement the calculations carried out with the device itself. Adelard also makes an important change to some of the technical data from his edition of the *zij al-Sindhind*, converting the meridian from that of Cordoba to that of Bath.[20]

Using an approach similar to that in his Euclid text, Adelard provides both Arabic names and Latin equivalents for the various parts of the astrolabe. He also integrates its operation completely with al-Khwarizmi's *zij* handbook, referring regularly to the data available in the star tables and thereby allowing the user to get the most out of the technology.[21] The other central Arab voice is that of Maslama al-Majriti, who first transposed the *zij al-Sindhind* to the meridian of Cordoba and replaced its Persian calendar with the Islamic one. At one point, Adelard mentions an *astrolabium doctoris Almirethi*, a reference to an instrument that once belonged to al-Majriti or came from his school of mathematical astronomers.[22]

In laying out the "opinions of the Arabs," Adelard devotes considerable space to the use of the circle to measure and depict the movements across the sphere of the universe, suggesting that this may still have been a novel idea among educated Western readers.[23] Such an understanding was vital, for the circle and sphere provide the basic building blocks for the study of the heavens. Here, *On the Use of the Astrolabe* comes into its own, introducing and explicating the common models behind the perceived movement of the heavens. These include the central notion of a concentric universe, nested spheres controlling the general movements of the celestial bodies, as well as the so-called eccentric orbits of the planets—identified since classical times as the sun, the moon, Mercury, Venus, Mars, Jupiter, and Saturn. Each planet is assigned its own sphere, and all of them are grouped around the earth, at the center, Adelard explains, but their circular orbits within the sphere fluctuate between a high and a low point, carving an eccentric path in their regular rotations.[24] And there are more spheres, including that of the fixed stars, as well as other refinements to keep the whole mechanism running like clockwork. *On the Use of the Astrolabe* is less a how-to on the astrolabe than a groundbreaking introduction to astronomy.

This complex theoretical apparatus reflects the heroic efforts by astronomers and philosophers over the centuries to address Plato's dictum to "save the appearances"—that is, to account for the increasingly precise observations of the scientists without violating the strict guidelines laid down by the Greeks and seemingly confirmed by common sense. In the fourth century B.C., Plato's creation myth, *Timaeus*, spelled out some of the central requirements: The world as rendered by the Creator must be a perfect whole; it must be unique, allowing the creation of no other; and it must be immune to decay or corruption. "Wherefore, he made the world in the form of a globe, round as from a lathe, having its extremes in every direction equidistant from the center, the most perfect and most like itself of all figures; for he considered that the like is infinitely fairer than the unlike."[25] For the Greek philosophers, the perfection of the celestial world should also be reflected in the course of the planets, each tracing eternal, perfect circles across the heavens.

Similar arguments were also advanced for the spherical shape of the earth. Common sense and everyday experience seemed to support this: the round image cast on the moon during a lunar eclipse; the observation of a ship's mast dropping below the horizon as it sailed from shore; or even the appearance or disappearance of the constellations as one moved north or south along the earth. The fact that a falling body, say an apple from a tree, appeared to plummet toward the center of the earth suggested that it must represent the center of the universe as well. There was no gravitational theory at the time to explain this phenomenon; besides, the notion that man inhabited the center of divine creation had obvious and long-lived religious and psychological appeal.[26] Surely a loving, all-powerful God would not exile his supreme creation, man, to some cosmological backwater.

Nor did placing the earth at the center of the stars and planets pose any practical difficulties for science. The observed motions of the heavens could generally be accounted for if the sun were seen to orbit a stationary earth in the opposite direction once a year, at a slight angle to the equator, and the "sphere of the fixed stars" were seen to rotate in a little less than twenty-four hours. Accurate calendars, almanacs, and timekeeping were all possible as a result. Even today, the basic principles of navigation and orientation all work perfectly well when based on an earth-centered model.

But there was one troubling issue, known since ancient times as "the problem of the planets," and the struggle to resolve it was central to the development of mathematical astronomy. Man had long noted that the planets—the word is derived from the Greek for "wanderer"—appear periodically to break their regular orbits, pause, and then reverse direction, before returning to their expected eastward route. Such retrograde motion occurs in Mercury every 116 days, while Mars reverses course just every 780 days. They also wander slightly north and south among the fixed stars, while generally remaining within the zodiac. The cause, of course, lies with the fact that both the individual planets and the earth itself are in constant motion— although very few in the classical and medieval worlds were prepared to consider that the earth was anything but fixed and central to the entire grand scheme. The moon, meanwhile, posed unique problems of its own; its irregular orbits around the earth, varying as much as seven hours from the average, long frustrated astronomers who sought to rely on this highly visible body as an easy way of marking time.[27]

Once again, Plato set the early tone, demanding "uniform and ordered movements" that would save the appearances. Soon a series of solutions involving interlocking spheres rotating on different axes around the central earth were advanced. The shelf life of this model was relatively brief, at least in scientific terms. Mathematical astronomy moved beyond it after only a century or so, but not before it had helped shape what was arguably the most long-lasting and influential cosmological vision in recorded history, that of Aristotle. His conception of the universe, that the planets are set in a series of rotating shells around the earth, survived more or less intact as a cosmological system until the early seventeenth century.[28] As far as the philosophers were concerned, the cosmos was defined by three general principles: It consisted of a series of rotating shells, with the earth at the center; it was shaped like that perfect solid, the sphere; and its bodies moved in perfect circles. There was, however, somewhat less unanimity concerning one other precept of Aristotle's cosmology: that the world was eternal. This matter would later come to haunt the great monotheist thinkers of Judaism, Christianity, and Islam alike.

With the work of Aristotle, the "problem of the planets" did not go away; it simply shifted from the realm of philosophy and cosmology to the smaller, more exclusive preserve of mathematical astronomy. In what might be viewed as an intellectual arms race, astronomers drew up ever-more-sophisticated mathematical models of planetary motion, only to find new problems cropping up almost immediately owing to new and better celestial observations and measurements. Two new weapons were introduced early on: the epicycle and the deferent. The deferent was defined as a circle that rotated around the earth, while the epicycle, which carried the planet, rotated around a point on the circumference of the deferent. Adjusted correctly, this combination of motions could approximate the periodic retrograde motion of each of the planets—that temporary reversal of direction—as seen from the earth.

Those minor discrepancies that could not be addressed by these techniques were at times resolved by shifting the center of the deferent circle slightly away from the earth. This created the so-called eccentric orbit, an approach that was particularly useful for the seemingly erratic movements of the sun. By shifting the center of the deferent ever so slightly, for example, astronomers could account for the observed fact that the sun spends almost six more days between the spring and autumn equinoxes than it does between autumn and spring.[29] One final innovation completed this complex mathematical edifice, the theory of the equant. According to this notion, the uniform motion of the planets, as demanded by Plato and his successors, was at times maintained not around the center of the deferent but around a displaced location. Seen from the earth, the course of the planet would appear unsteady or seem to wobble; seen from the off-center equant point, however, it would maintain uniform speed and distance, as required by the philosophers.

The Alexandrian mathematician Ptolemy took on the final job of assembling and refining this celestial machinery. He was also the architect of the equant theory. The system outlined in the *Almagest* was so successful at explaining and predicting the motions of the sun, the moon, and the planets as seen from the earth that scholars no longer referred to earlier works on the subject, many of which effectively disappeared. Gradually, Arab astronomers and philosophers began to voice unease about the equant and its violation of the principle of perfect, circular motion around a single center, the earth. A number of serious attempts were made to overhaul the Ptolemaic model, but these were based primarily on theoretical, not practical, grounds.

On the Use of the Astrolabe, accompanied by the earlier *zij al-Sindhind*, whetted the West's appetite for astronomy and opened the way for the later reception and eventual assimilation of the Ptolemaic system. The *Almagest* was translated into Latin from the original Greek in Sicily around 1160, but it was only with a version from the Arabic, completed in 1175, that it became known among Western scientists and philosophers.[30] Adelard's original treatise also helped make the bronze astrolabe all the rage in Europe, its use common as late as the seventeenth century. The instrument's great utility for casting a horoscope and other astrological operations, as well as its suitability as a teaching aid, fueled the relatively rapid diffusion of this new technology. Peter Abelard and Heloise, the most famous star-crossed lovers of the Middle Ages and accomplished scholars in their own right, had already named their love child Astrolabe. Sooner or later, every self-respecting scholar produced an astrolabe text; Chaucer left behind an unfinished essay on the device, dedicated to his nephew.

But *On the Use of the Astrolabe* contributed to one other important landmark— the early, tentative infiltration of pagan Greek cosmological thought into Western consciousness. Traditionally, early Latin texts on the astrolabe focused narrowly on just three topics: the theory of stereographic projection that displayed the three-dimensional universe on a two-dimensional surface (a map, a chart, or the disk of an astrolabe), the design and construction of the device, and instructions for its use. In his innovative enumeration and description of the concentric spheres of the universe, Adelard introduces for the first time one notable addition: an indiscernible outermost shell beyond the firmament that imparts power and gives form to things below.[31] So far, this is but a shadow of Aristotle's notion of the Unmoved Mover, who endows the celestial machinery with its eternal motion but otherwise takes no notice of man's affairs, an idea that would take increasing hold in the Christian West, much to the discomfort of traditional theologians and philosophers.

★　　★　　★

The order from the religious authorities at the University of Paris was enough to chill the blood, if not the actual pursuit of the new learning from the East: "Let the body of Master Amaury be removed from the cemetery and cast into unconsecrated ground, and the same be excommunicated by all the churches of the entire province." Moreover, the directive of 1210 commanded that the notebooks of a certain David of Dinant were to be handed over to the local bishop and burned forthwith. Another section of the same order gives a good idea of the nature of their offense: "Neither the books of Aristotle on natural philosophy nor their commentaries are to be read at Paris in public or in secret, and this we forbid under penalty of excommunication. He in whose possession the writings of David of Dinant are found after the Nativity shall be considered a heretic."[32]

Five years later, new statutes for the University of Paris, the West's leading center of theological studies, repeated the ban on the natural philosophy of Aristotle and the teachings of his two disciples, Master Amaury and David of Dinant. Apparently, the first decree had been generally evaded, or even ignored outright, in the faculty of arts—a tactic that would surface repeatedly in the increasingly contentious relationship between theologians and philosophers throughout the thirteenth century. The same order also spelled out more mundane rules of comportment for the teaching masters, including a ban on sartorial excess: "no round cope shoes that are ornamented or with elongated pointed toes." Masters were, however, allowed to invite friends and associates to university meetings and receptions, "but only a few."[33]

Church authorities had good reason to be concerned with the rapid pace of change in Paris and other fledgling centers of Western knowledge. The traditional clerical controls were starting to loosen, as the locus of advanced teaching began to move from the cathedral schools to the universities that were taking shape from among clusters of teachers and students in cities across Europe. Also beginning to die out was the centuries-old monopoly of the church fathers over philosophical and theological teachings. St. Augustine set the ground rules at the dawn of the Middle Ages when he taught that man should begin with faith and proceed from revelation to reason.[34] This established theology as the pinnacle of speculative thought and reduced philosophy, and with it natural science, to the role of "handmaiden" to the theologians—an approach that was beginning to come under fire from technological change and the accompanying trend toward more critical thinking. Still, the ban on Aristotle's natural philosophy—encompassing theories of nature, the origins of the universe, and similar topics—so early in the Arab-inspired awakening poses something of a riddle.

Europe's churchmen had long venerated the name of Aristotle in association with their beloved technique of logical argument, known as dialectic. In this way, they mirrored the earliest Abbasid encounter with his teachings, which were first mined for their logical systems to use in religious debate against non-Muslims. What philosophical instruction existed in twelfth-century Europe rarely moved beyond these methods of argument to encompass metaphysics or natural science. When it did so, it was often confronted with fragmentary texts and only half-baked understanding. The discipline itself was practiced primarily to enhance the mental acuity of students and to prepare them for the more serious study of theology; it was not designed to impart information, such as a coherent philosophical vision of the cosmos. In general, philosophical speculation, particularly cosmology, had been largely displaced for almost twelve centuries by the all-encompassing worldview of the church, which offered its own explanation of man's origins, his place in the universe, and his ultimate destiny.[35]

True, scattered Latin translations, primarily from the Arabic, of Aristole's major works of natural philosophy had already begun to appear some decades earlier in Spain and Italy, but it is hardly possible to speak in any meaningful way of an organized body of Aristotelian thought available in Latin. Members of the Paris faculty of theology, the driving force behind the bans of 1210 and 1215, would almost certainly have been hard-pressed to name any of Aristotle's offending texts, or to identify any of the vital Muslim commentaries needed to understand them.[36] No less an authority than Roger Bacon, who lectured at Paris, dates the real arrival there of the authentic natural philosophy of Aristotle to around 1230, one hundred years after many of the basic ideas and concepts of Greek and Arab natural science had already entered into circulation.[37] Surviving lecture notes from 1245 suggest that Roger himself was among the first to teach this natural philosophy at the University of Paris, although such works were already being debated at Oxford.[38]

So what precisely did the church have in mind as early as 1210 when it ordered a ban on Aristotle's natural science and suppressed the teachings of two of his more enthusiastic disciples, David of Dinant and Master Amaury? If Aristotle's thought was either unknown at the time or, at best, only poorly understood, then what was the threat to Christian orthodoxy? And whence did it come?

Here, as with the introduction of the Arabic Euclid and the star tables of al-Khwarizmi, the key lies with Adelard of Bath, whose hunt for the *studia Arabum* led him to the foremost classical authority on the subject of astrology, the ninth-century Persian scholar Abu Mashar al-Balkhi, commonly known among the Latins as Albumazar. Evidence from surviving manuscripts reveals that Adelard may have acquired Albumazar's *The Abbreviation of the Introduction to Astrology* while in Antioch, along with his copy of Thabit ibn Qurra's work on talismans. His Latin translations of the two texts appear together with a partial collection of astrological aphorisms, a clue that all three may have been completed around the same time and place.[39]

The work itself, essentially an astrological handbook, is not particularly remarkable. It is, rather, Albumazar's stripped-down and simplified version of his own encyclopedic *The Introduction to Astrology*, written in Baghdad in 848. The idea of the abridged text, the author tells us, was to bring this complex subject "closer to comprehension."[40] Missing is much of the rich philosophical explication and scientific detail that later made the larger work as popular in the West as it once was in the East. Still, it firmly established the importance of Arab astrological learning and incited a profound hunger for more among Latin scholars that lasted at least until the astronomical discoveries of Galileo and others in the seventeenth century.[41]

Astrology has long been in disrepute, but it was once seen as an important and legitimate field of study that promised a foretaste of human events from the movements of the stars and planets. This view rested on the widespread acceptance of the universal "law" whereby the entire natural world—the affairs of man; the life cycles of the animals and plants: phenomena such as earthquakes, floods, and weather—was directed by the movements of the heavens. This provided a coherent theory of nature that linked man and the cosmos into one single, satisfying whole. At its core lay the classical notion, celebrated in the title of Adelard's *On the Same and the Different*, that the eternal, perfect, and unchanging "superior" celestial bodies, the realm of the Same, governed the ever-changing, corruptible "inferior" region of man and the earth, that of the Different.

Such astrology served for centuries as a perfectly legitimate scientific theory: It appeared to account successfully for the observable world; it addressed the central questions of the day; and it proved fertile ground for further research and inquiry. Despite some misgivings among Muslim, Christian, and Jewish theologians that astrology imperiled man's freedom to choose good over evil and threatened individual accountability, its basic tenets were largely accepted without serious challenge. The philosopher Albertus Magnus found nothing amiss in reconciling astrology's fundamental principle with the biblical account of the sixth day of Creation, when the earth "brought forth" the living creatures. "Since the power to produce animals is not in the earth, but, according to astronomers, is in the heavens," Albertus concludes in his *Summa theologiae*, the earth must have provided the material principle for the animals, while the active part resided with the heavens.[42] It took another four hundred years, and Isaac Newton's universal law of gravitation, for the distinction among the learned between the heavens, on the one hand, and man's earthly home, on the other, to begin to blur and finally dissolve. Even then, it persisted in the fields of biology and medicine until Darwin's theory of evolution, published in 1859, finished it off forever.[43]

Given the central importance of astrology among the Arabs, it is little wonder that Adelard turned his own hand to what the West came to know as "the judgments of the stars"—as distinct from astronomy proper, which addressed the regular movements and positions of the heavens. "Here begins the smaller introduction to the science of the stars of Jafar the Astrologer, taken out of the Arabic by Adelard of Bath," reads the opening line of his Latin translation of Albumazar, the first complete Arabic astrology manual to appear in the West.[44] Adelard then goes on to introduce his readers to the fundamental import of astrology and its essential link to the mastery of the other sciences: "Whoever, seeking the higher science of philosophy with constant study, investigates the admirable effects of the celestial [beings] on the sensible universe—in that the likenesses of forms on high appear by certain natural motion over this lower world, and portend the foreknowledge of future things—can hardly achieve this without the knowledge of the degrees of the circle and the signs."[45]

The appearance of Adelard's *Abbreviation of the Introduction to Astrology*, completed around 1120, helped ensconce Albumazar in the West as the supreme authority on all aspects of astrological science.[46] Within two decades, translators working in Spain completed two different Latin versions of the full, unabridged astrology textbook, more than six times longer than Adelard's edition. These restored the philosophical and scientific underpinnings excised in the abbreviated text. This provided the West with its first real gateway to the natural science of the Arabic Aristotle. Albumazar had set out to justify and defend astrology in terms of general scientific understanding. In the world of ninth-century Baghdad in which he lived and worked, that meant linking it to the traditions of Greek physical science and metaphysics known as *falsafa*. And that meant, first and foremost, Aristotle—at least Aristotle as the Arabs understood him. The result is an eclectic work of Arab, Alexandrian, Persian, and Hindu astrological ideas, resting on a relatively solid footing of classical Greek scientific thinking.[47]

The Introduction to Astrology provided the budding natural philosophers of the Latin-speaking world with a compelling and comprehensive vision of the cosmos in which the machinery of the universe was governed by laws of motion and causality. Another popular work by Albumazar, also translated into Latin, showed how these same laws could be applied to the course of human history. In the preface to this second work, the Arab astrologer makes explicit the linkage between the heavens and events on earth, identified here in purely Aristotelian terms: "This is the book on the sum of the indications of the celestial bodies on terrestrial events occurring in the world of generation and corruption . . . It is called the *Book of Religions and Dynasties*."[48]

Today, the name of Albumazar has almost disappeared from sight, along with those of many of the other Arab scholars whose works were once common currency in both the East and the West. The tendency among Renaissance scholars and their successors, from the Enlightenment to the modern day, to dismiss the contributions of the Muslims and assign a classical Greek pedigree to the Western world of ideas led them to emphasize the influence of the astrological writings of the Greek astronomer Ptolemy.[49] However, the early work of Adelard of Bath and his immediate successors accorded Albumazar centuries of influence as one of medieval Christendom's leading authorities on science and philosophy. His teachings helped to establish almost universal acceptance for a vision of the cosmos as dominated by comprehensible laws.[50]

With its theoretical grounding in the classical Greek conception of the universe, *The Introduction to Astrology* proved an ideal vehicle for the transmission of science and philosophy in general to the Latin world, for it united the prestige of Aristotle with the undeniable lure of the occult. So influential was the philosophical basis of Albumazar's astrology that it served as the first important conduit to the West for Aristotle's natural philosophy.[51] A note in one medieval manuscript, possibly in Roger Bacon's own hand, says that the leading "authority in the science of the heavens" is not Aristotle himself but Albumazar.[52]

The first severe backlash by Christian theologians against the "new logic"— the Paris condemnation of 1210 aimed at Master Amaury and David of Dinant—was provoked for the most part by the growing popularity of Arab astrology and its undertones of pagan Greek philosophy. These two intellectual traditions, the Arab and the Greek, posed profound challenges to Christian orthodoxy that would come to occupy much of the theological and philosophical debate of the thirteenth and fourteenth centuries. These included questions of fundamental importance to the church: the role of man's free will; the immortality of the soul; God's knowledge of the particulars of human behavior, particularly apt given that he would preside over Judgment Day; and perhaps the most important for early science, the contentious matter of whether the earth was eternal, as asserted in Aristotle's natural philosophy, or created "in the beginning," as recorded in Genesis.

There was a general unease at this swelling invasion of ideas and thought seemingly in conflict with church doctrine, just as there had been two hundred years earlier at the Arab-based learning of Pope Sylvester II. One medieval Latin scribe appended his own succinct commentary to a fresh manuscript copy of Albumazar's great astrological textbook: "Finished, with praise to God for his help and a curse on Mahomet [Muhammad] and his followers."[53] The Western world could not simply adopt unaltered some of the fundamental precepts of this new natural philosophy; yet it could not afford to ignore any longer the bounties of science and other advanced learning that accompanied more suspect teachings. A reworking of natural philosophy would be essential before Christendom could begin to accept and fully exploit the new science now arriving from the East.

But for now, Aristotle's great works of cosmology and physics, already widely read in Arabic for centuries, remained largely unknown in the West, as did the insightful and provocative commentaries of the Muslim philosophers, particularly the peerless works of Avicenna and his rationalist successor Averroes. These texts, which reflected hundreds of years of debate within the Islamic tradition but were unknown in the West, would have an immediate

and powerful impact on young minds across Europe. Soon they would be all
the rage at Paris, Oxford, and other universities.

Adelard of Bath burst onto the European intellectual landscape as a young
man, straight out of the cathedral school in Tours, with his public denuncia-
tion of the teachings of "the moderns" and his equally public intention of
redressing the shameful state of Western learning by turning to the Arab world
for illumination. The vague outlines of his life and adventures—even his taste
in clothes, or at least in colors—can be gleaned from his translations and
original writings. The same cannot be said for the time or place of his death,
both of which remain obscured from modern view.

However, it may be possible to identify Adelard with the anonymous
astrologer responsible for a series of remarkable royal horoscopes carried out in
England in the middle of the twelfth century. Horoscopes from the Norman
period are extremely rare. By one estimate, there may be no more than fifteen
examples extant from the entire twelfth century, and there was just a handful of
Western astrologers alive—and perhaps only two in all of England at the
time—capable of performing the sophisticated calculations and determinations required to carry out these politically sensitive readings for the royal
house.[54]

Several aspects of the collection suggest that Adelard may be the author of
as many as nine of ten horoscopes preserved together in a single manuscript.[55]
In the first place, they rely on astronomical data similar to that from the *zij* of
al-Khwarizmi and reworked for the latitude of Cordoba, the very same material
Adelard first translated into Latin and introduced to the West. Second, the
work exhibits a considerable level of technical skill and experience, except for
the rather glaring problem that the astrologer should be using local data from
England, not Spain. And third, the horoscopes presume a trusted position
within the court, something Adelard seems to have enjoyed later in life. The
bulk of the collection can be dated to 1151, when he would have been around
seventy years old, a good number of years for his day but not an unreasonable
life span. After that, Adelard's paper trail disappears, suggesting that the well-
traveled scholar, court astrologer, and resident Arabist likely died some time
not long afterward.

Adelard's experience in the world of Arab science established him as a
respected scholar and intellectual elder statesman back home in England.

There he inspired a steady stream of brilliant scholar-adventurers, some of whom soon followed in his footsteps to consult the Arabs on everything from astrology to zoology. Exploiting his standing at court, Adelard used one section of *On the Use of the Astrolabe* to propose to Henry Plantagenet a radical model for his kingdom. It should be ruled, Adelard tells the future Henry II, by a philosopher-king, for philosophers speak the truth and are guided by natural justice and reason. It should be tolerant of all religions and beliefs. And it should recognize the authority of the Arabs—that is, of the scientists and thinkers—and not that of the rigid church fathers.[56]

Chapter Seven

"THE WISEST PHILOSOPHERS OF THE WORLD"

FIRED BY THE examples of Adelard of Bath, Stephen of Pisa, and other pioneers of the *studia Arabum*, adventurous Western scholars soon began to fan out across the former Muslim lands of Spain, Sicily and southern Italy, and the so-called Latin East in pursuit of newly available works of philosophy and the arts and sciences that accompanied them. Christian conquest and, to a far lesser extent, trade began to open up the vast Arab libraries to Western eyes, particularly in Spanish territory once held by the Muslims. Plenty of eager readers stepped forward. Centuries before the region's final Arab stronghold, the kingdom of Granada, fell to the armies of Ferdinand and Isabella in 1492, the Latins were busy poring over the invaluable works left behind as the Muslims were forced to withdraw gradually from the Iberian Peninsula. In what amounted to an intellectual gold rush, young scholars hurried into the unknown to uncover Arabic texts and then render them into Latin before someone else could beat them to it.

From the second quarter of the twelfth century, individual Western scholars set up shop wherever they could find reliable supplies of Arabic books and influential patrons to support them. In Spain—the most popular destination due to both its proximity and its enormous cultural wealth—many of the translators worked in teams, employing local Jewish intellectuals or Christians versed in both Arabic and the vernacular as intermediaries between the original text and the final Latin version. Others mastered Arabic and even Hebrew, determined to squeeze the most out of the rich milieu of al-Andalus, where Jewish learning had flourished alongside that of the Arabs.

By its very nature, this spontaneous translation movement meant that errors, misunderstandings, and misattributions were inevitable. Access and brevity were often more important than content in the selection of texts, and as a result some minor works won widespread circulation while important books were ignored.[1] Early Christian scholars commonly thought they were reading Aristotle when they were more likely studying bastardized versions filtered through Arab astrology. Likewise, works falsely attributed to Aristotle, the so-called Pseudo-Aristotle texts, circulated widely. A considerable number of "translations" have also come to light for which Arab or Greek originals remain unidentified, raising the possibility that some Latin scholars may have been concealing their own unorthodox views behind the newfound respectability of Arab learning.[2]

The translators more than made up for any such shortcomings with a flush of energy and enthusiasm that saw Arabic books rendered into Latin at an accelerating pace. Early interest in works of astrology prompted demand for an understanding of geometry, mathematics, and astronomy—all necessary to practice the art of celestial divination. Influential Arabic writings on the classification of the different sciences stimulated interest in a broader range of translations: on medicine, pharmacology, optics, alchemy, and ways to use the astrolabe and the *zij*. By the second half of the twelfth century, translations of major scientific works were being augmented by the teachings of the Arab philosophers.

The treasures that Western travelers found waiting for them owed much to the social, cultural, and intellectual traditions established under Muslim Spain's first great ruler, Abd al-Rahman, the refugee grandson of the tenth Umayyad caliph. Abd al-Rahman had escaped the Abbasid revolution and found refuge with his mother's Berber people in North Africa. From there, he set his eyes on the storied riches of nearby Spain, just across the strait. Within a few years, he patched together a coalition of Berbers, pro-Umayyad Arab fighters, and other disaffected groups and crossed into Europe in the autumn of 755.

A considerable chunk of the peninsula had already been under Arab control for more than four decades, ever since General Tariq bin Ziyad led a mostly Berber army of around seven thousand men from North Africa and defeated the Christian Visigoths. The general landed his invasion force in the spring of 711 and built a fortress on the mountain of rock that still bears his name—Jabal Tariq, or Gibraltar—before advancing well to the north and killing the Visigoth king, Roderic. But internal dissension plagued the new domain from the outset, and in the summer of 756 Abd al-Rahman exploited these weaknesses to capture the capital, Cordoba, and proclaim himself master of Muslim Spain.

Mindful of the sensitivities of his powerful Abbasid rivals back home, the new ruler was careful not to claim the title or religious authority held by the caliph—one of his successors would see to that almost two hundred years later. Instead, Abd al-Rahman settled for the unprepossessing title of amir, or military commander. During a reign of more than three decades, he set the ever-shifting geographic territory of Muslim Spain on a course to one day rival the glories of the eastern empire. The Muslims would remain a significant presence in Spain for almost eight centuries.

Like Abd al-Rahman himself, the raw materials for the transformation of what had been a Christian backwater under the Visigoths into Europe's undisputed cultural superpower owed much to their origins in the Arab heartland. The amir built a country villa just outside Cordoba, Munya al-Rusafa, named after his grandfather's estate in Syria from which the young prince had had to flee for his life. Exotic imports from the Middle East, such as pomegranates and peaches, soon graced this man-made oasis. So did Spain's first date palm, whose forlorn presence inspired Abd al-Rahman to write a nostalgic verse comparing its lot as an exile to his own: "I said to it: 'How like me you are, far away and in exile in long separation from family and friends. You have sprung from soil in which you are a stranger, and I, like you, am far from home.' "[3]

Yet this transposition, the source of the amir's melancholy, was by no means an aberration. The genius of the medieval Arabs lay in their extraordinary receptivity to new ideas, their ability to identify and adopt what they needed from foreign cultures—first Persian and Hindu, then Greek—and to modify and enhance these notions to fit the practical, intellectual, and, especially, religious demands of their own times. Ibn Khaldun, a masterful observer of the human condition whose family had been driven from al-Andalus by the Christian conquest, once noted that his fellow Arabs could simply not sit still: "All the customary activities of the Arabs lead to travel and movement."[4] The result was an almost dizzying transit of people, arts, technologies, even plants, across the enormous expanse of the known world that comprised the lands of Islam.

Even deep political divisions within this community of believers, whether the rise of al-Andalus in the eighth century, the later fragmentation of the

Abbasid Empire, or the eventual dissolution of Muslim Spain in the eleventh century into rival petty kingdoms, could not break the fundamental bonds provided by a common faith, language, and legal code and other shared cultural values. At the same time, Islam's presence on three continents gave it an extraordinary reach, capable of uncovering and then assimilating an array of traditions and cultures that might otherwise have remained isolated and apart. Arab scholars effectively enjoyed a global monopoly on knowledge of the far reaches of the world that remained unrivaled until Europe's Age of Discovery. In such an environment, it is no surprise that the celebrated physician and scientist al-Razi, known in the West as Rhazes, in the early tenth century could discuss intelligently the relative medicinal merits of different strains of saltwort grown as far apart as Spain and India.[5]

Over the course of four centuries, innovations of all kinds from India, Persia, and Iraq flowed steadily westward, through Egypt to the Muslims of the Maghrib—essentially modern-day Algeria, Morocco, and Tunisia; West Africa; and al-Andalus, the latter bordering directly on Christian Europe. For example, Arabs from Yemen who settled in North Africa and Spain brought along their established irrigation regulations and administrative procedures, as well as new crops, new technologies, and new systems to enhance land use and increase yields.[6] In time, this traffic would constitute somewhat less of a one-way street, but for now al-Andalus and the rest of the western Muslim world were the primary beneficiaries of this expanding store of innovation, science, and know-how emerging in the East.

Consider the common eggplant. Originating in India, the vegetable was apparently well established in Persia at the time of the Muslim conquest, and soon it was discussed in great detail in Arabic cookbooks and agricultural manuals. It was even celebrated in verse. The plant was then taken to Egypt, across the Maghrib, and into al-Andalus. One medieval account describes four different varieties known at the time in Spain: a "local" type, the Cordoban, the Syrian, and the Egyptian.[7] Watermelon, spinach, the hard wheat essential to the high art of Italian pasta, and many other foodstuffs now common on Western dinner tables followed similar patterns. Along the way, these imports had to be adapted to new climates and conditions and supported with often complex systems of cultivation and irrigation. Many important Andalusi crops—rice, sugarcane, and oranges and other citrus, to name just a few—had their origins in climates that did not suffer the summer droughts typical of the Mediterranean world. Irrigation schemes, based on advanced engineering techniques and backed by intricate legal and administrative procedures for implementing, sharing, and maintaining them, were vital to long-term success.

The farmers of Muslim Spain became expert in the diversion, collection, and distribution of water for farming, as witnessed by the rich Arabic linguistic trail they left behind in contemporary Spanish: The words for floodgate (*azuda*), irrigation ditch (*acequia*), waterwheel (*noria*), water mill (*aceña*), and related terms are all derivations from Arabic.[8] This same process of East-to-West progression and selective adaptation was repeated time after time, involving everything from the latest fashions in music, dress, and taste to sophisticated studies in astronomy, mathematics, medicine, and philosophy.

From its founding, the Arab court at Cordoba had set out to import books and attract scholars from the East in a deliberate bid to compete with the Abbasids. Among these works was the *zij al-Sindhind* of al-Khwarizmi, which arrived not long after it was completed in Baghdad. The prolonged struggle between al-Mamun and his brother for the Abbasid throne in the early ninth century left a number of court scholars, physicians, and poets temporarily without patronage or prospects; some were more than happy to try their luck in al-Andalus. Still, Spain battled a lingering reputation in the intellectual circles of Baghdad, Cairo, and Damascus as an uncultured, provincial outpost. It often took the threat of political or social unrest in the East, or promises of substantial financial reward, to convince hesitant scholars to make the trip.

One who did was the celebrated musician Ziryab, who arrived from Baghdad under mysterious circumstances; contemporary accounts hint darkly at royal intrigue and the poisonous jealousy of a less talented rival. Ziryab brought with him a repertoire of thousands of songs, and his talent and fame soon established him as Cordoba's leading arbiter of manners, taste, and popular culture. He is widely credited with introducing the locals to such niceties as toothpaste, underarm deodorant, eating meals in distinct courses, and fine cuisine in general. Among the other figures to appear on the scene was the eccentric inventor Abbas ibn Firnas, whose ill-fated attempt to fashion wings and then fly from the heights of the amir's palace ended in some serious injuries but not a broken spirit; he went on to perfect a technique for cutting crystal, build an in-home planetarium, and design a complex clepsydra, or water clock, that could approximate the changing times of the five daily prayers.[9]

The Muslim conquest had already brought the Arabic language to the western edge of Europe, and it quickly became the accepted medium of high culture and often of everyday life within and among the Muslim, Jewish, and Christian communities of al-Andalus. As early as the ninth century, the bishop of Cordoba bemoaned the fact that the Arabic tongue was endangering the survival of Latin, the language of the Catholic Church. He was aghast at the alarming rate at which his fellow Christians were devouring Arabic books and "building up great libraries of them at enormous cost . . . Hardly one can write a passable Latin letter to a friend, but innumerable are those who can express themselves in Arabic and can compose poetry in that language with greater art than the Arabs themselves."[10]

A handful of anti-Arab conservatives launched a campaign to incite Christians to slander the Prophet Muhammad in public, in the hopes that severe treatment of the militants would provoke a rebellion. A small number of these so-called Cordoba Martyrs were in fact executed, but only after Muslim and Christian leaders tried without success to defuse the crisis peacefully. The movement never caught fire, and good relations among the faiths were restored. Yet the bishop's deepest fears were not without foundation: The widespread use of Arabic did help break Latin's stranglehold on Europe's literary and learned speech, paving the way for the rise of the vernacular languages and the great works of "national" writers.[11] These include Cervantes, who uses the device of a lost Arab "original" author, Sidi ben Hamed, to frame his story of Don Quixote; Dante, whose description of Paradise and the Inferno almost certainly spring from Islamic models then in European circulation; and Shakespeare.

Andalusi innovations in Arabic love poetry spread into Christian Spain and southern France through diplomacy, intermarriage, war, and other contacts across the sectarian divide. The institution of the *qiyan*, a singing girl not unlike the Japanese geisha, carried on the tradition of Arabic lyrical poetry and song in the courts of al-Andalus. These slave girls presented their masters and patrons with an image of the beloved as capricious and often unattainable, in keeping with the erotic sensibility of the day: "For both by training and by innate instinct, her nature is to set up snares and traps for her victims," sighs one ninth-century Arab writer on the subject of the *qiyan*.[12]

These singers at times were given to Christian princes as diplomatic gifts or comprised part of a marriage dowry. They were also taken in battle. The seizure of the Muslim city of Barbastro by a force of Normans and knights from southern France in 1064 saw the capture of hundreds of these highly trained slave girls, many of whom ended up as entertainers and concubines in the royal households of southern France. One beneficiary was the young William IX of Aquitaine—often called the first troubadour, or lyric poet in a "modern" European tongue—who grew up surrounded by the songs and verses of the Arabs.[13] Readers of troubadour poetry will have no difficulty recognizing the recurrent themes—the lover's total submission to his beloved, the use of secret signs and intermediaries, the rapture induced by silent suffering and self-restraint—that run through the older repertoire of the *qiyan*.[14]

The geographer Ibn Hawqal, who visited Cordoba in 948, declared that the imperial capital "has no equal in the Maghrib, and hardly any in Egypt, Syria or Mesopotamia, for the size of its population, its extent, the space occupied by its markets, the cleanliness of its streets, the architecture of its mosques, the number of its baths and caravanserais [merchants' inns]."[15] Although figures vary wildly, the city's population has been estimated at more than one hundred thousand, roughly on par with the Byzantine capital Constantinople but towering over anything at the time in Christian Europe.

Other contemporary accounts say the caliphs maintained a library whose catalog alone filled forty-four large volumes. The collection was so big— commonly put at four hundred thousand volumes—that it took five days just to transport the works of poetry during one of the royal library's periodic moves to bigger quarters. Street lamps, paved city roadways, and other civic amenities were plentiful, seven hundred years before London could boast of any form of public illumination. Successful cataract operations, using instruments fashioned from sharpened fish bones, were carried out in the mosque by the city's surgeons.[16]

There were at least two fields where Andalusi men of science at times outdid their learned counterparts in the East. The first was the down-to-earth subject of agronomy, along with the related disciplines of botany, pharmacology, astrology, and meteorology. The second was the more rarefied matter of Aristotle's philosophy, encompassing cosmology, metaphysics, and elements of theology.

A number of factors drove what might be termed a Green Revolution carried out by the Muslims of the Iberian Peninsula—some seemingly accidents of history, others intimately bound up with the nature and experience of the Arabs themselves. First, the science of agriculture received a big boost from the timely appearance in Spain of several key scientific works. The sudden arrival in the tenth century of a Greek medical masterpiece by Dioscorides, a diplomatic gift of the Byzantine emperor, sparked intensive interest in the pursuit of botany and pharmacology. Also influential was the *Calendar of Cordoba*, a uniquely Andalusi work that combined a wealth of Arab astronomical tradition and intricate calculations with agricultural information, weather predictions, and even key elements of the religious calendar of Spain's large Arabic-speaking Christian community, the Mozarabs, from the Arabic for "those who follow the ways of the Arabs." Emblematic of the multi-confessional nature of al-Andalus, where Muslim rulers were generally tolerant of their Jewish and Christian subjects, one surviving example of the *Calendar of Cordoba* is written in standard Arabic but with Hebrew letters.[17] Entries for March in one text include the vernal equinox, the coming of Easter, astronomical events predicted in the *zij al-Sindhind*, and a storm warning for late in the month: "The winds which blow now damage, by their violence, the early figs and the formation of fruits."[18]

Second, there was a pervasive desire on the part of the Andalusis to match the glories of the Muslim heartland and even to surpass them. In the fine art of cuisine, for example, this meant at the very least replicating the large variety of fruits, vegetables, and herbs featured in the classical Arab repertoire developed in the East. And that required significant advances in collecting, introducing, acclimatizing, and successfully raising crops historically unknown in Spain. Much of the basic research was assisted by the vogue among the rich and powerful for experimental and ornamental gardens, patterned after Munya al-Rusafa, the country estate of the first amir. In such surroundings, specialists could adapt imported plants to the local conditions and improve existing varieties, by means of grafting or other techniques.[19]

The number of such "royal" gardens rose substantially in the early eleventh century, when the centralized caliphate collapsed and made way for dozens of petty kingdoms scattered across al-Andalus. The imperial capital never recovered from what the Arabs call the *fitna*, a state of social chaos. "Weep for the splendor of Cordoba," laments the historian Ibn Idhari. "Fortune made her a creditor and demanded payment for the debt."[20] But this dispersal of power into small, atomized states created opportunities for scholars of all sorts, as the new generation of individual rulers and petty dynasts sought to imitate the caliphs of old and to outdo one another at the same time.[21] With their political and military room to maneuver often circumscribed by internal weakness, as well as by treaty obligations with one another and with the Christians to the north, these so-called party kingdoms were left to fight it out in the cultural arena. Agronomists, poets, philosophers, and other court intellectuals were perhaps the only ones in al-Andalus to benefit directly from the *fitna*.

The shrinking geography of Muslim Spain, under steady pressure from Christian expansionism, introduced an added element of fluidity to this game of royal patronage. The ruler of Seville, for example, eagerly snapped up one of al-Andalus's leading agricultural authorities, Ibn Bassal, and appointed him director of the "Garden of the Sultan" after the fall of Toledo to the Christians forced the scholar and other members of the city-state's Muslim intellectual elite to scatter.[22] Seville soon emerged as the center of the science of agriculture, with much of the activity linked to the work of Ibn Bassal and his colleagues at the Garden of the Sultan.

Andalusi treatises on agronomy typically open with chapters on the varying types of soil, water, and fertilizers, followed by sections on veterinary science, the cultivation of plants and the rearing of animals. Many include timetables or calendars of agricultural activity, combined with important meteorologic advice and associated astronomical techniques, folk traditions, and even magic.[23] Perhaps the most remarkable extant work in the Seville tradition is the twelfth-century *Anonymous Botanist*. This treatise presents an ambitious attempt at the systematic classification of the plant kingdom along recogniz-ably modern lines many centuries before the Western works of Cesalpinus and Linnaeus.[24]

In contrast to the intellectual curiosity and cultural receptivity of the Arab world, the Christian West showed remarkably little interest in this Green Revolution. In the three regions of Western military success against the Muslims in the eleventh and twelfth centuries—Spain, Sicily, and the crusader states of the Near East—the agricultural innovations and crop introductions of the Arabs generally disappeared under the new European stewardship of the land. Christian peasants brought in to work the newly conquered territory were unable to master the skills needed to cultivate these specialized crops. This was aggravated further by the rigidity of the prevailing European feudal land system. Knowledge of vital irrigation techniques was also lost in the Arab retreat, and lower population densities created by the departure of Muslim refugees reduced economic incentives for intensive farming.[25]

Instead, the Christians tended to rely on familiar but less valuable old crops, chiefly cereals and vines, which they farmed in the old ways. Later attempts to follow Arab examples frequently failed for lack of know-how or proper organization, or else produced crops that were substandard. In the early thirteenth century, Frederick II of Sicily had to send to the Middle East for Arab experts to help him revive what had once been, before his ancestors drove out many of the Muslims, a thriving sugarcane industry.[26] It took centuries for Europe to demonstrate any real receptivity to the new crops, first as ornamental exotica and then as foodstuffs and industrial raw materials. Well into the late Renaissance, long after the last Muslims had been forcibly converted or expelled altogether, Spanish authorities had to translate an Arabic agronomy manual in order to get the most out of the land that was once al-Andalus.

In Spain, practical obstacles to the effective adoption of Arab innovations were augmented by an almost insurmountable ideological barrier—the notion that the Christians had a sacred duty to expel the Muslims, extirpate all traces of their faith and culture, and liberate the land from these foreign invaders. This was not conquest, but "reconquest," a divinely inspired return to the natural order of things, in which Spain was a strictly Catholic country, pure of blood and pure of heart. It was often called a Crusade, but the Spanish preferred the term *Reconquista*.

It took time, but the *Reconquista* proved an unstoppable military and political force, steadily rolling back the Muslims over the centuries. Yet Catholic Spain, alone among the major Western states, found it almost impossible to benefit directly from the riches of Arab science that were left virtually on its doorstep. When Seville fell in 1248, the forces of the Christian *Reconquista* were unaware that the minaret of the city-state's great mosque was also Europe's first observatory, built under the supervision of the mathematician Jabir ibn Afiah. Unsure what to do with the towering structure, the conquerors turned it into a belfry.

As the pace of the translation movement accelerated, aided by high-level patronage from church and state, the Muslims were helpless to prevent the appropriation of their cultural and intellectual heritage. In a sign of the frustration that this engendered in certain circles, one Muslim cleric from al-Andalus raged against his fellow believers for trafficking in Arabic texts. In an age when the modern practice of scholarly citation and other similar conventions were unheard of, it was easy for Arab ideas to be passed off as Western innovations. "You must not sell books of science to Jews and Christians," warned Ibn Abdun, ". . . because it happens that they translate these scientific books and attribute them to their own people and to their bishops, when they are indeed Muslim works."[27]

Two of the most prominent early translators, the Englishman Robert of Ketton and the Slav Hermann of Carinthia, teamed up in Spain to pursue a course of reading and study that they hoped would enable them one day to master the complexities of the *Almagest*. Along the way, Hermann translated Albumazar's *Introduction to Astrology*, taking up the complete version that Adelard had slighted in favor of the more basic *Abbreviation*, while Robert introduced the West to al-Khwarizmi's science of algebra and produced the first Latin text on the Arab art of alchemy. The pair regularly sent their translations to colleagues in France, where the texts enriched the curricula of the old cathedral schools. Clearly, the two felt they were making progress as they worked their way painstakingly through the imposing body of Arab learning. At one point, Hermann writes of "the trappings and decorations which long vigils and most earnest labor had acquired for [us] from the depths of the treasures of the Arabs."[28] Elsewhere, Robert recommends they turn next to a "book concerning ratios, so that a clearer way to the *Almagest* (which is the principal goal of our study) might be open to us."[29]

But in 1142, this intellectual idyll was disrupted by the unexpected arrival from France of Peter the Venerable, the abbot of Cluny, which at its height boasted more than six hundred monasteries and about ten thousand monks.[30] Peter approached the two scholars with an unusual commission—the first Latin translation of the Koran, as well as some other works on Muslim beliefs and practices. Neither Robert nor Hermann, working together somewhere in the vicinity of the Ebro River, had ever shown the slightest interest in religious questions. They were more than content to learn from the Muslim scientists and philosophers and to leave the crusading, whether military or literary, to others.

The abbot was forced to shell out an exorbitant sum to entice the two men to drop their beloved scientific research for this religious commission. Yet, it seems, he lacked complete confidence that his Latin translation team was up to the job. "I found them in Spain around the Ebro, studying the art of astrology, and brought them to do this business by means of a large remuneration," Peter later acknowledges in a letter to a church colleague. "In order that the translation should not lack the fullest fidelity, nor anything be taken away be deceit from our attention, I also added a Saracen to the Christian translators."[31]

Peter's project provides an intriguing counterpoint to the church's steadfast commitment to holy war, fifty years after Pope Urban II's call to crusade. Why was it, Peter wondered, that the church was so intent on killing Muslims rather than on saving their souls by converting them to Christianity? But to do that, the West would first have to address its woeful ignorance about the faith. "A flame was enkindled in my meditation. I was indignant that the Latins did not know the cause of such perdition, and by reason of that ignorance could not be moved to put up any resistance; for there was no one who replied [to it] because there was no one who knew [about it.]"[32]

Peter's indictment of the church's single-minded approach was also an indictment of the sad state of Latin learning, for he blamed the West's general disinterest in foreign languages and foreign ways. He also noted that the Muslims were "clever and learned men" whose collections of books on the liberal arts and the study of nature had drawn Christian thinkers to Spain.[33] Until Christian knowledge of the Muslims improved, any notion of intellectual crusade was unthinkable. It is not clear, however, whether Peter's money was well spent. Attempting to formulate a more accurate picture of Islam, so that he might convert Muslims to his faith, Peter fell into some of the same traps that would ensnare many later Christian commentators who lacked the abbot's resources.

For example, he saw in reports of the Muslims' practice of polygamy little more than a tactic to attract male followers and to satisfy Muhammad's own carnal desires under the guise of religion. Islam's sanction of an active sex life between husband and wife scandalized the abbot, who saw this as an open invitation to participate in "unnatural" practices. In the end, Peter could not decide if the Muslims were heretics or simply pagans. He was particularly disconcerted that the Muslims, like heretics, accepted Christ as a prophet while, like pagans, rejecting the church's sacraments. In the end, he concluded that they were probably heretics, although he seemed less than convinced.[34]

But Peter was certain that Christendom must do more than pick up the sword; it must pick up the pen as well. "Whether one gives the Muslim misconception the shameful name of heresy or the vile name of paganism, we must act against it, that is, we must write."[35]

Robert, who took the lead in the translation of the Koran, was less than enthusiastic about the entire project. Writing in the preface, he says he was willing "to overlook in the meantime, my principal study of astronomy and geometry" to take part in the translation but was determined to return at once to his life's work, one that would "penetrate . . . all the heavenly orbits, and their quantities, orders, and habits, and especially all manner of movement of the stars, their effects and natures."[36] Likewise, Hermann immediately resumed the life of a secular scholar. Still, the money, patronage, and prestige gained from the translation of the Koran, and the project's backing by the powerful Cluniac order, helped establish the translation of Arabic works as an endeavor worthy of church patronage.[37] That such support was forthcoming can be seen in the common practice of dedicating Latin renditions of Arab science and philosophy to leading clerics of the day.

That Robert and Hermann initially conceived their translation enterprise as an entryway to the *Almagest* was a testimony to the enormous gravitational pull that this as-yet-undigested work exerted on medieval Western thought. Such was its allure that just the rumored existence of Arabic copies in the Spanish libraries was enough to send Gerard of Cremona hurrying to see for himself. The most prolific figure among the translators of the second half of the twelfth century, Gerard remained in Spain to render into Latin more than seventy Arabic texts. Among his output was the original object of his intellectual desire: a Latin version of the *Almagest*. It proved by far the most popular edition among medieval scholars, and it was the first to be printed, appearing in Venice in 1515.[38]

A eulogy by Gerard's disciples reflected the influence on their master of Ptolemy's great work: "[He] trained from childhood at centers of philosophical study and had come to a knowledge of all of this that was known to the Latins; but for the love of the *Almagest*, which he could not find at all among the Latins, he went to Toledo; there, seeing the abundance of books in Arabic on every subject, and regretting the poverty of the Latins in these things, he learned the Arabic language, in order to be able to translate. In this way, combining both languages and science, . . . he passed on the Arabic literature in the manner of the wise man who, wandering through a green field, links up a crown of flowers, made from not just any, but the prettiest; to the end of his life, he continued to transmit to the Latin world (as if to his own beloved heir) whatsoever books he could . . . as accurately and as plainly as he could."[39]

Among the many translations attributed to Gerard and his team were medical textbooks and surgical manuals, including Avicenna's great *Canon of Medicine*; *The Calendar of Cordoba*; and assorted treatises on alchemy and chemistry, astrology, astronomy, mathematics, optics, and the science of weights.[40] In an important shift away from the purely technical concerns of the old French cathedral schools that shaped many of the earliest translations, Gerard and his colleagues began to expand the West's intellectual horizons through the introduction of a broader range of Greek philosophy and natural science, as well as the writings of the Arab philosophers and scientists themselves.

If the old ways were represented by the narrow demands of the cathedral curriculum based on the seven liberal arts, an approach that left no real place for study of the natural universe, then this Arab-inspired learning offered Christian thinkers new avenues for exploring the world around them. Introducing Avicenna's philosophical work *On the Soul*, the Jewish scholar and co-translator Avendauth made the case for this radical departure: "Latin readers will know with certainty something hitherto unknown, namely whether the soul exists, what are its nature and its qualities according to its essence and its activity, and this will be proved by true reasons . . . Here, then, is a book translated from the Arabic, whose author, you must know, has collected everything that Aristotle said in his book about the soul, sense-perception and the sensible, the intellect and the intelligible."[41]

Although the intellectual ferment bubbling out of al-Andalus in the mid-twelfth century attracted many of the best and the brightest from across Christendom—men like Gerard, Robert, Hermann, and Peter the Venerable—it seems the Iberian Peninsula held no particular allure for Adelard of Bath, just one generation before. With no mention of Spain in his extant writings, it is impossible to know for sure why Adelard did not simply head straight there from Laon, France, and instead made the more arduous journey south and east to Sicily and then on to the crusader principality of Antioch. One reason may lie with established ties between the prominent Benedictine community in Adelard's native Bath and those in Sicily, where he was hosted by the local Benedictine bishop, and Antioch's large Pisan quarter.

By contrast, the young scholar Daniel of Morley seems to speak for many of the newer generation when he recalls years later on his return home how he traveled to Spain after abandoning his studies in Paris in disgust at the masters' low level of learning. "When some time ago I took myself away from England for the sake of academic study and spent some time in Paris, there I saw beasts seated in scholarly chairs with grave authority . . . These masters were so ignorant that they stood as still as statues, pretending to show wisdom by remaining silent," Daniel writes some time after 1175. "But when I heard that the doctrine of the Arabs . . . was all the fashion in Toledo in those days, I hurried there as quickly as I could, so that I could hear the wisest philosophers of the world."[42]

After studying with Gerard of Cremona and others, Daniel went back to England with "a precious multitude" of Arabic books, extending a tradition first introduced by Adelard of Bath. On Daniel's return, Bishop John of Norwich, himself a student of astronomy, asked the well-traveled scholar to write a treatise on a revised *zij* known as the Toledan Tables. Instead of an essay on the latest in astronomical thinking, Daniel turned out an organized cosmology, the first in the West to be fully informed by "the doctrine of the Arabs," especially the Aristotelian worldview of the astrologer Albumazar.[43] One version features at least a dozen quotations from *The Introduction to Astrology*, citing Albumazar on everything from the makeup of the celestial bodies to perfect circular motion and the source of color.[44] Other references are drawn from different Arab works on the natural philosophy of Aristotle and from a close reading of Adelard's *On the Use of the Astrolabe*.[45]

Beginning in the early ninth century, the Arab scholars of the House of Wisdom worked their way through the classics of Greek philosophy and science, systematically laying a solid foundation for their own original research. Three hundred years later, the West was accorded no such luxury; instead, the translators began to inundate Christendom with ancient texts and more recent Arabic commentaries, scientific innovations, and philosophical advances. The shock arrival of this pagan philosophy, dressed in enticing Arab garb and leavened with the occult, shook Western scholars out of their narrow worldview and forced them to confront troubling questions about the nature of the universe, the definition of knowledge, and even the existence of God.

Arab thinkers soon dominated Latin learning. Traditional Christian authorities, such as Augustine and Bede, were often tossed aside, and Arabic words,
terms, and phrases—the names of the stars, for example, as well as dozens of
technical terms—were increasingly embedded in Western scholarly literature.

For the rising new class of scholars, wandering intellectuals like Daniel of
Morley, this made perfect sense: "Let us then borrow from them and, with
God's help and command, rob the pagan philosophers of their wisdom and
eloquence. Let us take from the unfaithful so as to enrich ourselves faithfully
with the spoils."[46] Such intellectual larceny was not without its practical
problems. The early translators, for example, discovered that Latin lacked the
vocabulary to keep up with the Arabs' philosophical and scientific language.

Adelard of Bath had already freely acknowledged the Arabs as his masters, a
tradition adopted by those who followed. Soon, the translator Hugh of
Santalla, a close colleague of Robert and Hermann, was urging his fellow
scholars to follow the Muslim lead in astronomy: "It befits us to imitate the
Arabs especially, for they are as it were our teachers and precursors in this
art."[47] Another scholar hailed the Arabs as the only people to truly understand
geometry. Such was the standing of the Muslims in twelfth-century England
that partisans of Henry II, Adelard's onetime pupil, threatened the pope that
their lord would convert to Islam in order to rid himself of that "meddlesome
priest," Thomas Becket, the archbishop of Canterbury.[48] In the event, the
murder of Becket did the trick.

Adelard of Bath's scholarly explorations largely ignored philosophical or
theoretical texts. For his translation of Albumazar, after all, Adelard chose
the author's abbreviated text, without its vital philosophical core. His strong
leanings toward the more technical disciplines of Arab astronomy and
astrology set the direction for the first wave of the Latin translations carried
out in Spain. By the thirteenth century, the West was awash in competing
astronomy texts, prompting Oliver of Brittany to complain, "A day would
scarcely suffice to completely tell of [astronomy's] innumerable books and
authors."[49]

But the growing sophistication of Western scholars meant it was only a
matter of time before they would venture from the mildly problematic matter
of astronomy and astrology, with their implied threat to the Christian notion
of free will, to the downright dangerous learning of Arab and Greek cosmology

and metaphysics. Bridging the gap between the two was the towering figure of Michael Scot, who in the first half of the thirteenth century shaped the course of philosophy, mathematics, and science more than any other Western figure. If Adelard of Bath had nibbled at the edges of the *studia Arabum* one hundred years before, then Michael Scot devoured Muslim learning whole—first in Toledo and then in Sicily, at the court of Frederick II, the Holy Roman emperor.

Little is known of Michael's early life.[50] He was born somewhere in Scotland in the late twelfth century, and his name appears in medieval manuscripts as Master Michael Scot, suggesting he had earned a degree of some sort and probably taught as well. This notion is supported by the gentle didacticism of some of his writings and translations. At one point, he promises his royal patron that he will produce an introductory work on astrology "in a popular grammar-school style,"[51] while his literary, scientific, and biblical references are all in keeping with the university conventions of his day. He had considerable medical knowledge, wrote about the influence of the heavens on human health, and may have had formal medical training. A sixteenth-century roll of famous physicians includes the following entry: "Michael by cognomen and *medicus* by profession, by nation a Scot."[52] One Latin manuscript offers alchemical recipes that it says come from "the book of MS, physician to Emperor Frederick."[53]

Over the centuries, many have poured fantasy and fable into the murky depths of Michael's life story. We are told, for example, that his astrological skills enabled him to predict the cause of his own death—that he would be struck on the head by a small rock. Michael took to wearing a metal helmet of his own design in an attempt to ward off the inevitable. One version says the prediction came good one day after he bared his head for Mass, when a pebble broke free from the vaulted ceiling of the church and grazed his head; Michael examined the missile and the seemingly minor wound, promptly went home to arrange his affairs, and died within days. Some time earlier, he warned Frederick, whom he served as both astrologer and physician, not to let the royal barber bleed him, then a common medical procedure. The king ignored the advice and almost died from infection after a freak accident.

Michael's forecasts of the outcomes of Frederick's military adventures were said to have been highly accurate. The poet Henry of Avranches, who had recently joined the Sicilian court, recalls how Michael predicted the emperor's success in a planned war against the Lombard cities, some time before the campaign began in 1236. The poet then offers his version of the astrologer's death:

> As he was about to say more, he became silent and,
> Not permitting his secrets to be published to the world,
> Bade that his breath be spent on thin air,
> Thus the inquisitor of the Fates submitted to Fate.[54]

Dante's *Inferno* places Michael Scot with the sorcerers in the lower depths of hell, saying he "truly knew every trick of the magical arts," while Shakespeare may have drawn on him for the character of Prospero in *The Tempest*. Two hundred years after the Bard, Sir Walter Scott's epic *The Lay of the Last Minstrel* still celebrates the persistent legend of his famed countryman:

> A wizard, of such dreaded fame,
> That when, in Salamanca's cave,
> Him listed his magic wand to wave,
> The bells would ring in Notre Dame![55]

In the course of his varied and colorful career, Michael emerged as the West's first real expert on Aristotle; the translator of seminal texts on Arabic astronomy and metaphysics; the mentor to one of the West's great mathematical geniuses; and an author of original works on astrology, human anatomy, physiology, and physiognomy. In an age of mass illiteracy, such esoteric book learning and association with Arab teachings was enough to see him branded a wizard.

For all the singular infamy ultimately attached to his name, Michael Scot was very much a product of the broad social and economic changes that had been taking shape gradually across the West since the tenth century or so, chiefly the emergence of a money economy and the associated rise of towns and cities.[56] Early medieval Europe knew nothing like the great Muslim political, cultural, and commercial hubs—Baghdad, Cairo, Damascus, and Cordoba. The Arabs had proved great builders of cities, and these urban centers were central to the Muslim enterprise. They provided the meeting place of ideas, the storehouses of books, the abodes of scholars, and the great mosques where the latter could lecture or teach. They housed the tradesmen of the intellectuals' craft, such as scribes, papermakers, librarians, and booksellers. Urban merchants and traders generated the surpluses of cash and leisure time that made the scholarly life possible in the first place. In the division of labor that characterized Arab city life, there was ample room for the thinker, the teacher, and the writer.

For their part, most medieval European cities were modest outgrowths of military encampments or ecclesiastical centers, or congealed gradually around market towns that dotted traditional trade routes. Some grew from settlements dating back to Roman times. But all that changed as the feudal order in the countryside started to unravel, and the peasants fled the land that kept them in bondage to make their own way in the growing urban centers. There they pursued commerce, taking advantage of a general upturn in the European economy driven in part by expanding foreign trade and the emergence of town life. The new urban communes soon organized to defend their interests against the nobility, the crown, and the church. Artisans and other professionals founded guilds and corporations to regulate membership, reduce competition, and protect their livelihood. This is the origin of the modern term *university*, which initially described the universe, or totality, of members of a guild or profession. Students and teaching masters who began to meet informally in the towns and cities adopted the institution of the university from the urban guilds; over time, the term's origins became obscured, leaving the word today with the sole meaning of an institution of higher learning.[57]

Europe's new intellectuals were distinct in medieval society for both their high degree of mobility and their urban origins.[58] The breadth of this movement can be seen in the extraordinary range of nationalities represented among the leading translators active in Spain: Germans, Englishmen, Scots, Frenchmen, Italians, Slavs, and others. Yet they all shared a number of important characteristics: They saw themselves as pioneers, had little time for established convention, and were prepared to roam far and wide to find the best teachers and the latest texts, or to take part in the most heated debates of the day. Many within the religious establishment had nothing but contempt for such "professional students." One twelfth-century monk lamented, "They are wont to roam about the world and visit all its cities, till much learning makes them mad; for in Paris they seek liberal arts, in Orleans classics, at Salerno medicine, at Toledo magic, but nowhere manners and morals."[59]

Some eked out a living as beggars or worked as servants to more well-off colleagues. Others literally sang for their supper. In what may be a rare autobiographical tidbit, Michael Scot touts the value of musical skill for the poor but educated traveler: "Nor is there a musical instrument that can better guide his life everywhere, whoever plays it, than the lyre, as is clear from the experience of anyone who goes from door to door playing it," he writes in one unpublished manuscript. "If they play it well, it pays their way everywhere in Christendom."[60]

The translation movement that helped make Michael Scot the leading public intellectual of his day was an export industry, carried out by educated, inquisitive, and independent "knowledge workers" drawn to Spain from foreign lands in pursuit of the *studia Arabum*. The finished goods, in the form of translations, commentaries, and original works, rarely remained behind where they were created. Instead, these were destined for the foreign markets of Italy, France, and England—home to groupings of scholars and students who came together by the early thirteenth century to create the West's earliest universities, in Bologna, Paris, and Oxford. The new Arabic texts pouring forth from the former al-Andalus were learned, coherent, and steeped in the authority of Aristotle and the Muslims' advanced sciences. They were not susceptible to the sort of allegorical interpretation that the Latin world had used in the past to deflect or absorb dangerous, non-Christian ideas.

Nowhere was their effect more profound than at the University of Paris, by now the leading center of Christian theology. Here at last, the students and young teaching masters seemed to say, was direct access to the teachings of philosophy, unencumbered by church orthodoxy or the ignorant Latin scholarship of yesteryear. Set in motion by Adelard and carried through by men like Michael Scot, the irresistible force of the new science was now headed for the immovable object of Christian teaching. Something would have to give.

PART IV

Al-Asr/Afternoon

Chapter Eight

ON THE ETERNITY OF THE WORLD

MICHAEL SCOT'S DUBIOUS reputation, a product of his association with the dangerous learning of the Arabs, was further clouded by his affiliation with Holy Roman Emperor Frederick II, who ruled his tumultuous domains from Sicily and southern Italy. Grandson of Roger II—the original "baptized sultan" and the sponsor of al-Idrisi's Map of the World—Frederick was twice excommunicated by the popes for disobedience and widely suspect in the West for his love of Muslim learning, his deep ambivalence toward Christian holy war, and his immoderate erudition. Frederick spoke half a dozen languages, followed a scandalous regimen of bathing and diet prescribed by his Arab physicians, and traveled with his own personal "dialectician"—a Muslim, no less—so he could pursue his philosophical studies on the road.

His running war of words with the popes, at times drifting into armed conflict, led to a church-inspired whisper campaign claiming that Frederick was actually the Antichrist, a rumor bolstered by the circumstances surrounding his birth. Frederick's mother was the posthumous daughter of Roger II, and it was said that she had been hidden away in a convent at an early age amid predictions that she would one day bring disaster to the land. At age thirty, she married Frederick's father, ten years her junior, and the pair were childless for almost a decade before her unexpected pregnancy. A popular superstition of the day said the Antichrist would be born by a nun, and soon many fingers were pointed at Frederick.[1]

This rumor campaign also fed on the emperor's well-known affinity for the world of Islam, which discomfited both the church and his own Christian subjects. One scandalized European contemporary wrote, "When the time came for the midday prayer and the muezzin's cry rang out, all his pages and valets rose, as well as his tutor, a Sicilian with whom he was reading Aristotle's *Logic* in all its chapters, and they offered the canonic prayer, for all were

Muslims."[2] This was a view more appreciated by a prominent Arab ambassador to Frederick's court: "He was distinguished among all the kings of the Franks for his talents and his taste for philosophy, logic, and medicine; he had an appreciation of the Muslims since he had been reared in Sicily where the majority of the inhabitants profess Islam."[3] Yet other Arab commentators were put off by his poor physical stature, ruddy face, balding head, and failing eyesight: "If he had been a slave, one would not have paid 200 drachmas for him," quipped one.[4]

Still, Frederick II was the subject of widespread popular awe; some called him *stupor mundi*, the wonder of the world. On a famous visit to the Italian city of Ravenna in 1231, Frederick marched through the streets with his personal menagerie of strange and wild beasts, many then unknown to the locals. These included elephants, camels, panthers, white falcons, and Europe's first giraffe—a present from al-Kamil, the sultan of Egypt.[5]

In the winter of 1229, the maverick emperor succeeded where previous crusaders had repeatedly failed: He reclaimed control of Jerusalem, captured from the Christians more than four decades before by the celebrated Muslim warrior Saladin. Frederick had arrived in the Latin East eight months earlier, albeit after much stalling and numerous delays, but he did not follow the course of the earlier Crusaders to attain his goal. In fact, no blood was shed at all. Instead, Frederick painstakingly negotiated the peaceful handover of Jerusalem and surrounding territory with Sultan al-Kamil, who then controlled the Holy Land.

Reports say the talks between the two sides, held in secret and subject to wild rumormongering by jealous church officials fearful that Frederick had lost all taste for religious warfare, dragged on and on. The patriarch of Jerusalem, a bitter enemy of the emperor, at one point lamented to his allies at the papal court in Rome, "It is with the greatest shame and disgrace that we report to you that it is said the sultan, hearing of the emperor's enjoyment of living in the manner of the Saracens, sent him singing girls and jugglers, persons who were not only of ill report but unworthy even to be mentioned among Christians."[6] A German poet, on crusade with the emperor, compared al-Kamil and Frederick to a pair of stubborn misers unable to agree on how to divide three pieces of gold.[7] At last, the two sides reached a settlement, and Frederick, the reluctant crusader, could claim success. The deal included formal Christian control of the city, including the historic burial place of Christ, but also guaranteed Muslim access to the Islamic holy sites. It stipulated a ten-year cessation of hostilities, much to the chagrin of the bellicose members of the papal party, who wanted no part of any diplomacy with the infidels.

Seen outside the narrow perspective of the papal curia, Frederick's achievement was a remarkable triumph—not for Christian arms but for a new standard of political, diplomatic, and intellectual commerce with the Arab world. The Holy Roman emperor never had enough troops at his disposal to take Jerusalem by force. Besides, the Arabs had patched up their latest internal disputes and were now more than a match for the Army of the Cross. Still, Frederick was desperate for some kind of victory. His struggle with the popes and other political pressures back home demanded that he return to Italy triumphant. Playing the only real card he had, the emperor reminded al-Kamil relentlessly that he had come to the region at the latter's request to help against a rival Muslim ruler in Damascus. That quarrel may have been resolved by the unexpected death of the sultan's adversary, Frederick noted, but he had set off in good faith. He could not go home empty-handed. "If he had not feared injury to his honor, he would not have demanded so great a sacrifice of the sultan," writes the medieval Egyptian historian al-Maqrizi.[8]

At first the sultan was unimpressed by such blandishments. He no longer needed the emperor's assistance, and the handover of Muslim-held territory would certainly unnerve his subjects and anger the clergy. But Frederick slowly wore down the sultan with months of patient diplomacy, backed by a clever cultural offensive. The emperor closeted himself with al-Kamil's special envoy, engaging him in fluent Arabic in rambling discussions of science, philosophy, and religion. He sent mathematical puzzles and philosophical riddles to the sultan's court in Cairo, where they were discussed by leading Arab scholars. Apparently moved by Frederick's persistence and his knowledge of, and respect for, Arab learning and the Muslim faith, the sultan at last relented. Frederick's well-known battles with the popes in Rome may also have played a part; by assisting Frederick, the Arabs would indirectly deal a blow to these "Christian caliphs," the leading proponents of the anti-Muslim Crusades.

Much had changed since the time of Peter the Hermit and the First Crusade, more than 125 years earlier. The Muslim was no longer simply the faceless enemy of Christendom. Islamic learning had already begun to make deep inroads into the European consciousness. Peter the Venerable, the powerful abbot who had ordered the translation of the Koran the better to attack the "heresy" of Islam, had conceded publicly that the Arabs were particularly clever at science and philosophy. General enthusiasm for the Crusades was also on the wane among the European public. England and France, once reliable founts of crusading zeal, were busy fighting each other. A recent expedition against the Muslims, led at the pope's insistence by a prelate and not an experienced military or political figure, had ended in disaster. Critical verses, sung by the troubadours, ridiculed that campaign and further undercut popular support for the entire venture.[9] Frederick himself only went along in the face of unrelenting pressure from the popes, with whom he was eager to prevent a final, irreparable rupture in relations.

By now, a growing network of commercial, political, and intellectual ties had slowly begun to bind East and West. Known among the Arabs as al-Emberor, Frederick II was a product of this emerging Europe—engaged with the broader world, its ideas, and its culture. Patterning his court after that of his grandfather and the Arab rulers of his own day, al-Emberor offered generous financial rewards to draw top intellectual talent into his retinue. He supported Muslim and European scholars and corresponded with learned figures and rulers throughout North Africa, al-Andalus, and other centers of Arab science. Nor was his patronage limited to Christians and Muslims. Jacob Anatoli, the prominent Jewish translator of Arab science and philosophy, newly arrived from Provence, praised the emperor as a "friend of wisdom and its votaries" for his financial support.[10] Judah ben Solomon ha-Cohen, an Andalusi Jew and the author of an encyclopedia of philosophy, corresponded with the court and even visited Frederick in northern Italy.[11]

Frederick's overbearing personality and autocratic style left him suspicious of any institution he could not control completely. Universities in his realm developed only slowly and never really competed with the great early centers in Paris and Oxford. Frederick saw the university at Naples and the famed medical school at Salerno as little more than reliable sources of trained administrators and courtiers, rather than as independent institutions of learning.[12] As an incubator of the arts and sciences, however, the court of Frederick II played an important role in the transmission to the West of the *studia Arabum*. The great Catholic thinker Thomas Aquinas began his university career at Naples— founded by Frederick in 1224—before moving on to Paris, then the center of European theological and philosophical thought. And it was certainly at Naples that Thomas was first exposed to the Arab philosophical tradition.

On March 18, 1229, the Holy Roman emperor made his symbolic entrance into Jerusalem, where he spent a single night. His only regret, he later said, was that local Muslim officials had suspended the calls to prayer out of respect for the Christian monarch; he had longed to hear the summons of the muezzin ring out across the old city before dawn. Such respect for al-Emberor was not shared by the local Franks. The citizenry of Acre pelted him with garbage as he boarded his ship for the homeward voyage. Even after his return to Italy, Frederick remained in touch with Sultan al-Kamil. The pair continued to exchange correspondence and diplomatic gifts, and the sultan even sent his friend one of his most learned philosophers to instruct the Christians further.[13]

Michael Scot joined this Arabized court sometime in the mid-1220s on the strength of a reputation earned in Spain. He had arrived in Toledo around 1217 and set about translating an important Arab treatise on the heavens and three of Aristotle's most influential works, *On Animals, On the Heavens,* and *On the Soul,* from the Arabic versions. As Frederick's science adviser and court astrologer, Michael later published a translation of Avicenna's work on zoology and wrote widely on astrology, meteorology, and physiognomy— all of the works dedicated to al-Emberor. These works show Michael's acquaintance with medicine, music, and alchemy, as well as Aristotelian philosophy in general. Pope Honorius III called Michael "singularly gifted in science among men of learning," while another pope testified to his facility with Arabic and Hebrew.[14] The papal court was instrumental in securing support for this roaming scholar and occasional minstrel in the form of stipends from the revenue of church properties. We are told he also had respectable knowledge of Arab astronomy and its applications and prided himself on his meticulous calculations.[15]

His ties to Frederick now put Michael at the intellectual and cultural heart of the new Europe, and after the difficulties he had faced as an impoverished student and young master, he was determined to make the most of it. "One who wishes to have honor among the peoples of the world will gain it either by divine providence such as becoming bishop, abbot, or patriarch by perfect election, or by perfect work, which is had by genius of nature or art, such as being an approved master of some faculty," he writes in one illuminating passage.[16] Clearly, Michael had traded in his transitory skill with the lute for the hope of lasting fame through the written word.

Michael used the platform afforded by the imperial court to promote radical ideas, new learning, and novel technologies. Among his protégés was Leonardo of Pisa, also known as Fibonacci and today considered one of the greatest mathematicians of all time. Like Michael and his lord Frederick, Leonardo was the product of an increasingly worldly Europe. His father was a Pisan merchant in the city-state's North African enclave, in modern-day Algeria, and he sent his young son to learn the latest arithmetic and accounting methods, including the basis for the Italian art of double entry bookkeeping, from the local Muslim traders.[17] Leonardo later traveled to Sicily, Egypt, southern France, and Constantinople, before returning to his native Italy. There, in 1202, he completed *The Book of Calculation*—the first comprehensive work in Christian Europe on algebra and geometry.[18] It also provided the most detailed Latin account to date of working with the Arabic number system, first spelled out by al-Khwarizmi: "Here Begins the First Chapter," writes Leonardo. "The nine Indian figures are: 9 8 7 6 5 4 3 2 1. With these nine figures, and with the sign 0 which the Arabs call zephyr (*al-sifr*), any number whatsoever is written."[19]

Leonardo's work came to the attention of Michael, who sent the mathematician a detailed commentary, including proposed changes and corrections to *The Book of Calculation*. Michael also ensured that the Italian scholar would have the backing of the emperor, who delighted in Leonardo's ability to solve mathematical puzzles that had stumped some of the leading Arab experts with whom Frederick was in regular correspondence. A later edition of *The Book of Calculation* thanks Michael on both scores: "You, my Master Michael Scott, most great philosopher, wrote to my Lord [Frederick II] about the book on numbers which some time ago I composed and transcribed to you; whence complying with your criticism, your more subtle examining circumspection, to the honor of you and many others, I with advantage corrected this work . . . Further, if in this work is found insufficiency or defect, I submit it to you for correction."[20]

Leonardo produced major treatises on geometry, second-degree equations, and the practical needs of a growing international mercantile class—converting multiple currencies, allocating shares in commercial partnerships, working with varying units of measure—and he anticipated the coming use of decimal fractions. In an unusual departure from the conventions of his day, Leonardo omitted references to mystical numerology, and he was more than willing to acknowledge Arab contributions to his art.[21] "In solving problems there is a certain method called 'direct' that is used by the Arabs, and that method is a laudable and valuable method, for by it many problems are solved."[22] A number of his books addressed in detail some of the very puzzles that Frederick had posed to him and other contestants in court-sponsored mathematics tournaments, but none enjoyed anything like the popularity accorded the more derivative *Book of Calculation*.

Leonardo also developed what has come to be known as the Fibonacci sequence, based on his solution to a puzzle on the breeding fortunes of rabbits. *The Book of Calculation* poses this riddle as follows: "A certain man had one pair of rabbits together in a certain enclosed place, and one wishes to know how many are created from the pair in one year when it is the nature of them in a single month to bear another pair, and in the second month those born to bear also."[23] The resulting pattern of numbers Leonardo generated in his solution has been found to address an entire range of scientific and mathematical problems. Today, application of this famous sequence is the subject of its own scholarly journal, the *Fibonacci Quarterly*, and it has been used for decades by technical market analysts trading stocks, bonds, and other instruments.

Frederick's reign—he was crowned in 1198 as a boy of four and died in 1250—marked an important way station in the West's long journey toward the great scientific advances of the seventeenth century. Perhaps unique among contemporary European rulers, this second of the "baptized sultans" sought to ground his worldview in reason, a hallmark of the coming scientific method. This approach was at the heart of the emperor's decision to abolish trial by ordeal—the same system of justice once ridiculed by Usama ibn Munqidh, the Syrian commentator on the early crusaders. It was, Frederick concluded, a method that did not lead to truth and could not be justified by reason.[24]

In an original treatise on falconry, Frederick goes well beyond a somewhat cursory study one hundred years earlier by Adelard of Bath by incorporating material from Arabic sources as well as the latest translations by Michael Scot of Aristotle and Avicenna on zoology. For example, he introduces to the West the Arab practice of hooding falcons, and he turns to Egyptian experts for an attempt to incubate ostrich eggs with the heat of the sun.[25] Like Adelard, he has freed himself from the "halter" of authority; al-Emberor was more than prepared to correct no less an authority than Aristotle whenever his own observations or extensive experience with falcons demanded it.[26] Frederick writes with the same note of intellectual self-confidence that would later prevail more broadly in the West: "Our work is to present things that are as they are."[27]

Few of his contemporaries were sympathetic to his scientific bent and reliance on reason. Pope Gregory IX, who battled Frederick for power and influence at every turn, bitterly accused the emperor of disregarding church teachings and, by extension, papal authority by accepting only that which could be proved by rational thinking.[28] Popular tales—some concocted by his many enemies, such as the thirteenth-century Franciscan monk Salimbene, who detested the emperor—cataloged Frederick's supposed scientific excesses. One held that the monarch had ordered that infants be raised in total silence in an effort to learn whether they would grow up to speak Hebrew, thought of at the time as man's "natural" language. In another episode, we are told, the emperor directed that a condemned man be allowed to suffocate in a sealed room, which was then opened carefully to see if his soul had escaped after death.

Frederick was also a voracious reader, ready to take what he needed from scholars of different traditions or faiths, whether Muslim, Jewish, or Byzantine Christian, with an openness that clearly shocked the staid churchmen back in Rome. The fear of change that for centuries had effectively paralyzed the collective intellect of the Christian Middle Ages was remarkably absent in Frederick's makeup.[29] By his own account, he had been eager for knowledge since childhood, "inhaling tirelessly its sweet perfumes." That same open and inquisitive nature, colored by a certain unbridled enthusiasm and scattershot quality of mind, informed the so-called Sicilian Questions, a rambling series of philosophical, metaphysical, and scientific questionnaires that Frederick enthusiastically forwarded to his large network of mostly Arab scholars. "Tell us . . . just where are hell, purgatory, and the heavenly paradise, whether under or on or above the earth?"[30] Frederick asked his correspondents. Other topics had to do with optics—why did an object appear to bend when partly immersed in water?—and the size and structure of the universe.

Some Arab respondents had their doubts about the depth of Frederick's understanding of philosophical matters, yet the fact remains that the emperor was an important figure in the scientific development of the West—not least because he exhibited a new spirit of inquiry and cultural receptivity that broke with centuries of self-imposed intellectual isolationism. His Sicilian Questions prefigured one of the major battlegrounds for the conflict between traditionalist Christian theologians and a new generation of Western philosophers, inflamed by the works of the leading Arab thinkers: "Aristotle the sage in all his writings declares clearly the existence of the world from all eternity. If he demonstrates this, what are his arguments, and if not, what is the nature of his reasoning on this matter?"[31]

Earlier, Frederick posed a similar question to Michael Scot. It is not clear whether al-Emberor was satisfied with the answers from his enigmatic science adviser, but there can be no doubt that his intense curiosity about the subject was inspired by the latest in Arab philosophical thinking to reach his court. Here, too, Michael's hand was crucial, for his reputation for black magic surely pales beside the profound and lasting shock waves from his translations of the works of Abul-Walid Ibn Rushd, the greatest in a long line of eminent medieval Arab philosophers. Ibn Rushd was known to the Latins as Averroes, but his explanations of Aristotelian philosophy were so fundamental to the West's emerging understanding of science, nature, and metaphysics that he was commonly referred to simply as the Commentator.

The son and grandson of famous Muslim jurists in the Andalusi capital of Cordoba, Averroes could bring to bear both a first-rate Arab education—he was trained in medicine, religious law, and theology and even dabbled in astronomy—and the political acuity gleaned from his family's long experience in senior state and religious posts. Despite widespread suspicion toward philosophy among the mainstream local clerics, it is clear that Averroes also received competent instruction in the discipline, which had quietly made its way to al-Andalus from the eastern Muslim lands. Following the family tradition, Averroes served as the qadi, or religious judge, of Seville from 1169 to 1172, when he was appointed chief justice of Cordoba.

Unable to open the gates of heaven to non-Christians, Dante nonetheless celebrated Averroes by placing him in limbo, alongside Aristotle and members of his "philosophic family." The Italian poet and philosopher also referred to him approvingly as the one "who made the Great Commentary." Raphael's masterful fresco *The School of Athens* has given Averroes a permanent home inside the Vatican's Apostolic Palace. But it was Michael Scot's translations, underwritten, transcribed, and forwarded to the universities at Frederick's command, that did more than anything to bring the Commentator's comprehensive views on philosophy, particularly his reading of Aristotle, to the immediate attention of the Latin-speaking world.

For Averroes's Western readers, who tended to take his often-subtle positions to their most extreme conclusions, these works were a revelation. Among his most incendiary philosophical teachings was his insistence on the doctrine of the Eternity of the World, in contradiction to the traditional Muslim, Christian, and Jewish understanding that God made the universe at a time of his choosing and then controlled each and every event in it. After all, Genesis tells us, "In the beginning, God created heaven and earth." The Christian world, following the lead of the Jews and followed in turn by the Muslims, generally took this to mean the universe had a distinct starting point and was created "from nothing." Against this, Averroes laid out the Aristotelian view that both time and matter were eternal and that the Creator had simply set the entire process in motion.

Implicit in the teachings of this Arab philosophical tradition was the notion that God did not bother with the details of everyday human life, that he was blissfully unaware of what the medieval theologians called "particulars." Likewise, God was effectively removed—prevented, even—from day-to-day management of the universe. Instead, he relied on the timeless functioning of universal laws of nature that stemmed from his own perfection. In the eyes of their many critics, such notions contravened the scriptural promise of Judgment Day, when God would personally assess each man's adherence to the moral code spelled out by revelation. They also raised serious doubts about scriptural accounts of miracles. But they helped create the necessary opening for man to pursue and uncover the laws of existence, otherwise known as natural science.

Centuries earlier, St. Augustine had quipped that a place in hell had been set aside for anyone who dared to ask what God was up to before the Creation.[32] But the growing legion of Averroes's followers in the West would not be put off so lightly. Adelard of Bath had already given the Christian world permission to explore the universe. Now, with the help of Michael Scot, Averroes opened the door to a brave new world. For this Arab thinker, like Aristotle before him, God had created the universe but then left it to man to make his own way through it.

The doctrine of the Eternity of the World has a long history in Christianity. The faith itself was born into a world still very much under the sway of Greek philosophy, and it enjoyed much of its initial success within the Greek cultural sphere. Thus, it was important for the early church to adopt and preserve as much as it could of this rich classical inheritance, particularly where it might be used to support the church's claim for the truth of Christ's revelation. However, the problematic issue of the Eternity of the World lay mostly dormant for centuries at a time, obscured by the complexity of the writings of the leading Greek authorities. On those occasions when it was examined, the church fathers and some later Christian theologians effectively conspired to assert, notwithstanding the evidence to the contrary, that there was no real contradiction between scripture and Aristotle's natural philosophy.[33]

True engagement with the natural world was possible only once this intellectual fiction had begun to unravel, but first Christendom would have to follow doggedly the trail blazed earlier by the Arab thinkers in their own attempts to harmonize the demands of philosophy with the demands of religious faith. Writing in the ninth century, the philosopher al-Kindi acknowledges his debt to the Greeks. But he also makes it clear that the Arab thinkers were intent on advancing classical wisdom and adapting it to the needs of Muslim culture: "It is fitting then to remain faithful to the principle which we have followed in all our works, which is first to record in complete quotations all that the Ancients have said on the subject, secondly to complete what the Ancients have not fully expressed, and this according to the usage of our Arabic language, the customs of our age, and our own ability."

Al-Kindi goes on to note that "research, logic, preparatory sciences, and a long period of instruction" are the only way for ordinary people—meaning those who are not blessed by God with prophecy—to attain knowledge.[34] This proved of enormous value to the Latin scholars of the late Middle Ages, for much of the debate that later roiled Paris, Oxford, and other centers of church teachings had already been well rehearsed for them. All they had to do was master the Arabic texts and follow along.

The Greek teachings on the origins of the universe are often couched in difficult language and are not entirely without equivocation. Nonetheless, there are passages in Aristotle's major works that make it clear what he had in mind. Writing in *Metaphysics*, for example, Aristotle says; "There is something which is always moved with an unceasing motion; but this is circular motion. And this is not only evident from reason, but from the thing itself. So that the first heaven will be eternal. There is, therefore, something which moves. But, since there is that which is moved, that which moves, and that which subsists as a medium between these, hence there is something which moves without being moved, which is eternal, and which is essence and energy."[35] This is Aristotle's famous Unmoved Mover. The full implications of his position—if they were even fully understood at the time—either did not really penetrate the early Christian consciousness or were conveniently ignored.[36]

For Aristotle, the whole question of the Eternity of the World was also bound up with his conceptions of infinity and time, the latter of which he defined as the measure of bodies in motion. Here, Augustine and some later Christian thinkers felt they had enough wiggle room to absolve Aristotle of contradicting the word of God, as spelled out in Genesis. They argued that the universe was created not "in time" but together "with time."[37] Before the Creation, there were no bodies or anything else to provide the change and movement that Aristotle's notion of time required. With the creation of the necessary bodies, however, time could now be said to exist, providing the "beginning" that the book of Genesis demanded. Augustine wrote in his *Confessions*, "If there was no time before the creation of heaven and earth, the question, 'What were you [God] doing then?' is meaningless, for when there was no time, there was no then."[38] Augustine may have distorted Aristotle's views, but he did manage to keep the problem at bay in the West for eight hundred years.

Among the first works to shake Christendom's complacency were the writings of the prolific Persian polymath Avicenna, who enjoyed enormous popularity among Western philosophers and theologians well into the thirteenth century and beyond. Of particular interest were Avicenna's discussions of metaphysics and the notion of the soul, excerpted from his comprehensive *Kitab al-Shifa*, or *The Book of Healing*, begun in 1021.[39] These excerpts were first rendered into Latin in Toledo no later than 1166, but as with most of the other translations of major Arabic texts, it took considerable time before their full impact was felt. More than one hundred extant Latin manuscripts of Avicenna's philosophical writings were copied after 1250— three times the figure in circulation before that date, despite a head start of almost one hundred years.[40]

Avicenna's teachings had much to commend them to Christian thinkers. Faced with the daunting task of parsing Aristotle's own work on the subject, particularly the notoriously opaque *Metaphysics*, Avicenna appeared to offer a familiar way into such a complex matter. He himself says he read *Metaphysics* forty times—enough to memorize it—but understood the author's true intent only after he stumbled on a short guide by his predecessor Abu Nasr al-Farabi in the booksellers' bazaar. "I returned home and hastened to read it, and at once the purposes of that book were disclosed to me because I had learned it by heart. I rejoiced at this and the next day I gave much in alms to the poor in gratitude to God Exalted."[41]

Avicenna defines the "full fruit" of metaphysics as establishing the existence and attributes of God, a notion that would have had the enthusiastic backing of his newfound Christian readers. As a Muslim—and thus, a committed monotheist—Avicenna is naturally far more interested than the pagan Aristotle in connecting metaphysics to the study of God. But thanks to the fortuitous help from al-Farabi's primer, Avicenna also broadens this notion of metaphysics to encompass the full Aristotelian tradition as well as Islamic theology.[42] Throughout, Avicenna attempts to accommodate both philosophy and his fundamental religious convictions, beliefs that dovetailed with many of the concerns of medieval Christendom. This was particularly the case with his complex account of the creation of the world, which was designed to preserve a distinction between an eternal God, perfect in his simplicity, and the transitory and imperfect world of material things.[43] The fact that this attempt ultimately incited such opposition in both East and West cannot obscure its inherent worth or the considerable influence that it wielded throughout the late Middle Ages.

The teachings of Avicenna on the soul, and on psychology in general, also entered Western tradition through his voluminous studies of medicine and biology. Michael Scot, who translated Avicenna's *On Animals*, absorbed the philosopher's views in the context of his own work as a physician. He freely adopted Avicenna's ideas on the sensory faculties, the distinction between perception and motion, and the difference between man's practical and contemplative intellects.[44] Avicenna's comprehensive *Canon of Medicine*, meanwhile, contained important contributions to the scientific method, including keen clinical observations of various diseases.[45] It also uncovered a world where man could understand and even use the laws of nature for his own benefit, a central characteristic that would come to define the new world of Western science.[46] So pervasive was his influence that *The Incoherence of the Philosophers*, by the theologian Abu Hamid al-Ghazali, the foremost attack on Avicenna and perhaps the single most important work of medieval Muslim theology, was generally mistaken in the West as an affirmation of Avicenna's philosophical views.[47]

For Avicenna, God is the only thing in the universe without a cause; he alone is necessary and everything else is contingent upon him. God's own necessity sets in motion a complex chain of events through a series of intelligent agents, who in turn create the heavenly bodies and the terrestrial world in the best and only way possible. This idea, which runs from the late Greek commentators of the third century A.D. through to Avicenna's Arab predecessors, held out some promise for Muslims, Jews, and Christians alike: It attributes everything in the universe to a single source, and it provides some sort of rational framework for the Creation.[48] But Avicenna also argues that God would not be God had he not created the world instantaneously; it was not, as common readings of scripture seem to suggest, an act of divine will in which the idea of Creation and its implementation took place separately. This yields an eternal universe but one that was "created" in that it relies on the first cause, here synonymous with God.[49]

Born in 1058, twenty-one years after Avicenna's death, Al-Ghazali famously complains in his *Incoherence of the Philosophers* that Avicenna's teaching on the Eternity of the World and related matters leaves God with almost nothing to do. Once events are set in motion, God cannot intervene in the subsequent unfolding of his own creation. Nor is he aware of the pulse of daily life among men, the so-called particulars. And any decision to create the universe flows from his very nature and is completely removed from God's own hands. Al-Ghazali, a brilliant polemicist and notable among the Muslim theologians for his readiness to take on the philosophers on their own terms, asks pointedly whether Avicenna's God really is God in any meaningful sense of the word.

Al-Ghazali's biting critique of the Eternity of the World is an assertion of God's infinite power against what he sees as Avicenna's impious restrictions on divine freedom of action. Here, the traditional theologians must have felt they were on solid scriptural footing, for they could draw on a literal reading of the Holy Book to support their arguments for God's absolute knowledge of all things. "There does not escape him the weight of an atom in the heavens or in the earth," says the Koran (34:3). For al-Ghazali, such knowledge and its attendant power mean the world is in a constant process of divine re-creation, with the atoms that comprise the universe instantaneously reshuffled again and again by God's hand. Reality is actually a continuing series of "new" realities, each one deliberately created by God but none of them dictated by necessity. If a ball of cotton burns when thrust into a flame, al-Ghazali argues, it is only because God at that instant wills it to burn, and not because burning is a necessary and natural outcome of the introduction of the flame. Our notion of cause and effect, he says, is an illusion.

He includes the doctrine of the Eternity of the World in one of his three allegations of infidelity against the philosophers, a hint of the full-scale attack on the grounds of heresy that would be mounted against the same notion in the Christian West more than 150 years later. It was, perhaps, both al-Ghazali's great luck and his great misfortune to have come after his first major adversary, in the person of Avicenna, but before his second, the rationalist Averroes. To a remarkable degree, however, al-Ghazali's *Incoherence of the Philosophers* anticipates many of the arguments that will feature in the later works of Averroes, particularly his direct response to al-Ghazali, tartly titled *The Incoherence of the Incoherence.*

Frederick II, the *stupor mundi,* was not the only medieval ruler tantalized by the Eternity of the World, for it was a similar question, posed fifty years earlier by the Muslim master of al-Andalus, that led to the commentaries on Aristotle that would one day rattle the intellectual foundations of Christendom. Sometime around 1168, Averroes was ushered into the presence of the sultan, Abu Yaqub Yusuf. To his alarm, Averroes found himself drawn into the sultan's discussion of creation. Abu Yaqub had spent his earlier years as governor of Seville, where he immersed himself in that city's great libraries and surrounded himself with scientists and philosophers. He had assumed the sultanate in 1163 and was now prepared to indulge his abiding personal interest in a slightly more public fashion. "The first thing that the Prince of Believers said to me, after asking my name, my father's name and my genealogy, was: 'What is their opinion about the heavens'—referring to the philoso-phers—'are they eternal or created?'" Averroes later recalled.[50]

This was dangerous territory. Philosophy, and even its sparring partner theology, had never really enjoyed more than a tenuous hold on intellectual life in al-Andalus. Islamic Spain had long been under the influence of the conservative Maliki school of religious jurisprudence, whose founder had once declared that human wisdom could not go beyond the writings of the Koran and the teachings of the sunnah, the lived example of the Prophet and his early companions: "Knowledge is threefold: the clear Book of God, past Tradition, and 'I know not.'"[51] As a result, scholars generally operated discreetly, or under the direct protection of the local rulers, who shielded them from censure by the clerical authorities. These conservative jurists saw no need for theology, let alone philosophy. Even the books of al-Ghazali—seen today as the great defender of Muslim theological orthodoxy against the Arab and Greek philosophers—were burned on the say-so of the conservative jurists. The first real Andalusi philosopher, known in Latin as Avempace, once compared himself to a lonely weed—unwanted, isolated, and unappreciated.[52]

Things began to improve somewhat with the arrival from North Africa in 1146 of the Berber Almohad dynasty, whose founder, Ibn Tumart, quietly began to loosen the reins on theology and even philosophy. Ibn Tumart believed in a strict literal reading of the Koran and had little time for the formularized interpretations of the legal schools, such as the Malikites, that had grown up around the religious texts. For him, man was endowed with reason that would allow him to make sense of religious teaching. Ibn Tumart and other like-minded Muslim thinkers believed that reason and revelation were complementary and in no way stood in opposition to each other. The faculty of reason established the grounds for man's belief in revelation. Thus, reason could establish the existence of God.[53] The Almohad leader and his successors, however, remained cautious in public lest they anger the powerful religious jurists.

No wonder Averroes was terrified when the sultan first broached a taboo subject like the Eternity of the World: "Confusion and fear took hold of me, and I began making excuses and denying that I had ever concerned myself with philosophic learning." However, Averroes had been introduced at court by his friend and mentor Ibn Tufayl, a philosopher and the physician to the sultan, and the ruler then launched a discussion of the very topic, exhibiting considerable knowledge of the matter. "Thus he continued to set me at ease until I spoke, and he learned what was my competence in that subject," reports Averroes. "And when I withdrew he ordered for me a donation in money, a magnificent robe of honor, and a steed."[54]

By the time of his meeting with the sultan, Averroes had already written works on religious law and philosophy, as well as a major medical textbook, which enjoyed great popularity for centuries among Christian, Jewish, and Muslim doctors. Years later, he would be summoned to replace his aging friend

Ibn Tufayl as the sultan's personal physician. But first, Abu Yaqub charged him with a fateful commission, with Ibn Tufayl acting as go-between. Averroes later recalled for one of his students: "Ibn Tufayl summoned me one day and told me, 'Today I hear the prince of Believers [the sultan, Abu Yaqub] complain of the difficulty of expression of Aristotle and his translators, and mention the obscurity of his aims, saying if someone would tackle those books, summarize them and expound their aims, after understanding them thoroughly, it would be easier for people to grasp them.'" Ibn Tufayl at once recommended the sultan assign the task to Averroes, who leaped at the offer of royal patronage for his philosophical work. "This is what led me to summarize the books of the philosopher Aristotle."[55]

Despite a full roster of duties as a jurist, Averroes threw himself into the Aristotle project. With the political and financial backing of the sultan, he turned out three types of works devoted to explicating specific texts for his Muslim readers: the epitomes, summarizing Aristotle's central points; the so-called middle commentaries, which paraphrased and explained the material; and the "great" commentaries, which examined the text line by line and brought to bear a wide range of Arab and Greek philosophical writings as well as his own interpretations. In all, thirty-eight commentaries are extant in Latin, Arabic, or Hebrew, covering most of Aristotle's major works.[56] Together, they represent a remarkable effort to reveal the "true" Aristotle, shorn of many of the accretions of later Greek commentators and the esoteric tendencies of Avicenna, and to assert an Andalusi philosophical tradition as opposed to that of the Muslim East.[57] This was in keeping with Averroes's own inclinations as well as those of the rationalist Almohad sultans, who were determined to establish the place of reason alongside revelation.

At the core of this collection is the Great Commentary on Aristotle's *Metaphysics*, an exhaustive study of the science of being and the key, in Averroes's eyes, to understanding both God and the natural world. In writing on the Creation, Averroes advances Aristotle's view that the world is eternal and concludes that the accepted view of Muslim, Christian, and Jewish theologians that it was created in time—and from nothing—is absurd. The Commentator rejects the literal reading of scripture and argues that it places unacceptable limits on God's power and perfection. What did God do before he created the universe, he prods his readers, sit by idly? And why did God elect to create the world at one particular time and not another? This suggests the unthinkable—

that God, who is perfection itself, either made a mistake or had a change of heart.

The Great Commentary also identifies among Aristotle's most important precepts the notion that the route to primary knowledge is through an understanding of causality.[58] In another work, Averroes spells out his argument that accepting the philosophers' approach to cause and effect, without direct recourse to God, provides the only basis for man's knowledge of his surroundings: "Denial of cause implies denial of knowledge, and denial of knowledge implies nothing in this world can be really known."[59]

This sets him on a collision course with the theologians, who claim that the philosophers' understanding of Creation, and their attendant views on cause and effect, leaves God powerless. In response, Averroes says that God can apprehend our lowly world of generation and corruption without a change in the state of his perfect knowledge. This gives him access to the particulars. The theologians' cardinal error lies in confusing man and God and casting the latter as a sort of superman. "He who believes this makes God an eternal man and man a mortal God," Averroes writes in *The Incoherence of the Incoherence*, his direct reply to al-Ghazali.[60] "It becomes clear that they [the theologians] only made God an eternal man, for they compared the world with the products of art wrought by the will and knowledge and power of man . . . But this theory is nothing but a metaphor and a poetical expression."[61]

Averroes's defense of God's knowledge of the particulars preserves his vision of the Eternity of the World without undermining the Muslim articles of faith concerning Judgment Day and related questions. And it is this running dispute over Creation that forms the bulk of the "exchange" between Averroes and al-Ghazali. Like the struggle over the particulars, the battle over the Eternity of the World boils down to a question of God's divine attributes, chiefly his knowledge, power, and will. The theologians fight tooth and nail to preserve a maximalist reading of God, while the philosophers led by Averroes seek to create metaphysical space for reason and for a natural world governed by immutable laws—both essential ingredients for true science.

In the world of late twelfth-century Islam, politics tipped the balance against Averroes and in favor of the theologians. With the Berber sultans of al-Andalus facing a deadly threat from the Christian armies of northern Spain, the palace sought to rally the conservative Muslim clerics and the people at large with public displays of orthodox religious zeal. Averroes was disavowed in 1195 and banished to the predominantly Jewish town of Lucena, outside Cordoba. His philosophical works were burned, and the study of his teachings was banned by a tribunal of his fellow religious judges.

Averroes's formal exile lasted just two years before he was recalled to the Almohad court in Marrakesh. He died not long afterward, on December 9, 1198. Fourteen years later, Spanish Islam suffered a mortal defeat at the hands of a powerful Christian coalition in the battle of Las Navas de Tolosa. Muslim al-Andalus never really recovered. The same cannot be said for Averroes. Within little more than half a century of his death, he was the undisputed star of an intellectual drama playing out along Paris's Street of Straw, the legendary scholars' lane that ran through the theological heart of western Christendom.

Averroes's Herculean effort to fulfill the sultan's commission bequeathed Europe a thoroughly rationalist approach to philosophy that changed forever the landscape of Western thought. This put Averroes almost five centuries ahead of Descartes, whose mathematical rationalism has made him the West's traditional candidate for founder of modern philosophy.[62] Centuries before, St. Augustine had made philosophy subordinate to theology. The arrival in the West of Averroes's writings began to turn this state of affairs on its head. Averroes takes as his starting place the assertion that Aristotelian philosophy is a fully demonstrative science capable of attaining absolute truth from ironclad first principles. For him, philosophy is as reliable a source of truth as revelation, and the two can never be in any real opposition to each other. Where necessary, an allegorical interpretation of scripture can reveal an inner meaning in accordance with philosophical proof. Both theology and philosophy lead man to the same truth.[63]

There was much more to Averroes than first met the medieval Western eye. Missing almost completely from the early Latin translations was the pious Muslim thinker who wrote compelling works on religious law and produced specific treatises exploring the place of philosophy and its relationship to a great monotheistic faith like Islam. Caught up in its unbridled enthusiasm for the commentaries on Aristotle, the Christian world at the time saw little or no value in those of Averroes's works that addressed overtly Islamic themes. As a result, they were not translated into Latin until centuries later, although medieval Jewish thinkers, including the masterful Moses Maimonides, proved far more receptive. Among these "unknown" texts was Averroes's landmark assertion of the rightful place of philosophy within a religious context, *On the Harmony of*

Religion and Philosophy.[64] Introducing the work, Averroes notes, "The purpose of this treatise is to examine, from the standpoint of the study of the [Divine] Law, whether the study of philosophy and logic is allowed by the Law, or prohibited, or commended—either by way of recommendation or as obligatory."[65]

Averroes concludes that philosophy and revelation are different approaches to the same answers. Reaching into the holy texts, he finds ample support in Islam for the use of man's reason, and even takes it as the religious duty for those few truly capable of philosophizing. "Now since this religion is true and summons to the study which leads to knowledge of the Truth, we the Muslim community know definitely that demonstrative study [i.e., philosophy] does not lead to [conclusions] conflicting with what scripture has given us; for truth does not oppose truth but accords with it and bears witness to it."[66] Averroes then goes on to argue for the superiority of the demonstrative knowledge of qualified philosophers over and above the dialectical knowledge of the theologians or the rhetorical knowledge of the pious masses.

This Averroes—sincere believer in God and defender of the Muslim faith—was all but invisible to thirteenth-century Western thinkers hungry for new ways to look at the world. Rather, the Averroes of the Latin imagination was almost as much a product of men like Michael Scot and Frederick II as he was of his own pen. Michael translated four of the great commentaries, including those on the seminal *Metaphysics* and *On the Soul*; two middle commentaries; and one epitome.[67] Frederick saw to it that these and other translations were sent to the Italian universities, whence they soon made their way to Paris. A manuscript at the Bibliothèque Nationale, dated 1243, contains almost all the works of Averroes known to the medieval West.[68] In a cover letter, addressed to "you men of learning" at Bologna, Frederick declares his wish to share this priceless material with the world. "We will not conceal those fruits, gathered with so great effort, nor can we find satisfaction in thinking of them as our own property unless first we share with others so great a good . . . Therefore deign to accept these books as a gift from your friend, the emperor, and, at his request and through the kindness of your hearts, make known to him what you discover as a result of your research."[69]

At first reactions to Frederick's gift were rather muted. The works of Averroes seemed to slip naturally into the running Christian debate over the Eternity of the World and the reception of Aristotle in general. Some churchmen even welcomed the Commentator as someone who could shed much-needed light on the convoluted world of Aristotelian thought. But such a steady state of affairs was clearly doomed. Europe's universities, despite their proud origins as semiautonomous corporations, were at heart religious institutions and had to answer to the highest church officials. It was only a matter of time before the secular masters, chiefly the philosophers at the University of Paris, realized that they could deploy the Latin Averroes as their champion against the theologians. His assertion that proper philosophy was superior to theology and that both offered legitimate paths to the same eternal truths doomed Augustine's notion that philosophers were mere handmaidens to the men of God. Soon enough, the forces of faith and reason were at one another's throats, and it would take the patience of a philosopher-saint—in this case, one steeped in the teachings of Averroes and his school—to craft a truce between those who upheld the traditional church teachings and the new generations of early modern scientists, as shaped by the Arabs.

Chapter Nine

THE INVENTION OF THE WEST

WHEN THOMAS AQUINAS, theologian and future saint, arrived in Paris in early 1269, he found the university almost paralyzed by a persistent problem: What to do with the philosophers? Aristotle's instructive texts on logic, the beloved dialectic of the medieval churchmen, had long since been endorsed by a religious establishment eager to demonstrate the truth of Christian revelation. However, natural philosophy, as explicated and amplified by the leading Arab thinkers, was another matter altogether. The full force of the *studia Arabum*, in particular with the arrival in the 1230s of Michael Scot's translations of Averroes, turned what had been a mostly genteel tug-of-war over the world-view of medieval Christendom into a philosophical, theological, and scientific free-for-all.

The seven liberal arts had easily given way before the Arab intellectual onslaught, but theology—the queen of sciences, its medieval exponents called it—still retained its dominance over St. Augustine's "handmaiden," philoso-phy, and the attendant natural sciences. As long as this new philosophy failed to present anything like a coherent metaphysics, a proper science of "being as being," there were few points of conflict with Christian faith. For all the early novelty of the abacus, the astrolabe, and the alembic, theology's position as the primary way to understand the natural world appeared secure. When the first hints of a unified cosmology did appear, beginning in the mid-twelfth century, they generally reflected the user-friendly ideas of Plato, which the church had little difficulty assimilating as its own.[1] All that changed irrevocably with Averroes, whose steadfast advocacy of Aristotelian thought within the context of his own monotheism overwhelmed Christian intellectuals of the day. Suddenly the handmaiden turned on her mistress.

Christendom had already detected the gathering threat. Beginning with the first "condemnations" at the University of Paris in 1210, the church attempted to safeguard its teachings and wall them off from the insidious effects of intemperate philosophizing. Over the course of the thirteenth and fourteenth centuries, the authorities in Paris would issue more than a dozen lists of banned ideas, meticulously detailed in an official register of errors. The frequency with which these orders were issued, however, suggests just how ineffective the condemnations must have been at deterring the curiosity of scholars and theologians alike.

This was a losing battle, as many in the church recognized. Among the first to do so was Thomas Aquinas's own Dominican order, whose charter of 1228 authorized its students to consult the works of pagans and philosophers, albeit only "briefly." This was an early recognition that science was here to stay and must be mastered, or at least addressed intelligently.[2] Soon enough, Dominican thinkers would seek to harness these new ideas to defend and strengthen the faith. Even the papacy was compelled to find ways in which natural philosophy might be made compatible with Christian doctrine. Pope Gregory IX, notwithstanding his stinging rebuke of Frederick II's reliance on "reason," modified the standing ban on the natural philosophy of Aristotle and his Arab commentators to allow the formation of a special commission to purge the works in question of their errors.

"But since, as we have learned, the books on nature which were prohibited . . . are said to contain both useful and useless matter," the pope writes, "lest the useful be vitiated by the useless, we command your discretion . . . that, examining the same books as is convenient subtly and prudently, you entirely exclude what you shall find there erroneous or likely to give scandal or offense to readers, so that, what are suspect being removed, the rest may be studied without delay or offense."[3] In another concession, Gregory annulled the excommunication of any scholars who had been caught violating the old prohibition. The promised papal commission never met, but by 1255 all works of natural philosophy available in Latin had been made part of the university's official arts curriculum. Since an arts degree was a prerequisite to more advanced study, this meant that entire cohorts of medieval university graduates, including all future theologians, were steeped in the teachings of natural philosophy.

The startling success of natural philosophy and its expanding hold on the Western imagination throughout the thirteenth century was accelerated by the steady transformation of the medieval university into a powerful social, intellectual, and cultural institution in its own right. The university remained within the general orbit of the church for centuries, but it was first and foremost a product of the growing need for trained clerks, lawyers, doctors, and secular officials and bureaucrats.[4] The bounties of the *studia Arabum* offered a ready-made curriculum to help meet this demand.

It is easy to see why philosophy, as put forward by the Arabs and the Greeks, held enormous appeal for the late medieval mind as it slowly began to shed its isolationism and confront the natural world. This new science was breathtaking in its scope and offered a coherent explanation of just about everything. While it covered elements of the traditional Christian view that it confronted, it also contained much new material on questions left effectively untouched by religious teachings, such as the workings of the physical world and the inner mind of man. It proceeded logically from basic assumptions and self-evident principles, promising order in a seemingly haphazard world.[5] Best of all, it carried the powerful Aristotle "brand," already well established through the practice of dialectics and through the underlying principles of Arab astrology, popularized by the Latin translations of Albumazar.

At Paris, Europe's leading center of higher learning and preeminent seat of religious studies, the arts faculty swelled dramatically until it dwarfed those of theology, law, and medicine. Within one hundred years of Michael Scot's translations of Averroes there were more than eight times as many arts masters as there were teachers in the other faculties combined.[6] Early figures are sketchy, but modern estimates put the total number of students who matriculated at Europe's universities between 1350 and 1500 at 750,000.[7] The exciting new ways of university life, with its loose guilds of masters, its rough-and-tumble student associations, and its heated rivalries among the faculties and between individual professors, challenged the sleepy monopoly long enjoyed by the cathedral schools and, by extension, the control over advanced education by the church.

Such a state of affairs alarmed many traditional theologians who saw the rising influence of the arts masters—for all practical purposes now professional philosophers—as a danger to the faith and to their own standing. Armed with the translations of Averroes and Avicenna, these masters were actively promoting a number of problematic ideas that questioned established Christian doctrine. Adding to the rancor between the arts and theology faculties was the growing presence in the latter of the mendicant orders, the

Dominicans and the Franciscans, who were widely suspected of putting loyalty to Rome ahead of the academic interests of the university. Nor were religious orders exempt from a bitter rivalry of their own, which further roiled the university scene.

By the time of Thomas Aquinas's arrival in the late 1260s, things in Paris had deteriorated still further. Many among the arts masters were openly asserting their right to pursue philosophical speculation wherever it might take them. This generally meant incursions into territory the theologians guarded jealously for themselves, including speculation on the Creation, the soul, and the attributes of God. In response, the theologians, backed by the more cautious secular scholars, went on the attack against these growing Aristotelian tendencies. Their inspiration was the Franciscan John of Fidanza, later canonized as St. Bonaventure, who reminded his rivals that theology remained the queen of sciences and that reliance on philosophy as anything but preparation for more advanced study guaranteed a "fall into darkness."[8] One of Bonaventure's allies, meanwhile, warned his theological colleagues, such as Thomas, not to indulge in philosophizing: "It is not seemly that a theologian should have recourse to the errors of the philosophers."[9]

In their zeal, this conservative faction greatly inflated the threat from a maximalist reading of Arab philosophy at its most hostile to the Christian religion, a reading Western scholars later dubbed "Latin Averroism." According to their critics, the militant philosophers left no role for God or revelation and denigrated theology in the cause of advancing science. The theologians even accused these so-called Averroists of hiding their secret secularist leanings behind professions of faith.

Certainly, Averroes himself believed that no such sleight of hand was required. The Commentator was unequivocal in asserting that the truth of the philosophers and that of the theologians was one and the same, although he was never in any doubt that philosophical thinking was superior. Besides, he respected revelation and the prophets Moses, Jesus, and Muhammad, who could reach the masses in ways philosophy never could. But Averroes's actual views were rarely discussed in any detail, and even his most faithful Latin readers still had no access to his important works on the relationship of philosophy and religion. What mattered was the way both sides, the clergy and the independent-minded arts masters, saw Averroes and the entire Arab tradition as the fulcrum of their own struggles with each other.

As it had with the Muslims before, the question of the Eternity of the World provided the medieval Christians with one of their central intellectual battlegrounds. Bonaventure used Lenten conferences in 1267 and 1268 to denounce philosophy not illuminated by faith, and he listed the Eternity of the World among the most dangerous errors of the day. Such a notion was heretical, he argued, and could not possibly be proved by reason. Bonaventure and his supporters then went a step further. They asserted that they could demonstrate, with the help of philosophy, that the world had been created "in time" in accordance with their reading of the book of Genesis. In December 1270, the hard-line bishop of Paris followed Bonaventure's lead and issued a list of thirteen condemned errors that could not be taught or held in any way. Singled out for special attention were the Eternity of the World and God's indifference to particulars. Like earlier condemnations, they were generally ignored in both the arts and the theological faculties.

The Dominicans dispatched Thomas, their star theologian, from Rome to Paris in the hopes of addressing the main sources of turmoil at the university. These included the growing radicalism of the Averroists in the arts faculty and the general hostility of the secular masters toward the mendicant orders. The Dominicans also saw a serious threat from conservatives opposed to all natural philosophy, which included teachings the Dominicans believed were invaluable in combating heretics, such as the Cathars, whom the church eventually crushed in a bloodthirsty Crusade in southern France. Before joining the Dominicans, Thomas studied at Frederick II's University of Naples, where he first encountered natural philosophy in an environment shaped by the works of the Arab and Jewish thinkers favored by the emperor. These included Avicenna and Averroes, as well as the Jewish scholar Maimonides, who wrote his philosophical treatises in Arabic. One of Thomas's first teachers later joined a circle of Christians and Jews studying Maimonides, whose *Guide for the Perplexed* and other works may have been translated or summarized at the Sicilian court by Michael Scot.[10]

Several early treatises by Thomas from the 1250s reveal a careful and thoughtful engagement with both Avicenna and Averroes, a feature that would run through all his writings, even when he disagreed violently with his Arab predecessors. Avicenna was at the time still the leading authority for Western philosophers, and the list of his ideas that can be found in Thomas's works is an impressive one. These include two proofs of God's existence and the distinction between divine and human knowledge.[11]

Similarly, Maimonides's approach to the Eternity of the World provided a powerful impetus for Thomas's later thinking on the subject and its broader implications for philosophy and faith. In his *Guide for the Perplexed*, Maimonides argues that one could accept Creation in time on faith but still admit the existence of knowable natural causes. Like Averroes a native of al-Andalus, Maimonides sought to reconcile reason and revelation by arguing that the Aristotelian laws of nature took over only after God created the world from nothing.[12]

Thomas had already sided decisively with his fellow theologians—and against Averroes—in a dispute with the radical philosophers over the immortality of the soul, but his *On the Eternity of the World*, written in 1270 toward the height of the troubles in Paris, was a bitter disappointment to many in the theology faculty. In a direct blow to Bonaventure and his circle, Thomas dismisses as "fragile" the church's accepted view that reason can demonstrate with certainty that the world was created in time. Proponents argued, for example, that God, as the cause of all things, must have come before the world that he created, thus establishing the Creation as a specific temporal event. Drawing on the formulation that Averroes adopted earlier in *The Incoherence of the Incoherence*, Thomas responds that these traditionalists fail to understand that both God's creative actions and his will must be seen as instantaneous.[13]

"Since people are accustomed to think of productions that are brought about by way of motion, they do not readily understand that an efficient cause [that is, God] does not have to precede its effect in duration. And that is why many, with their limited experience, attend to only a few aspects, and so are overhasty in airing their views." He also dismisses fears that this would deprive God of his will, which likewise does not have to precede its effect in duration. "The same is true of the person who acts through his will, unless he acts after deliberation. Heaven forbid that we should attribute such a procedure to God!"[14]

Such reasoning leads Thomas to acknowledge the logical possibility that the Arab philosophers were correct: The world is both eternal and created by God. What is more, his approach avoids the danger of making the world co-eternal with God—a notion that Jews, Christians, and Muslims would all abhor as polytheism. Of course, Thomas notes at the very outset of *On the Eternity of the World* that it is an absolute article of Catholic faith that the world was created by God at a specific time, but he concludes somewhat testily that the traditionalists' tiresome philosophical arguments do no credit to the cause: "Some of them are so feeble that their very frailty seems to lend probability to the opposite side."[15]

Thomas revisited the question of the Eternity of the World throughout his lifetime, addressing the subject in at least six different works.[16] Only one philosophical challenge to eternal creation, first investigated by al-Ghazali in the eleventh century, ever seemed to give Thomas pause: If the world had existed always, then the number of souls left behind by the dead would be of infinite magnitude, something that medieval thinkers saw as a logical impossibility. Thomas concedes that the matter is indeed "difficult," but then brushes it aside by suggesting that perhaps God made men some time after the creation of an eternal world. "Besides, no demonstration has as yet been forthcoming that God cannot produce a multitude that is actually infinite."[17]

Debate over the eternal creation served as a platform for Thomas's undoubted scholastic virtuosity, but it also went to the heart of one of the most pressing questions of the late Middle Ages, the relationship between revelation and reason. For the theologians and philosophers in Paris, this effectively meant the relationship between the powers of an omnipotent God, as spelled out in scripture, and the laws of nature, as cataloged by the new men of science. Such disparate figures as al-Ghazali and Bonaventure, one a revered Muslim theologian and the other a Christian saint, allowed for no real distance between God and the natural world. In their eyes, what science perceived as natural laws were in fact the continuous creative powers of God, processes that could be interrupted and even reversed at any time and without warning.

By contrast, Thomas afforded the natural philosophers far more freedom, an approach that effectively narrowed the field for theology at the same time. This reflected, perhaps, an abiding respect for the great Greek, Arab, and Jewish philosophers, dating back to his university days in Naples.[18] In *On the Eternity of the World*, Thomas points out with a certain satisfaction that none of these great thinkers saw any contradiction in the idea of an eternal universe created by God. With characteristic sarcasm, he does not show the same respect for his contemporary rivals: "Thus only they who so cleverly detected this inconsistency are men with whom wisdom is born!"[19]

But Thomas also astutely recognized the pressing need to hammer out an intellectual and theological compromise that defended the fundamental doctrine of the church yet still made room for the science unleashed by the Arabs. Anything else would condemn the church to a debilitating and possibly fatal struggle with the forces of reason. Directed in 1271 by the head of the Dominican order to rule on a mixture of doctrinal and cosmological questions, Thomas was cautious in his response: "A number of these articles pertain more to philosophy than to faith. We do a great disservice . . . [to holy doctrine], when we affirm or we reprove in its name things that do not belong to it."[20] Likewise, he says, it is no concern of doctrinal faith how one interprets Aristotle.[21]

For Thomas, only a few areas were off-limits to philosophy, and then only because man could never hope to penetrate the mysteries of the divine will. He found just three articles of faith that could not be proved by reason and that had to simply be accepted by all Christians: God's creation of the world at a specific time; the Trinity; and Jesus's role in the salvation of mankind.[22] By implication, virtually the entire natural world and even what might appear to be traditional theological questions—for example, regarding God's existence— were proper subjects for the philosophers and could be adjudicated by reason. For Thomas, as for Averroes before him, philosophy and religion could never truly contradict each other.

In his unfinished masterwork, *Summa theologiae*, Thomas returns to the Eternity of the World to argue that preserving the separate realms of science and revelation is imperative to protect Christian faith: "That the world had a beginning . . . is an object of faith, but not of demonstration or science. And we do well to keep this in mind; otherwise, if we presumptuously undertake to demonstrate what is of faith, we may introduce arguments that are not strictly conclusive; and this would furnish infidels with an occasion for scoffing, as they would think that we assent to truths of faith on such grounds."[23]

At the time of Thomas's death, in March 1274, there was certainly no sign that his monumental effort to harmonize faith and reason—an effort guided by the spirit of Averroes, tempered by Christian tradition—would outlast the tumultuous decade, let alone one day become the teaching of the Catholic Church. Many of his fellow theologians were aghast at this "natural theology." The more prescient recognized that Thomas had opened the way to almost unbridled philosophical speculation, and they feared deeply what might come next.

The Franciscans, no doubt driven by conviction as well as by their historic rivalry with the Dominicans, led a furious assault on Thomas. They helped engineer a new round of condemnations—the fiercest ever—on the third anniversary of his death, which took aim at Thomas in spirit, although not in name. They also produced a polemic, *The Correction of Brother Thomas*, and included it in the order's curriculum. At Paris and at Oxford, a Franciscan stronghold, several masters sympathetic to Thomas's views were persecuted or excluded from teaching. The Dominicans fired off a treatise of their own in defense of their champion and made his work part of their own course of studies. However, Thomas Aquinas's views gradually prevailed at the highest levels of the church, and he was canonized in 1323. Two years later, church officials in Paris formally cleared St. Thomas of any heresy in connection with the condemnations.

The internal battle over Thomas's legacy, however bitter, was not the only worry facing the church. The era had also seen the emergence in Paris of a powerful new generation of secular intellectuals, led by the street fighter turned metaphysician Siger de Brabant. As a young student, Siger was the leader of the Picard nation, a student association that literally fought for the interests of the natives of the Low Countries. Brawls with the royal gendarmes and members of the three other "nations"—the French, the Normans, and the English, which included the large German contingent—were a regular feature of student life along the Street of Straw, and Siger was instrumental in some of the worst of the fighting. At one point, he was on the verge of expulsion for his part in the kidnapping of a French rival. Nevertheless, he managed to secure his master of arts degree by 1265 and became an instructor at the faculty of arts.

Siger immediately turned his combative spirit, as well as his impressive intellect, on the more orthodox colleagues in his own department and on the faculty of theology. Like Averroes, Siger and his supporters saw the pursuit of philosophical truth as the supreme human endeavor. But the members of this circle, while devout Christians all, were indifferent to the religious implications of their philosophizing. Instead, they set out to establish a firm distinction between philosophy and theology, each with its own methods and its own concerns.

In the eyes of the hard-liners in Paris, fed up with these upstart Averroists and already leery of the direction in which Thomas was seeking to take the church, such independence of mind was the arts masters' greatest sin. The thirteen condemnations of 1270 had been a warning shot in response to the militancy of Siger, who by now had a significant following among the arts students, but like previous church bans they had had little effect. The next year, Siger led a breakaway faction of masters who refused to accept defeat in elections for a new rector of the arts faculty. The dissidents effectively created their own parallel department, named their own rector, and awarded their own arts degrees.[24] Meanwhile, the orthodox majority in the arts faculty took an oath not to discuss theological matters in their classrooms. The pope's personal representative, the papal legate, finally intervened in 1275 to confirm the elected rector, and Siger left the university for good. Soon teaching in private anything except grammar and logic was also banned, suggesting that discreet study of illicit material had been rampant.

The church was not done with the rebels. Siger and two colleagues were summoned to appear before the Inquisition on January 18, 1277, to face charges of heresy. However, there is no record of any convictions, suggesting that all three were eventually acquitted. Three months later, the bishop of Paris published his infamous list of 219 condemned propositions, the same compilation that indirectly implicated Thomas Aquinas. Among the allegations against the arts masters was adherence to the Double Truth: "For they say these things are true according to philosophy but not according to the Catholic faith, as if there are two contrary truths and as if the truth of the Sacred Scripture were contradicted by the truth in the sayings of the accursed pagans."[25]

These condemnations of 1277, drafted by a committee of church bureaucrats, paint a curious and often distorted portrait of the intellectual scene in Paris. Yet they reveal the anxiety among the ecclesiastics that they were losing the intellectual high ground to the secular philosophers and their Arab mentors. Almost a dozen "errors" on the bishop's list concern the Arabs' notion of the Eternity of the World, with the authors of the bans also insisting, against the teachings of Thomas Aquinas, that Creation in time can be proved by reason. Several entries reflect the church's deep concern with determinism, inherent in Arab astrology's link between celestial activity and events on earth. Still others condemn accepted Christian positions, or else they hopelessly mangle the controversies of the day beyond recognition. In places, the banned propositions read like taunts between playground rivals; for example, the masters are specifically proscribed from asserting "that there is no more excellent state than the study of philosophy" and "that the only wise men in the world are the philosophers."[26]

The tragic and talented Siger—one of his students called him "the most distinguished teacher of philosophy"[27]—never returned to the lecture hall. In truth, his views had never strayed far from those of Thomas, whom he had clearly read and admired, but his unyielding insistence that the philosophers go where reason took them, an early defense of intellectual freedom, cost him his career and possibly his life. A chronicle from his native region of Brabant tells us that he died at the hands of a crazed cleric: "This Siger, a Brabantine by birth, as a consequence of holding certain opinions against the faith, was no longer able to remain in Paris, and went to the Roman court, where after a short while he died of stabbing by his half-mad secretary." The date of his murder must have been sometime before November 1284, when a letter from the archbishop of Canterbury makes mention of his death.[28]

The condemnations of 1277 dampened enthusiasm in Paris for rationalist speculation and natural philosophy, but they failed to weed out the influence of Thomas, or that of Averroes and his pugnacious acolyte, Siger de Brabant. The locus of scientific and philosophical activity in many cases simply shifted elsewhere, and the influence of the Averroist tendency took root as far away as Poland and England. Theology historically enjoyed little prestige or influence at the Italian universities, such as Padua and Bologna, and Averroes's teachings flourished there into the seventeenth century. Even at Paris, it was not so long before such matters were again openly read and debated. The men of science were clearly here to stay.

It is tempting to attribute their success to the raw power of natural philosophy and to the inability of the church to stamp out this competing "theory of everything" in the same way it had destroyed the Cathar heresy. Yet to do so is to overlook the crucial role of the Arabs as master architects—not simply as midwives—of the emerging Western worldview. This was no mere "recovery" of classical wisdom by the medieval Latins, with the Arabs cast in the role of benevolent guardians, as most Western histories of the period tell us. Rather, it represented the enormous transfer—some might even say cultural theft—of invaluable Arab knowledge and technology directly to the Christian West.

The case of Aristotle's natural philosophy is but one prominent example of the Arab influence at work. The great philosopher never had much time for God, and certainly did not conceive of a deity like the one who governed the monotheistic faiths of Judaism, Christianity, and Islam. The same could not be said of the medieval Arab philosophers, from al-Kindi to Averroes, who painstakingly subjected Aristotle to the demands of their belief in the one true God. And it was this "Arab Aristotle," not so much the pagan thinker of classical Greece, who ultimately triumphed in the West. Once in place, much of this Aristotelian worldview—particularly its rigid, even doctrinaire, conception of the cosmos—would face centuries of critical study by Christian scholars, a reevaluation that ultimately would lead to something resembling modern science.

As it happened, a similar process had long since been under way in the lands of Islam.

Just as Avicenna and Averroes "corrected" Aristotelian metaphysics to make room for God, so from the eleventh century onward the Arab scientists— the successors to Baghdad's House of Wisdom—assembled their own critical response to Greek astronomy and cosmology. The result was a theoretical and practical assault on the accepted architecture of the universe, codified by Ptolemy in the second century A.D. Gradually, the way was paved for that system's complete overthrow, proposed by the Polish astronomer Nicolaus Copernicus in the mid-sixteenth century and completed by Isaac Newton 150 years later. This celestial revolution put the sun, rather than the earth, at the center of the universe and affirmed the predominant position of science in Western society.[29] The transformation of man's place in the heavens—from the center of attention to just one among many— required not only a profound psychological shift but also some high-powered scientific innovation. Here, too, the West got some vital help from the Arabs.

Specifically, the only "original" theorems in Copernicus's monumental *De Revolutionibus*, published in 1543 as the scientist and churchman lay on his deathbed, have been traced directly to the earlier work of highly sophisticated Arab scientists unhappy with the teachings of the *Almagest*, Ptolemy's great astronomical textbook. In the early years of Arab science, Abbasid scholars gently edited and revised this classic work. Supported by al-Mamun and some of the other early caliphs, these astronomers corrected Ptolemy's calculation of the length of the solar month and greatly improved his measurement of the angle of the sun's course around the earth, known as the ecliptic. Such initial changes, important but not fundamental to the underlying theory of the original work, were generally incorporated into updated Arabic translations of the Greek text.[30]

Other improvements to the *Almagest* were more significant, such as the introduction of the Arab trigonometric functions to replace or supplement the more cumbersome chords used in the Greek tradition. "I say, since the method of the moderns, which uses the sines at this point instead of the chords, is easier to use, as I will explain below, I wish to refer to it as well," writes the astronomer Nasir al-Din Tusi in his *Redaction of the Almagest* in 1241.[31] Such was the importance of this process that the medieval Latin translators got better results working with Arabic editions of the *Almagest*, rather than starting all over again with the unedited Greek original.

This gradualist approach was joined by more ambitious efforts to evaluate Ptolemy's model of the universe on theoretical grounds. Here, the main sticking point was the *Almagest*'s readiness to violate, when necessary, one of the cardinal rules of natural philosophy, as taught by Aristotle and accepted by Ptolemy and his successors, including the Arabs: that celestial objects all moved in uniform circular motions, with the earth at their center. Ptolemy had already tried to account for the irregular movement of the celestial bodies with his notorious equant point, but he then shifted this theoretical axis of rotation away from the center of the earth—and thus from the center of the universe— in order to reflect centuries of observational data on how the planets actually moved when seen from the earth. By suggesting that some of these orbs effectively rotated around an axis that did not pass through the center of the universe, the *Almagest* introduced planetary motion that was neither perfect nor uniform.

This, said the early Arab critics, meant that Ptolemy's account of planetary motions was "false," giving rise to the theoretical literature known as *shukuk*, or "objections."[32] The oldest detailed critique dates to the mid-eleventh century, completed one hundred years before Hermann of Carinthia and Robert of Ketton struggled mightily in Spain to even understand the science of the *Almagest* well enough to translate it into Latin.

It was not long before the critique of Greek astronomy spread from the realm of science to that of natural philosophy. Avicenna took note of Ptolemy's theoretical shortcomings, as did Averroes and Maimonides. These latter philosophers, along with Averroes's mentor Ibn Tufayl and others, were part of a sustained critical tradition centered in al-Andalus that sought to replace the model of the *Almagest* with a nest of hollow spheres all centered on the earth.[33] The effort failed—although Avicenna hinted that he had found a separate way to save the model by eliminating the offending equant point, a claim that even his most loyal student dismissed[34]—but it nonetheless reveals the extent to which the Arabs were demanding that science not only account for observed phenomena but also accord with its own understanding of reality. In other words, science had to be both predictive and consistent, central tenets of the modern scientific method. "The science of astronomy of our time contains nothing existent, rather the astronomy of our time conforms only to computation and not to existence," complains Averroes.[35]

Astronomers connected with an observatory at Maragha, in what is today northwest Iran, produced a number of significant breakthroughs to address the deficiencies found in classical astronomy. This research center was built in 1259 on the orders of Genghis Khan's grandson, Hulegu, who one year earlier had led the Mongol forces in the sack of Baghdad and the execution of the last of the Abbasid caliphs. Baghdad's authority had long since been whittled down from its once-great expanse, and the caliphs, whose religious significance remained important, had been reduced to little more than political figureheads by the Mamluk warlords who had once served them. But the end of empire did not extinguish the scientific traditions once animated by the early Abbasids. As with the diffusion of scholarly learning into scattered Muslim courts after the collapse of central rule in al-Andalus, so, too, did other centers in the East exhibit remarkable intellectual activity after the loss of Baghdad. These included Diyarbakir, in southeast Turkey, as well as Isfahan, Damascus, and Cairo.[36] Such was the case at Maragha, which brought together an extraordinary collection of astronomers, engineers, and other experts and included a state-of-the-art science library.

Nasir al-Din Tusi, now the observatory's director and scientific adviser to Hulegu, had already devised an ingenious approach to the problem of the equant, one that generated linear motion from the uniform rotations, in opposite directions, of two spheres. Modern scholars have dubbed this the Tusi Couple. Not only did this address a major shortcoming within Ptolemaic astronomy, but it also helped later Arab scientists, as well as later Western ones, mount serious challenges to the authority of Aristotelian physics.[37] Meanwhile, Tusi's assistant and the designer of the observatory's specialized instruments solved the same problem in a different manner. Over time, the theorems developed by Tusi and his colleague were introduced into a range of planetary models by the Arab astronomers, most elegantly by the official timekeeper at the Umayyad mosque in Damascus, Ibn al-Shatir, who used them to account for the movements of the moon, the so-called upper planets, and the lower planet, Mercury.

Ibn al-Shatir died in 1375, but 168 years later his use of the theorems of the Maragha astronomers turns up in the groundbreaking work of Copernicus, suggesting that the Polish astronomer must have been familiar with the work of his Arab predecessors.[38] No means of direct transmission has yet been established, and there is no evidence that Copernicus knew Arabic or that these theorems were ever published in Latin. There are only hints: From 1496 to 1503, he studied in Italy, where Arab science and philosophy avoided the backlash experienced in Paris; there were in his day a number of Western Arabists capable of explaining such advanced works to Latin scientists; and Copernicus, who had studied Greek, may also have had access to late Byzantine borrowings from Arab astronomy. Adding to the mystery, Tusi's proof of his couple, made around 1260, and the proof included by Copernicus in his *De Revolutionibus* three centuries later use identical designations for the same geometric points, an indication to modern scholars that Copernicus had firsthand access to Tusi's work.[39]

Neither Ibn al-Shatir nor Tusi ever suggested anything as radical as transposing the Ptolemaic model to place its center at or near the sun, the defining feature of what became known as the Copernican revolution, although some Greek and Arab scholars had already pondered the idea. The enormous obstacles facing any theory of a sun-centered universe—established religious teaching and philosophical tradition, common sense and daily human experience, and the lack of a gravitational theory to make the whole thing work— testify to the genius of Copernicus's insight and to the brilliance of the Western men of science who later perfected his work. Yet it is worth nothing that Ibn al-Shatir had already imposed uniform circular motion on Ptolemy in such a way that all planetary movements now revolved around a single point, the earth. This made Copernicus's conceptual breakthrough that much easier by allowing him to shift that center toward the sun without having to reinvent an entire model of the heavens from scratch.[40]

The scientific, philosophical, and theological struggles over Copernicus's proposal of a heliocentric universe, which was buried in his famously difficult treatise under a mountain of complex mathematics, continued for many years.[41] The birth pangs of the new world of independent science included Galileo's heresy conviction in 1633 for his support of Copernicus, the earlier burning at the stake of the freethinking philosopher Giordano Bruno, and the persecution of countless others by the Catholic Church, at disastrous and lasting cost to its reputation and authority.

Nonetheless, the fearsome inquisitors never managed to put the jinn of Arab science back in the bottle. The findings of Johannes Kepler on elliptical planetary orbits and Isaac Newton's later theory of gravitation, published in 1687, effectively completed the work of Copernicus and helped guarantee the success of the scientific revolution. The church was forced to abide by the verdict of natural philosophy, its former handmaiden, and accept that the earth in fact revolved around the sun. Galileo was eventually rehabilitated, and in 1979 Pope John Paul II expressed regret for the mistreatment of the great Italian scientist and inventor at the hands of the church.

The verdict of history on this entire episode has been harsh, and rightly so. This is all the more the case because the church willfully ignored the prescriptions of its own St. Thomas—and through him those of Aver-roes—for the peaceful and productive coexistence of faith and reason. Under the direct influence of the Arab Aristotelians, Thomas had carved out a truce between traditional church teachings and the discoveries of the emerging generations of modern Western scientists. That compromise defines the rules of engagement to this day between the realms of faith and reason. And it stakes the Arabs' claim as inventors of the West, a debt that Adelard of Bath identified many centuries ago on his return from Antioch: "Of course God rules the universe," he assures his readers. "But we may and should enquire into the natural world. The Arabs teach us that."[42]

ACKNOWLEDGMENTS

Like the wandering intellectuals whose singular dedication helped bring Arab learning to the West, the present work, too, has had something of a peripatetic history. Little did I realize it at the time, but many of the ideas and thoughts that would find their way to these pages had been slowly crystallizing in my mind over the years and throughout my extensive travels, mostly in the Muslim world. Along the way, many people contributed to my effort to meld so many disparate elements into a comprehensive and meaningful narrative—far too many to thank individually. Yet they do all have my sincere thanks. Worthy of particular mention are Michelle Johnson, who read every word with care, insight, and good humor; Professor Paul Cobb, whose willingness to share his expertise and advice was invaluable; and Will Lyons, whose support and enthusiasm never wavered. Y. S. Chi gave the project a timely push. Needless to say, any shortcomings in the final text are solely the responsibility of the author.

I would also like to thank the staff at the Library of Congress, particularly in the Main Reading Room, where much of the research for this book was carried out in grand old-world style. While the extensive collection was of course immensely helpful, I also took considerable inspiration from the depiction in the great dome over my head of Human Understanding as she lifts her veil and glances up gratefully from Finite Intellectual Achievement. Among the twelve figures she credits is an Arab bearing the knowledge of "Physics"—that is, natural philosophy. Fittingly, he stands next to the figure of the Christian Middle Ages.

Further down the marble walls is an anonymous quotation that I adopted as a personal epigraph: "We taste the spices of Arabia yet never feel the scorching sun which brings them forth." It seemed a useful commentary on the work at hand. Alas, none of the sixteen bronze statues of famous thinkers along the balustrade of the upper galleries represents any Arab or Muslim figures. Yet their absence, too, is part of the story.

Finally, I would like to thank my agent, Will Lippincott, for recognizing the destination from a long way off and my editors at Bloomsbury, Peter Ginna in New York and Michael Fishwick in London, for helping me get there.

NOTES

Prologue: Al-Maghrib/Sunset

1. *Walter the Chancellor's The Antiochene Wars: A Translation and Commentary*, trans. and ed. Thomas S. Asbridge and Susan B. Edington (Brookfield, VT: Ashgate, 1999), 78.
2. Ibid., 79.
3. Ibid., 80–81.
4. *Adelard of Bath, Conversations with His Nephew: On the Same and the Different, Questions on Natural Science and On Birds*, trans. and ed. Charles Burnett (Cambridge: Cambridge University Press, 1998), 69–71.
5. Steven Runciman, *The First Crusade* (Cambridge: Cambridge University Press, 1980), 157.
6. Ibn al-Qalanisi, *The Damascus Chronicle of the Crusades*, trans. and ed. H. A. R. Gibb (Mineola, NY: Dover Publications, 2002), 89.
7. Geneive Abdo, "America's Muslims Aren't as Assimilated as You Think," *Washington Post*, Outlook sec., August 27, 2006.
8. Aziz S. Atiya, *Crusade, Commerce, and Culture* (Bloomington: Indiana University Press, 1962), 220.
9. Roger Bacon, *Opus Majus*, trans. Robert Belle Burke (Philadelphia: University of Pennsylvania Press, 1927), 815.
10. Brian Stock, "Science, Technology, and Economic Progress in the Early Middle Ages," in *Science in the Middle Ages*, ed. David C. Lindberg (Chicago: University of Chicago Press, 1978), 12.
11. Francesco Petrarch, *Letters of Old Age*, trans. Aldo S. Bernard, Saul Levin, and Reta A. Bernard (Baltimore: Johns Hopkins University Press, 1992), 2: 472.
12. In this view, salient geopolitical, environmental, and economic factors are generally ignored. For a thoughtful analysis of the decline of Muslim science and innovation, see Ahmad Y. al-Hassan, "Factors Behind the Decline of Islamic Science After the Sixteenth Century," in *Islam and the Challenge of Modernity: Historical and Contemporary Contexts*, ed. Sharifah Shifa Al-Attas (Kuala Lumpur: International Institute of Islamic Thought and Civilisation, 1996), 351–89. The notion that the faith was ultimately antithetical to science has come under increasing attack by historians of Islamic science. See the works of George Saliba, most recently, *Islamic Science and the Making of the European Renaissance* (Cambridge, MA: MIT Press, 2007); Roshdi Rashed; A. I. Sabra; and Ahmad Dallal.

Chapter I: The Warriors of God

1. Anna Comnena, *The Alexiad*, quoted in *The First Crusades: The Accounts of Eyewitnesses and Participants*, trans. and ed. August C. Krey (Princeton, NJ: Princeton University Press, 1921), 70.

2. Albert of Aix, "Historia Hierosolymita," in *First Crusades*, Krey, 48.

3. Guibert of Nogent, "Gesta Dei per Francos," in *Translations and Reprints from the Original Sources of European History*, vol. I, trans. and ed. Dana C. Munro (Philadelphia: University of Pennsylvania Press, 1895), 20.

4. There is no extant text of Urban's speech in Clermont. However, a number of medieval chronicles contain accounts, including some drawn from those present. This version is from Fulcher of Chartres, "Gesta francorum Jerusalem expugnantium," in *A Source Book for Medieval History*, ed. J. Thatcher and Edgar Holmes McNeal (New York: Scribners, 1905), 517. See also *Fulcher of Chartres: Chronicle of the First Crusade*, trans. Martha Evelyn McGinty (Philadelphia: University of Pennsylvania Press, 1941), 16.

5. Christopher Tyerman, *God's War: A New History of the Crusades* (Cambridge, MA: Harvard University Press, 2006), 77–78.

6. Ibid., 47–48.

7. Jonathan Riley-Smith, *The First Crusade and the Idea of Crusading* (Philadelphia: University of Pennsylvania Press, 1986), 4–5.

8. Ibid., 7.

9. Anna Comnena, *The Alexiad*, quoted in E. O. Blake and C. Morris, "A Hermit Goes to War: Peter and the Origins of the First Crusade," *Studies in Church History* 22 (1985): 90.

10. "Le Chanson d'Antioch," in *First Crusade: The Chronicle of Fulcher of Chartres and Other Source Materials*, ed. Edward Peters (Philadelphia: University of Pennsylvania Press, 1998), 302–06.

11. *Annales Rosenvaldenses*, quoted in Blake and Morris, "Hermit Goes to War," 93.

12. Guibert of Nogent, in *Translations and Reprints*, Munro, 20.

13. Albert of Aix, *Historia Hierosolymita*, in *First Crusades*, Krey, 56.

14. Albert of Aix, *Historia Hierosolymita*, quoted in Norman Daniel, *The Arabs and Medieval Europe* (London: Longman, 1979), 123.

15. *The Chronicle of Solomon bar Simson*, in *The Jews and the Crusaders: The Hebrew Chronicles of the First and Second Crusades*, trans. and ed. Shlomo Eidelberg (Madison: University of Wisconsin Press, 1977), 21.

16. Eidelberg, *The Jews*, 4.

17. Anonymous of Mainz, in Eidelberg, *The Jews*, 110.

18. Eidelberg, *The Jews*, 5–6.

19. *Solomon bar Simson*, in Eidelberg, *The Jews*, 30.

20. Atiya, *Crusade*, 58 (see Prologue, n. 8).

21. Anna Comnena, *The Alexiad*, in Krey, *First Crusades*, 70.

22. Carole Hillenbrand, *The Crusades: Islamic Perspectives* (Chicago: Fitzroy Dearborn, 1999), 270.

23. A. al-Azmeh, "Barbarians in Arab Eyes," *Past and Present* 134 (1992): 7.

24. Al-Masudi, *Kitab al-Tanbih wa'l-ishraf*, in *Islam from the Prophet Muhammad to the Capture of Constantinople*, trans. and ed. Bernard Lewis (New York: Oxford University Press, 1987), 2: 122.

25. Runciman, *The First Crusade*, 139–49 (see Prologue, n. 5).

26. E. S. Bouchier, *A Short History of Antioch* (Oxford: Basil Blackwell, 1921), 231–32.

27. Raymond of Aguilers, *Historia francorum qui ceperint Jerusalem*, quoted in R. B. Yewdale, *Bohemond I, Prince of Antioch* (Amsterdam: Adolf M. Hakkert, 1970), 53.

28. *Fulcher of Chartres*, 43–44.

29. Thomas S. Asbridge, *The Creation of the Principality of Antioch, 1098–1130* (Woodbridge, UK: Boydell Press, 2000), 48.

30. Abu Saad al-Harawi quoted in Amin Maalouf, *The Crusades Through Arab Eyes*, trans. Jon Rothschild (New York: Schocken Books, 1984), xiii. Maalouf notes that not all Arab historians attribute these exact words to al-Harawi. Ibn al-Athir, for example, attributes them to a poet who had been inspired by al-Harawi's lament.

31. Usama ibn Munqidh, *The Book of Contemplation: Islam and the Crusades*, trans. Paul M. Cobb (Harmondsworth, UK: Penguin Classics, 2008), 144.

32. Maalouf, *Crusades Through Arab Eyes*, 39–40.

33. Ibid., 39–40.

34. Hillenbrand, *Crusades*, 260.

35. Ibn Munqidh, *Book of Contemplation*, 146.

36. Ibid., 144.

37. Ibid., 153.

38. Hillenbrand, *Crusades*, 258.

39. Ibn al-Arabi, quoted in Hillenbrand, *Crusades*, 49. Ibn al-Arabi was a religious scholar from al-Andalus, not the more famous Muslim mystic of the same name.

40. Raymond of Aguilers, "Historia Francorum," in *First Crusades*, Krey, 261.

41. *First Crusade*, Peters, 14–15.

42. *Cronica de Alfonso III*, quoted in Phillip F. Kennedy, "Christian-Muslim Frontier in al-Andalus," in *The Arab Influence in Medieval Europe*, ed. Dionisius A. Agius and Richard Hitchcock (Reading, UK: Ithaca Press, 1994), 86.

43. Norman Daniel, *Islam and the West: The Making of an Image* (Oxford: One World, 1993), 135–36.

44. Ibid., 133.

45. Raymond of Aguilers, "Historia Francorum," in *First Crusades*, Krey, 260.

46. "Le Chanson d'Antioch," in *First Crusade*, Peters, 305.

47. Nikita Elisseeff, "The Reaction of the Syrian Muslims After the Foundation of the First Latin Kingdom of Jerusalem," in *Crusaders and Muslims in Twelfth-Century Syria*, ed. Maya Shatzmiller (Leiden, Netherlands: E. J. Brill, 1993), 163.

48. Hillenbrand, *Crusades*, 72.

49. Ibid., 73–74.

50. Daniel, *Islam and the West*, 137.

51. Atiya, *Crusade*, 171 (see Prologue, n. 8).

52. David Abulafia, "The Role of Trade in Muslim-Christian Contact During the Middle Ages," in *Arab Influence*, Agius and Hitchcock, 1.

53. Ibid., 10.

Chapter 2: The Earth Is Like a Wheel

1. *Adelard of Bath*, Burnett, 3 (see Prologue, n. 4).

2. Riley-Smith, *First Crusade*, 8 (see chap. 1, n. 7).

3. A. C. Crombie, *Augustine to Galileo* (Cambridge, MA: Harvard University Press, 1979), 1: 32.

4. Louise Cochrane, *Adelard of Bath: The First English Scientist* (London: British Museum Press, 1994), 24.

5. The eight prayers as spelled out in the Rule of St. Benedict are as follows: matins or vigils, lauds, prime, terce, sext, none, vespers, and compline. See Gerhard Dohrnvan Rossum, *History of the Hour: Clocks and Modern Temporal Orders*, trans. Thomas Dunlap (Chicago: University of Chicago Press, 1996), 35.

6. Kenneth F. Welch, *Time Measurement: An Introductory History* (London: G. Bell and Sons, 1924), 17.

7. Stephen C. McCluskey, *Astronomies and Cultures in Early Medieval Europe* (New York: Cambridge University Press, 1998), 105–08.

8. Ibid.

9. Welch, *Time Measurement*, 15.

10. McCluskey, *Astronomies and Cultures*, 112.

11. Ibid., 111.

12. For a discussion of the impact of monastic timekeeping on the creation of modern, capitalist society, see Lewis Mumford, *Technics and Civilization* (New York: Harcourt, Brace and World, 1963), 12–17.

13. McCluskey, *Astronomies and Cultures*, 85.

14. G. R. Evans, *Fifty Key Medieval Thinkers* (London: Routledge, 2002), 42.

15. McCluskey, *Astronomies and Cultures*, 115.

16. David C. Lindberg, *The Beginnings of Western Science: The European Scientific Tradition in Philosophical, Religious, and Institutional Context, 660 B.C. to A.D. 1450* (Chicago: University of Chicago Press, 1992), 39.

17. Notker the Stammerer, *Notatio*, quoted in Michael Idomir Allen, "Bede and Frechulf at Medieval St Gallen," in *Beda Venerabilis: Historian, Monk & Northumbrian*, ed. L. A. J. R. Houwen and A. A. MacDonald (Groningen: E. Forsten, 1996), 65.

18. Charles Burnett, *The Introduction of Arabic Learning into England* (London: British Library, 1997), 17.

19. Cochrane, *Adelard of Bath*, 5–6.

20. Burnett, *Introduction of Arabic Learning*, 13.

21. Ibid., 13–17.

22. Ibid., 3.

23. Donald R. Hill, *Studies in Medieval Islamic Technology* (Brookfield, VT: Ashgate, 1998), 22.

24. Burnett, *Introduction of Arabic Learning*, 12–13.

25. Gerbert d'Aurillac, *The Letters of Gerbert, with His Papal Privileges as Sylvester II*, trans. and ed. Harriet Pratt Lattin (New York: Columbia University Press, 1959), 37.

26. Emilie Savage-Smith, "Celestial Mapping," in *The History of Cartography*, vol. 2, bk. 1, *Cartography in the Traditional Islamic and South Asian Societies*, ed. J. B. Harley and David Woodward (Chicago: University of Chicago Press, 1987), 24–25.

27. School of Gerbert, *De utilitatibus astrolabii*, quoted in McCluskey, *Astronomies and Cultures*, 165. As McCluskey points out, this work has been attributed variously to Gerbert and to one of his students, among several others.

28. Bruce Dickey, "Adelard of Bath: An Examination Based on Heretofore Unexamined Manuscripts" (Ph.D. diss., University of Toronto, 1982), 25.

29. Fulbert of Chartres, *The Letters and Poems of Fulbert of Chartres*, trans. and ed. Frederick Behrends (Oxford: Clarendon Press, 1976), 261. See also McCluskey, *Astronomies and Cultures*, 177, n. 34. On the earliest use of Arabic words, see Burnett, *Introduction of Arabic Learning*, 5.

30. McCluskey, *Astronomies and Cultures*, 177.

31. Cochrane, *Adelard of Bath*, 6.

32. William of Malmesbury, *History of the Kings of England*, trans. John Sharpe (London: Longman, Hurst, Rees, Orme, and Brown, 1815), 199.

33. Quoted in Burnett, *Introduction of Arabic Learning*, 16.

34. Michael Scot, *Liber introductorius*, quoted in Lynn Thorndike, *Michael Scot* (London: Thomas Nelson and Sons, 1965), 93–94.

35. Richard Erdoes, *A.D. 1000: Living on the Brink of the Apocalypse* (New York: Harper and Row, 1988), 90.

36. McCluskey, *Astronomies and Cultures*, 177–78.

37. Cochrane, *Adelard of Bath*, 3.

38. Ibid., 3–5.

39. *Adelard of Bath*, Burnett, xvii–xviii (see Prologue, n. 4).

40. Ibid., 71.

41. Ibid.

42. Ibid., 73.

43. Crombie, *Augustine to Galileo*, 35.

44. Eugen Weber, *Apocalypses: Prophecies, Cults, and Millennial Beliefs Through the Ages* (Cambridge, MA: Harvard University Press, 1999), 34–45.

45. *The Confessions of St. Augustine*, trans. F. J. Sheed (New York: Sheed and Ward, 1942), 247.

46. Ibid., 247–48.

47. Thomas of Chobham, MS Cambridge, Corpus Christi College 455, fos. 81–82, quoted in D. L. d'Avray, *The Preaching of the Friars: Sermons Diffused from Paris Before 1300* (Oxford: Clarendon Press, 1985), 232–33.

48. Debra Hassig, *Medieval Bestiaries: Text, Image, Ideology* (Cambridge: Cambridge University Press, 1995), xvii.

49. Ibid., 40ff.

50. Arthur Koestler, *The Sleepwalkers: A History of Man's Changing Vision of the Universe* (London: Arkana, 1989), 89.

51. Cosmas Indicopleustes, *The Christian Topography*, trans. and ed. J. W. McCrindle (London: Haklyut Society, 1887), 6. See also Koestler, *Sleepwalker*, 93.

52. Isidore of Seville, *The Etymologies*, trans. and ed. Stephen A. Barney, W. J. Lewis, J. A. Beach, and Oliver Berghof (Cambridge: Cambridge University Press, 2006), 286.

53. Ibid.

54. Koestler, *Sleepwalkers*, 105.

55. Ibid., 101–02.

56. René Girard, *The Girard Reader*, ed. James G. Williams (New York: Herder and Herder, 2004), 100.

57. Guillaume de Machaut, *Judgment of the King of Navarre*, quoted in Girard, *Girard Reader*, 100.

58. Samuel K. Cohn Jr., "The Black Death and the Burning of Jews," *Past and Present*, 196 (2007): 8–9.

59. Erdoes, *A.D. 1000*, 1–7.

60. Ibid., 8.

61. Cochrane, *Adelard of Bath*, 11.

62. Ibid., 11–12.

63. Crombie, *Augustine to Galileo*, 33–34.

64. For a discussion of what he calls medieval "double-think," see Koestler, *Sleepwalkers*, 97–106.

65. *The Venerable Bede's Ecclesiastical History of the English People*, ed. J. A. Giles (London: Henry G. Bohn, 1847), 291.

66. Maxime Rodinson, *Europe and the Mystique of Islam*, trans. Roger Veinus (Seattle: University of Washington Press, 1987), 4.

67. David R. Blanks, "Islam and the West in the Age of the Pilgrim," in *The Year 1000: Religious and Social Response to the Turning of the First Millennium*, ed. Michael Frassetto (New York: Palgrave Macmillan, 2002), 259.

68. Ibid., 260–61.

69. Rodinson, *Europe and the Mystique*, 7.

70. Norman Daniel, "Crusade Propaganda," in *A History of the Crusades*, vol. 6, *The Impact of the Crusades on Europe*, ed. Harry W. Hazard and Norman P. Zacour (Madison: University of Wisconsin Press, 1989), 54–55.

71. Allison Drew, "The De Eodem et Diverso," in *Adelard of Bath: An English Scientist and Arabist of the Early Twelfth Century*, ed. Charles Burnett (London: Warburg Institute, 1987), 17–23.

72. *Adelard of Bath*, Burnett, 91.

Chapter 3: The House of Wisdom

1. Ibn al-Nadim, *The Fihrist of al-Nadim*, trans. and ed. Bayard Dodge (New York: Columbia University Press, 1970), 650.

2. Pier Giovanni Donini, *Arab Travelers and Geographers* (London: Immel, 1991), 21.

3. Al-Yaqubi, *Le Pays*, trans. Gaston Wiet (Cairo: L'Institut Français d'Archéologie Orientale, 1937), 10.

4. Dimitri Gutas, *Greek Thought, Arabic Culture: The Graeco-Arabic Translation Movement in Baghdad and Early Abbasid Society* (London: Routledge, 1998), 19.

5. Ibid., 13–14.

6. Atiya, *Crusade*, 209 (see Prologue, n. 8).

7. Jonathan Bloom, *Paper Before Print: The History and Impact of Paper in the Islamic World* (New Haven, CT: Yale University Press, 2001), 48–51. On the city's first paper factory, see Gaston Wiet, *Baghdad: Metropolis of the Abbasid Caliphate*, trans. Seymour Feiler (Norman: University of Oklahoma Press, 1971), 70.

8. Johannes Pedersen, *The Arabic Book*, trans. Geoffrey French (Princeton, NJ: Princeton University Press, 1984), 116–17.

9. Ibid., 115–16.

10. Ruth S. Mackensen, "Four Great Libraries of Medieval Baghdad," *Library Quarterly* 2 (1932): 280.

11. Pedersen, *Arabic Book*, 52.

12. Saleh Ahmad El-Ali, "The Foundation of Baghdad," in *The Islamic City*, ed. A. H. Hourani and S. M. Stern (Oxford: Bruno Cassirer, 1970), 89–90.

13. Guy Le Strange, *Baghdad During the Abbasid Caliphate* (Westport, CT: Greenwood Press, 1983), 17.

14. El-Ali, "Foundation of Baghdad," 93–94.

15. Ibid., 94.

16. Sayyid Maqbal Ahmad, *A History of Arab-Islamic Geography* (Amman: Al al-Bayt University, 1995), 25.

17. Michael Cooperson, *Al Ma'mun* (Oxford: Oneworld, 2005), 19–21.

18. Al-Yaqubi, *Le Pays*, 4.

19. Ibid., 5–6.

20. Quoted in El-Ali, "Foundation of Baghdad," 96–97.

21. Gutas, *Greek Thought, Arabic Culture*, 33–46.

22. Ibid., 43.

23. Ibn Khaldun, *The Muqaddimah: An Introduction to History*, trans. and ed. Franz Rosenthal (Princeton, NJ: Princeton University Press, 1967), 3: 113–14.

24. Said al-Andalusi, *Science in the Medieval World: "Book of the Categories of Nations,"* trans. and ed. Semaan I. Salem and Alok Kumar (Austin: University of Texas Press, 1991), 44.

25. Al-Masudi, *The Meadows of Gold*, trans. and ed. Paul Lunde and Caroline Stone (London: Kegan Paul, 1989), 388.

26. Aydin Sayili, *The Observatory in Islam* (Ankara: Turk Tarih Kurumu Basimevi, 1960), 53.

27. Hunayn ibn Ishaq, *Risalat*, quoted in Max Meyerhof, "New Light on Hunain ibn Ishaq and His Period," *Isis* 8, no. 4 (1926): 690.

28. Gutas, *Greek Thought, Arabic Culture*, 2.

29. For a detailed discussion of the profound and lasting impact of this competition, see Saliba, *Islamic Science*, 27–72 (see Prologue, n. 12).

30. Pedersen, *Arabic Book*, 21–22.

31. Al-Biruni, *The Determination of the Coordinates of Cities: Al-Biruni's Tahid al-Amakin*, trans. and ed. Jamil Ali (Beirut: Centennial Publications, 1967), 191.

32. Gutas, *Greek Thought, Arabic Culture*, 137.

33. J. H. Kramers, "The Language of the Koran," in *Analecta Orientalia*, vol. 2 (Leiden, Netherlands: E. J. Brill, 1954), 164–65.

34. Gutas, *Greek Thought, Arabic Culture*, 65–69.

35. Pedersen, *Arabic Book*, 28.

36. Al-Masudi, quoted in Cooperson, *Al Ma'mun*, 22.

37. Ibn al-Nadim, *Fihrist of al-Nadim*, 254.

38. Abu Qurra, quoted in Mark N. Swanson, "The Christian al-Mamun Tradition," in *Christians at the Heart of Islamic Rule*, ed. David Thomas (Leiden, Netherlands: E. J. Brill, 2003), 67.

39. Gutas, *Greek Thought, Arabic Culture*, 108–09.

40. Lynn Thorndike, "The True Place of Astrology in the History of Science," *Isis* 46, no. 145 (1955): 277.

41. Abu-Sahl, *Kitab an-Nahmutan*, quoted in Gutas, *Greek Thought, Arabic Culture*, 46.

42. Cooperson, *Al Ma'mun*, 1–4 and 111–12.

43. Sayili, *Observatory in Islam*, 4–7.

44. Habash al-Hasib, quoted in David A. King, "Too Many Cooks . . . A Newly-Rediscovered Account of the First Islamic Geodetic Measurements," *Suhayl—Journal for the History of the Exact and Natural Sciences in Islamic Civilisation* 1 (2000): 217.

45. Al-Biruni, *Determination of the Coordinates*, 183.

46. Bernard R. Goldstein, "The Making of Astronomy in Early Islam," *Nuncius: Annali di Storia Della Scienza* 1 (1986): 87.

47. Habash al-Hasib, quoted in Sayili, *Observatory in Islam*, 56–57.

48. Sayili, *Observatory in Islam*, 57.

49. Arin was the Arab designation, apparently based on a faulty transliteration of Hindu texts. It is associated with the Indian city of Ujjain, in Madhya Pradesh state.

50. *Ibn al-Muthanna's Commentary on the Astronomical Tables of al-Khwarizmi*, trans. and ed. Bernard R. Goldstein (New Haven, CT: Yale University Press, 1967), 3–4.

51. D. A. King and J. Samsó, "Astronomical Handbooks and Tables from the Islamic World (750–1900): An Interim Report," *Suhayl—Journal for the History of the Exact and Natural Sciences in Islamic Civilisation* 2 (2001): 31.

52. David Eugene Smith and Louis Charles Karpinski, *The Hindu-Arabic Numerals* (Boston: Ginn and Co., 1911), 6.

53. Georges Ifrah, *The Universal History of Numbers: From Prehistory to the Invention of the Computer*, trans. David Bellos, E. F. Harding, Sophie Wood, and Ian Monk (New York: John Wiley, 2000), 529.

54. Owen Gingerich, "Islamic Astronomy," *Scientific American* 254 (April 1986): 70A.

55. *Ibn al-Muthanna*, Goldstein, 4.

56. Ibn al-Nadim, *Fihrist of al-Nadim*, 625.

57. King and Samsó, "Astronomical Handbooks and Tables," 14.

58. Bernard R. Goldstein and David Pingree, "The Astronomical Tables of al-Khwarizmi in a 19th Century Egyptian Text," *Journal of the American Oriental Society* 98, no. 1 (1978): 96–99.

59. Smith and Karpinski, *Hindu-Arabic Numerals*, 92.

60. Al-Khwarizmi, *Kitab al jam wa'l tafriq bi hisab al hind*, quoted in Ifrah, *Universal History of Numbers*, 364–65.

61. J. J. Berggren, *Episodes in the Mathematics of Medieval Islam* (New York: Springer-Verlag, 2003), 7.

62. Al-Khwarizmi, *The Algebra of Mohammad ben Musa*, trans. and ed. Frederic Rosen (Hildesheim, Germany: George Olms Verlag, 1986), 3.

63. Berggren, *Episodes in the Mathematics*, 63–64.

64. Ibid., 7.

65. Roshdi Rashed, *The Development of Arabic Mathematics: Between Arithmetic and Algebra*, trans. A. F. W. Armstrong (Dordrecht, Netherlands: Kluwer Academic Publishers, 1994), 14.

66. O. Neugebauer, "The Astronomical Tables of Al-Khwarizmi," *Det Kongelige Danske Videnskabernes Selskaber Historisk-Filosofiske Skrifter* 4, no. 2 (1962): 46.

67. Ibid., 23.

68. James Evans, *The History and Practice of Ancient Astronomy* (New York: Oxford University Press, 1998), 23–34.

69. Goldstein, "The Making of Astronomy," 86–87.

70. Gutas, *Greek Thought, Arabic Culture*, 75–85.

71. Ibid., 88.

72. Al-Masudi, *Muruj al-dahab*, quoted in Gutas, *Greek Thought, Arabic Culture*, 89.

73. Ibn al-Nadim, *Fihrist of al-Nadim*, 583–84.

Chapter 4: Mapping the World

1. Translations from the Koran are from Marmaduke Pickthall, *The Meaning of the Glorious Koran: An Explanatory Translation* (New York: Alfred A. Knopf, 1909). Pickthall's somewhat archaic use of English has on occasion been modernized.

2. J. H. Kramers, *Analecta Orientalia: Posthumous Writings and Selected Minor Works* (Leiden, Netherlands: E. J. Brill, 1954), vol. 2, 235–38.

3. Alfred T. Welch, "Muhammad: Life of the Prophet," *Oxford Encyclopedia of the Modern Islamic World* (New York: Oxford University Press, 1995), vol. 3, 159.

4. W. Montgomery Watt, *Muhammad at Medina* (London: Oxford University Press, 1956), 195.

5. Ibid., 198–201.

6. Watt, *Muhammad at Medina*, 205.

7. Ibid., 202.

8. Ibn Yunis, from a prose translation of a poem in David A. King, *In Synchrony with the Heavens: Studies in Astronomical Timekeeping and Instrumentation in Medieval Islamic Civilization* (Leiden, Netherlands: E. J. Brill, 2004), 215. King notes that the poem has been attributed to both Ibn Yunis and the famous legal scholar al-Shafi, but he prefers the former based on an analysis of its contents.

9. King, *In Synchrony*, 547.

10. Ibid., xvii.

11. Ibn al-Ukhuwwa, *Ma'alim al-qurba*, quoted in King, *In Synchrony*, 637–38.

12. Zayn al-Din al-Dimyati, Oxford, Bodleian Library MS March 592, quoted in David A. King and Richard P. Lorch, "Qibla Charts, Qibla Maps, and Related Instruments," in *The History of Cartography*, vol. 2, bk. 1, *Cartography in the Traditional Islamic and South Asian Societies*, ed. J. B. Harley and David Woodward (Chicago: University of Chicago Press, 1987), 190.

13. King and Lorch, "Qibla Charts, Qibla Maps," 189, n. 3.

14. A. J. Wensinck, "Kibla," in *The Encyclopedia of Islam*, vol. 5 (Leiden, Netherlands: E. J. Brill, 1960), 87.

15. Ibid., 189–93.

16. David A. King, "The Sacred Direction in Islam: A Study of the Interaction of Religion and Science in the Middle Ages," *Interdisciplinary Science Reviews* 10 (1985): 321.

17. Suliman Bashear, "Qibla Musharriqa and Early Muslim Prayer in Churches," *The Muslim World* 81, no. 3–4 (1991): 268.

18. A. J. Wensinck, "Kibla," in *The Encyclopedia of Islam*, vol. 5 (Leiden, Netherlands: E. J. Brill, 1960), 87.

19. David A. King, *Astronomy in the Service of Islam* (Brookfield, VT: Variorum, 1993), 257.

20. Carl Schoy, "The Geography of the Muslims of the Middle Ages," *Geographical Review* 14, no. 2 (1924): 261.

21. Fuat Sezgin, *Mathematical Geography and Cartography in Islam and Their Continuation on the Occident* (Frankfurt am Main: Institute for the History of Arabic-Islamic Science, 2005), 1: 159–60.

22. Peter J. Lu and Paul K. Steinhardt, "Decagonal and Quasi-Crystalline Tilings in Medieval Islamic Architecture," *Science* 315 (2007): 1106.

23. Donald R. Hill, "Arabic Fine Technology and Its Influence on European Mechanical Engineering," in *Arab Influence*, Agius and Hitchcock, 29–30 (see chap. 1, n. 42).

24. Ibid., 27.

25. A. Jon Kimerling, "Cartographic Methods for Determining the Qibla," *Journal of Geography* 101 (2002): 20–22.

26. Al-Masudi, *Muruj al-dahab* quoted in Donini, *Arab Travelers and Geographers*, 24 (see chap. 3, n. 2).

27. Donini, *Arab Travelers and Geographers*, 30.

28. Ibid., 31.

29. Al-Masudi, *Kitab al-Tanbih wa'l-israf*, quoted in Sezgin, *Mathematical Geography*, 78.

30. Abu Abdallah al-Zuhri, *Kitab al-gughrafiyah*, quoted in Sezgin, *Mathematical Geography*, 79.

31. Donini, *Arab Travelers and Geographers*, 36.

32. Sezgin, *Mathematical Geography*, 99.

33. Nafis Ahmad, *Muslims and the Science of Geography* (Dacca: University Press, 1980), 4.

34. Al-Muqaddasi, *The Best Divisions for Knowledge of the Regions*, trans. and ed. Basil Anthony Collins (Reading, UK: Garnet Publishing, 1994), 3.

35. Ibid., xxv.

36. Ibid., 45.

37. Sayyid Maqbul Ahmad estimates the weight of the silver planispheric map based on al-Idrisi's own account. See Ahmad, "Cartography of al-Sharif al-Idrisi," in *History of Cartography*, vol. 2, bk. 1, 159, n. 32.

38. Ibn Jubayr, *The Travels of Ibn Jubayr*, trans. R. J. C. Broadhurst (London: J. Cape, 1952), 348.

39. Hiroshi Takayama, "Law and Monarchy in the South," in *Italy in the Central Middle Ages, 1000–1300*, ed. David Abulafia (Oxford: Oxford University Press, 2004), 64–67.

40. Hubert Houben, *Roger II of Sicily: A Ruler Between East and West*, trans. Graham A. Lound and Diane Milburn (Cambridge: Cambridge University Press, 2002), 18.

41. Edmund Curtis, *Roger of Sicily and the Normans in Lower Italy, 1016–1154* (New York: G. P. Putnam's Sons, 1912), 308.

42. David Abulafia, "The Crown and the Economy Under Roger II and His Successors," *Dumbarton Oaks Papers* 37 (1993): 8.

43. Houben, *Roger II of Sicily*, 107.

44. Curtis, *Roger of Sicily*, 297.

45. J. F. P. Hopkins, "Geographical and Navigational Literature," in *Religion, Learning and Science in the Abbasid Period*, ed. M. J. L. Young, J. D. Latham, and R. B. Serjeant (Cambridge: Cambridge University Press, 1990), 318.

46. Al-Safadi, quoted in Sayyid Maqbal Ahmad, *History of Arab-Islamic Geography*, 163.

47. Al-Idrisi, *Opus geographicum*, quoted in Ahmad, "Cartography of al-Sharif al-Idrisi," 163.

48. Ahmad, "Cartography of al-Sharif al-Idrisi," 167–69.

49. George H. T. Kimble, *Geography in the Middle Ages* (London: Methuen and Co., 1938), 57.

50. Curtis, *Roger of Sicily*, 316.

51. "The Horizons of al-Idrisi in the Eleventh Century," in *Other Routes: 1500 Years of African and Asian Travel Writing*, ed. Tabish Khair and others (Bloomington: Indiana University Press, 2005), 86.

52. Sezgin, *Mathematical Geography*, 342.

53. Ibid., 541–42.

54. Ibid.

55. Ibid., 309. Details of Vasco da Gama's report on his journey to India can be found in Joao de Barros, *Ásia* (Lisbon: Nacional-Casa da Moeda, 1988), 152.

56. For a discussion of the Arab influence on Columbus, see J. H. Kramers, "Geography and Commerce," in *Religion, Learning and Science*, 93–94. See also Donini, *Arab Travelers and Geographers*, 37.

57. Smith and Karpinski, *Hindu-Arabic Numerals*, 139 (see chap. 3, n. 52).

58. Curtis, *Roger of Sicily*, 309.

59. Houben, *Roger II of Sicily*, 179.

60. Al-Idrisi, *Opus geographicum*, quoted in Karla Mallette, *The Kingdom of Sicily, 1100–1250: A Literary History* (Philadelphia: University of Pennsylvania Press, 2005), 146.

61. Al-Idrisi, *Opus geographicum*, quoted in Ahmad, "Cartography of al-Sharif al-Idrisi," 159.

62. Ibid., 163.

63. Kent Ljungquist, "Poe's Nubian Geographer," *American Literature* 48, no. 1 (1976): 73.

64. Kramers, "Geography and Commerce," 82.

65. Houben, *Roger II of Sicily*, 179.

66. Romuald of Salerno, ibid., 179.

Chapter 5: The First Man of Science

1. Allison Drew, "De Eodem et Diverso," 20 (see chap. 2, n. 71).

2. Stephen of Pisa, *Haly filius abbas*, quoted in Charles Burnett, "Antioch as a Link Between Arabic and Latin Culture in the Twelfth and Thirteenth Centuries," in *L'Occident and le Proch-Oriente au temps des crusades: actes du colloque de Louvain-la-Neuve, 24 et 25 mars 1997*, ed. Isabelle Draelants and others (Louvain-la-Neuve, Belgium: Brepols, 2000), 6.

3. Stephen of Pisa, *Haly filius abbas*, quoted in Charles Homer Haskins, *Studies in the History of Mediaeval Science* (Cambridge, MA: Harvard University Press, 1927), 135.

4. Burnett, "Antioch as a Link," 6.

5. *Adelard of Bath*, Burnett, 83 (see Prologue, n. 4).

6. Ibid., 91.

7. Charles Burnett, "Talismans: Magic as Science? Necromancy Among the Seven Liberal Arts," in *Magic and Divination in the Middle Ages: Texts and Techniques in the Islamic and Christian Worlds* (Aldershot, UK: Variorum, 1996), 7.

8. For a full text in English and Latin, see Charles Burnett, "Magister Iohannes Hispalensis et Limiensis and Qusta ibn Luqa's '*De differentia spiritus et animae*': A Portuguese Contribution to the Arts Curriculum?," in *Mediaevalia, textos e estudos* 7–8 (1995): 252–55. As Burnett notes, Richard Joseph Lemay first identified this "certain Antiochene" with Adelard of Bath. See Lemay, "The True Place of Astrology in Medieval Science and Philosophy: Towards a Definition," in *Astrology, Science, and Society: Historical Essays*, ed. Patrick Curry (Woodbridge, UK: Boydell Press, 1987), 70.

9. Burnett, "Talismans: Magic as Science?," 13.

10. Lynn Thorndike, "Traditional Medieval Tracts Concerning Engraved Astrological Images," in *Mélanges Auguste Pelzer* (Louvain, Belgium: Bibliothèque de l'Université, 1947), 231.

11. Adelard of Bath, *Liber prestigiorum*, quoted in Burnett, *Introduction of Arabic Learning*, 41 (see chap. 2, n. 18).

12. Emilie Savage-Smith, ed., *Magic and Divination in Early Islam* (Burlington, VT: Ashgate, 2004), xxiii.

13. Adelard of Bath, *Liber prestigiorum*, quoted in Burnett, "Talismans: Magic as Science," 10.

14. S. J. Tester, *A History of Western Astrology* (Woodbridge, UK: Boydell Press, 1987), 23.

15. Richard Kieckhefer, *Magic in the Middle Ages* (Cambridge: Cambridge University Press, 1990), 122.

16. Cyril Stanley Smith and John G. Hawthorne, trans. and eds., *Mappae Clavicula: A Little Key to the World of Medieval Techniques* (Philadelphia: American Philosophical Society, 1974), 9.

17. Cochrane, *Adelard of Bath*, 37 (see chap. 2, n. 4).

18. Charles Burnett and Louise Cochrane, "Adelard and the *Mappae Clavicula*," in *Adelard of Bath: An English Scientist and Arabist of the Early Twelfth Century* (London: Warburg Institute, 1987), 29–31. See also Cochrane, *Adelard of Bath*, 36–39.

19. Cochrane, *Adelard of Bath*, 36–37.

20. Bruce T. Moran, *Distilling Knowledge: Alchemy, Chemistry, and the Scientific Revolution* (Cambridge, MA: Harvard University Press, 2005), 11–12.

21. For a discussion of the religious aspects of Islamic alchemy and its relationship to modern chemistry, see Seyyed Hossein Nasr, "Islamic Alchemy and the Birth of Chemistry," *Journal for the History of Arabic Science* 3, no. 1 (1979): 40–45.

22. Nasr, "Islamic Alchemy," 40–45.

23. Roger Bacon, *Opus Tertium*, quoted in Crombie, *Augustine to Galileo*, 69 (see chap. 2, n. 3).

24. Moran, *Distilling Knowledge*, 33.

25. Ibid., 32–33.

26. Smith and Hawthorne, *Mappae Clavicula*, 4.

27. Robert of Ketton, *The Book of the Composition of Alchemy*, quoted in Eric John Holmyard, *Makers of Chemistry* (Oxford: Clarendon Press, 1931), 86. Robert was also known as Robert of Chester, among other names.

28. William R. Newman, trans. and ed., *The* Summa perfectionis *of Pseudo-Geber: A Critical Edition, Translation and Study* (Leiden, Netherlands: E. J. Brill, 1991), 5.

29. Moran, *Distilling Knowledge*, 9.

30. Lindberg, *Beginnings of Western Science*, 87 (see chap. 2, n. 16).

31. Thomas L. Heath, *A History of Greek Mathematics* (Oxford: Clarendon Press, 1921), I: 365.

32. Jeremy Gray, "Geometry," in *New Dictionary of the History of Ideas* (Detroit: Thomson Gale, 2005), 3: 92.

33. H. L. L. Busard, *The First Latin Translation of Euclid's Elements Commonly Ascribed to Adelard of Bath* (Toronto: Pontifical Institute of Mediaeval Studies, 1983), 3.

34. Gutas, *Greek Thought, Arabic Culture*, 120.

35. Scholars of medieval science have identified at least three early Euclid texts, known by convention as *Adelard I*, *Adelard II*, and *Adelard III*. Textual analysis, cross-references, and

other clues have fueled a lively debate that continues to run. Marshall Clagett first established the basic approach. See Clagett, "The Medieval Latin Translations from the Arabic of the *Elements* of Euclid, with Special Emphasis on the Versions of Adelard of Bath," *Isis* 44 (1953): 16–42.

For further studies and contrasting views, see Busard, *First Latin Translation*; Richard Lorch, "Some Remarks on the Arabic-Latin Euclid," and Menso Folkerts, "Adelard's Version of Euclid's *Elements*," both in *Adelard of Bath: An English Scientist*, 45–54; and Busard and Folkerts, *Robert of Chester's (?) Redaction of Euclid's* Elements, *the So-called Adelard II Version*, 2 vols. (Basel, Switzerland: Birkhauser Cerlag, 1992).

36. Clagett, "Medieval Latin Translations," 23.

37. Haskins, *Studies*, 25.

38. Jean Jolivet, "The Arabic Inheritance," in *A History of Twelfth-Century Western Philosophy*, ed. Peter Dronke (Cambridge: Cambridge University Press, 1988), 122.

39. For a comparative list of the use of technical terminology, see Busard, *First Latin Translation*, 391–96.

40. Burnett, *Introduction of Arabic Learning*, 42.

41. Folkerts, "Adelard's Version," 58–59.

42. A. C. Crombie, "Science," in *Medieval England*, ed. Austin Lane Poole (Oxford: Clarendon Press, 1958), 580.

43. *Adelard of Bath*, Burnett, xi (see Prologue, n. 4).

44. Herman the German, quoted in F. M. Powicke, "Robert Grosseteste and the Nichmachean Ethics," *Proceedings of the British Academy* 16 (1930): 88. See also Roger French and Andrew Cunningham, *Before Science: The Invention of the Friars' Natural Philosophy* (Aldershot, UK: Scolar Press, 1996), 231.

45. French and Cunningham, *Before Science*, 232. French and Cunningham go on to argue that Robert's interest in geometry with respect to nature is not about measuring and calculating, but about extending his neoplatonic view of nature. Nonetheless, the introduction of geometry to discussions of nature marked an important development in the emergence of scientific thinking. For more on Robert's innovations in the early scientific method, see A. C. Crombie, *Robert Grosseteste and the Origins of Experimental Science, 1100–1700* (Oxford: Clarendon Press, 1971).

46. Jeremiah M. Hackett, "Adelard of Bath and Roger Bacon: Early English Natural Philosophers and Scientists," *Endeavour* 26, no. 2 (2002): 73.

47. Cochrane, *Adelard of Bath*, 65–66.

48. John H. Harvey, *The Medieval Architect* (London: Wayland, 1972), 96.

49. John H. Harvey, "Geometry and Gothic Design," *Transactions of the Ancient Monuments Society* 30 (1986): 47–48.

50. E. H. Gombrich, *The Story of Art* (Englewood Cliffs, NJ: Prentice Hall, 1995), 185–86.

51. Ivor Bulmer-Thomas, "Euclid and Medieval Architecture," *Archaeological Journal* 136 (1979): 141–44.

52. Cooke MS, British Museum MS 23198, 145–47, quoted in Bulmer-Thomas, "Euclid and Medieval Architecture," 145.

53. Jean Gimpel, *The Cathedral Builders*, trans. Teresa Waugh (New York: Grove Press, 1983), 82–84.

54. Cochrane, *Adelard of Bath*, 81.

55. Raymond Mercier, "Astronomical Tables in the 12th Century," in *Adelard of Bath: An English Scientist and Arabist of the Early Twelfth Century*, 87.

56. Margaret Gibson, "Adelard of Bath," in *Adelard of Bath: An English Scientist and Arabist of the Early Twelfth Century*, 14.

57. Mercier, "Astronomical Tables," 88.

58. Ibid. See also Burnett, *Introduction of Arabic Learning*, 3.

59. Burnett, *Introduction of Arabic Learning*, 2.

60. Al-Andalusi, *Science*, 64 (see chap. 3, n. 24).

61. *Adelard of Bath*, Burnett, 69.

62. Ibid.

63. Mercier, "Astronomical Tables," 99–100.

64. John of Worcester, *Chronicon Iohannis Wigornensis*, trans. and ed. Patrick McGurk (Oxford: Clarendon Press, 1998), 3: 259–60.

65. John of Salisbury, *Policraticus*, 2, quoted in Gibson, "Adelard of Bath," 16.

66. *Adelard of Bath*, *Questions on Natural Science*, 99.

67. Ibid., 225.

68. Ibid., 227.

69. Ibid., 91.

70. Ibid., 227.

71. *Adelard of Bath*, Burnett, xxxi–xxxii.

72. Mercier, "Astronomical Tables," 89.

73. Charles Burnett has suggested that perhaps Adelard's level of Arabic was very low or virtually nil and that he relied on Arab informants and teachers rather than Arabic texts. This is difficult to square with some of the translations ascribed to Adelard, which Burnett and others generally accept, although it might have been possible with the help of reliable intermediaries. Still, the case "against" Adelard relies heavily on the absence of written Arabic material in some of his surviving works. Adelard's crucial role as a transmitter of Arabic learning, as well as his revolutionary stance on the importance of direct experience and reason over written authority, remains untouched by any debate over his level of linguistic skill. See Burnett, "Adelard of Bath and the Arabs," in *Rencontres de cultures dans la philosophie medievale* (Louvain-la-Neuve: Cassino, 1990): 89–107. For the opposite view, see the classic work of Haskins, *Studies*, 5–42.

74. *Adelard of Bath*, *Questions on Natural Science*, 105.

75. Ibid., 83.

76. Ibid.

77. Ibid., 103.

78. Adelard of Bath, *Questions on Natural Science*, quoted in Cochrane, *Adelard of Bath*, 45.

Chapter 6: "What Is Said of the Sphere . . ."

1. Charles Homer Haskins, "The Reception of Arabic Science in England," *English Historical Review* 30, no. 117 (1915): 56–57.

2. Richard W. Southern, *Medieval Humanism* (New York: Harper and Row, 1970), 167, n. 1.

3. Walcher of Malvern, Oxford, Bodleian Library MS Auct. F. 1. 9, f. 90, quoted in Southern, *Medieval Humanism*, 167.

4. Southern, *Medieval Humanism*, 163–64.

5. Burnett, *Introduction of Arabic Learning*, 15–16 (see chap. 2, n. 18).

6. Southern, *Medieval Humanism*, 169.

7. Mercier, "Astronomical Tables," 99–100.

8. María Rosa Menocal, *The Ornament of the World: How Muslims, Jews, and Christians Created a Culture of Tolerance in Medieval Spain* (Boston: Little, Brown, 2002), 151.

9. For example, see Bernard Septimus, "Petrus Alfonsi on the Cult at Mecca," *Speculum* 56, no. 3 (1981): 517–33.

10. Paul Kunitzsch, "Al-Khwarizmi as a Source for the Sententie astrolabii," in *From Deferent to Equant*, eds. David A. King and George Saliba (New York: New York Academy of Sciences, 1987), 227–36.

11. Burnett, *Introduction of Arabic Learning*, 16.

12. McCluskey, *Astronomies and Cultures*, 186–87 (see chap. 2, n. 7).

13. Haskins, "Reception of Arabic Science," 58.

14. McCluskey, *Astronomies and Cultures*, 180.

15. Ibid., 180–83.

16. There has been considerable scholarly debate about the date of *On the Use of the Astrolabe*. Its apparent dedication to Prince Henry Plantagenet, the future Henry II, at "the age of discretion" would suggest Henry was around sixteen years old at the time. That would place the work around 1149 or 1150. For this view, see Dickey, "Adelard of Bath," 64–70 (see chap. 2, n. 28). Charles Homer Haskins prefers somewhat earlier, 1142–1146. See Haskins, *Studies*, 28–29 (see chap. 5, n. 3). It was clearly one of Adelard's later works, for it refers to several of his earlier texts and assumes the reader is familiar with them.

17. Adelard of Bath, *On the Use of the Astrolabe*, quoted in Cochrane, *Adelard of Bath*, 98 (see chap. 2, n. 4).

18. Adelard of Bath, *On the Use of the Astrolabe*, quoted in Dickey, "Adelard of Bath," 11–12.

19. Dickey, "Adelard of Bath," 8.

20. Haskins, *Studies*, 28.

21. Dickey, "Adelard of Bath," 27.

22. Ibid., 13.

23. Cochrane, *Adelard of Bath*, 98.

24. Dickey, "Adelard of Bath," 19–20.

25. Plato, *Timaeus*, in *The Dialogues of Plato*, trans. and ed. Benjamin Jowett (Oxford: Oxford University Press, 1953), 3: 719.

26. Thomas S. Kuhn, *The Copernican Revolution: Planetary Astronomy in the Development of Western Thought* (Cambridge, MA: Harvard University Press, 1957), 29–38.

27. Ibid., 45–48.

28. Ibid., 55–59.

29. Ibid., 70.

30. Tester, *Western Astrology*, 153 (see chap. 5, n. 14).

31. Emmanuel Poulle, "Le Traite de l'Astrolabe d'Adelard de Bath," in *Adelard of Bath: An English Scientist*, 121.

32. *Chartularium universitatis Paresiensis*, quoted in Lynn Thorndike, *University Records and Life in the Middle Ages* (New York: W. W. Norton, 1975), 26–27.

33. Ibid., 78–79.

34. Etienne Gilson, *Reason and Revelation in the Middle Ages* (New York: Charles Scribner's Sons, 1938), 17.

35. Fernand van Steenberghen, *Aristotle in the West: The Origins of Latin Aristotelianism*, trans. Leonard Johnston (Louvain, Belgium: E. Nauwelaerts, 1955), 32–39.

36. For a discussion of the limited impact of Aristotle's natural philosophy in the early twelfth century, see John Marenbon, *Later Medieval Philosophy (1150–1350)* (London: Routledge and Kegan Paul, 1987), 54–56.

37. Roger Bacon, *Opus Majus*, 63 (see Prologue, n. 9).

38. Van Steenberghen, *Aristotle in the West*, 109.

39. Burnett, "Antioch as a Link," 3–4 (see chap. 5, n. 2).

40. Abu Mashar, *The Abbreviation of the Introduction to Astrology: Together with the Medieval Translation of Adelard of Bath*, trans. and ed. Charles Burnett, Keiji Yamamoto, and Michio Yano (Leiden, Netherlands: E. J. Brill, 1994), 13.

41. Richard Joseph Lemay, *Abu Mashar and Latin Aristotelianism in the 12th Century* (Beirut: American University of Beirut Press, 1962), xxxvii.

42. Albertus Magnus, *De vegetabilis et plantis*, quoted in Thorndike, "True Place of Astrology," 275 (see chap. 3, n. 40).

43. Thorndike, "True Place of Astrology," 277.

44. Adelard of Bath, quoted in *Abbreviation of the Introduction*, 15.

45. Ibid.

46. Lemay, *Abu Mashar*, 3–4.

47. Lemay, "True Place of Astrology," 68 (see chap. 5, n. 8).

48. *Abu Mashar on Historical Astrology: The Book of Religions and Dynasties (On the Great Conjunctions)*, trans. and ed. Keiji Yamamoto and Charles Burnett (Leiden, Netherlands: E. J. Brill, 2000), 3.

49. Lemay, "True Place of Astrology," 57.

50. Ibid., 58–59.

51. Edward Grant, *God and Reason in the Middle Ages* (Cambridge: Cambridge University Press, 2001), 89.

52. Lemay, "True Place of Astrology," 58–59.

53. Tester, *Western Astrology*, 153.

54. J. D. Lipton, "The Rational Evaluation of Astrology in the Period of the Arabo-Latin Translations, ca. 1126–1187 A.D." (Ph.D. diss., University of California, Los Angeles, 1978), 211–17. See also J. D. North, "Some Norman Horoscopes," in *Adelard of Bath: An English Scientist and Arabist of the Early Twelfth Century*, 149.

55. For a detailed analysis of the horoscopes and estimates of their dates and locales, see North, "Some Norman Horoscopes". (147–61), on which this account is based. North proposes Robert of Ketton, the prominent translator and scientist, as the only other possible candidate but quickly dismisses him for his lack of known connections to the throne.

56. Burnett, *Introduction of Arabic Learning*, 46.

Chapter 7: "The Wisest Philosophers of the World"

1. Edward Grant, *The Foundations of Modern Science in the Middle Ages* (Cambridge: Cambridge University Press, 1996), 24.

2. Anthony Pym, *Negotiating the Frontier: Translators and Intercultures in Hispanic History* (Manchester, UK: St. Jerome Publishing, 2000), 48.

3. Abd al-Rahman, "The Palm Tree," trans. in D. Fairchild Ruggles, *Gardens, Landscape, and Vision in the Palaces of Islamic Spain* (University Park: Pennsylvania State University Press, 2000), 42.

4. Ibn Khaldun, *The Muqaddimah, An Introduction to History*, trans. and ed. Franz Rosenthal (Princeton: Princeton University Press, 1967), I: 303.

5. Andrew M. Watson, *Agricultural Innovation in the Early Islamic World: The Diffusion of Crops and Farming Techniques, 700–1100* (Cambridge: Cambridge University Press, 1983), 92.

6. Ibid., 80–84.

7. Ibid., 70–71.

8. The respective terms are *asdad, saqiya, naura,* and *saniya.* See Expiración García Sánchez, "Agriculture in Muslim Spain," in *The Legacy of Muslim Spain*, ed. Salma Khadra Jayyusi (Leiden, Netherlands: E. J. Brill, 1994), 996.

9. J. Vernet, "Natural and Technical Sciences in al-Andalus," in *Legacy of Muslim Spain*, 939.

10. Alvaro, quoted in Robert Hillenbrand, "The Ornament of the World: Medieval Cordoba as a Cultural Center," in *Legacy of Muslim Spain*, 115.

11. Menocal, *Ornament of the World*, 42–43 (see chap. 6, n. 8).

12. Al-Jahiz, "Epistle on Singing Girls," quoted in Roger Boase, "Arab Influences on European Love Poetry," in *Legacy of Muslim Spain*, 466.

13. Menocal, *Ornament of the World*, 124–25.

14. Roger Boase, "Arab Influences," 466–73. For a detailed analysis of the extent of Arab influence on the troubadours, which remains controversial in scholarly circles, see also

María Rosa Menocal, *The Arabic Role in Medieval Literary History: A Forgotten Heritage* (Philadelphia: University of Pennsylvania Press, 1987).

15. Ibn Hawqal, quoted in Richard Fletcher, *Moorish Spain* (New York: Henry Holt, 1992), 65.

16. Luce López-Baralt, "The Legacy of Islam in Spanish Literature," in *Legacy of Muslim Spain*, 511–12.

17. Miquel Forcada, "Books of Anwa in al-Andalus," trans. Michael Kennedy, in *The Formation of al-Andalus: Language, Religion, Culture and the Sciences*, ed. Maribel Fierro and Julio Samsó (Aldershot, UK: Ashgate, 1998), 311.

18. *Calendar of Cordoba*, quoted in McCluskey, *Astronomies and Cultures*, 166–68 (see chap. 2, n. 7).

19. García Sánchez, "Agriculture in Muslim Spain," in *Legacy of Muslim Spain*, 997.

20. Ibn Idhari, *al-Bayan al-mughrib*, quoted in Robert Hillenbrand, "Ornament of the World," 127.

21. W. Montgomery Watt, *A History of Islamic Spain* (Edinburgh: Edinburgh University Press, 1965), 92.

22. García Sánchez, "Agriculture in Muslim Spain," 990.

23. Ibid., 992–93.

24. Rafael Valencia, "Islamic Seville," in *Legacy of Muslim Spain*, 145. See also García Sánchez, "Agriculture in Muslim Spain," 997.

25. Watson, *Agricultural Innovation*, 82–83.

26. Ibid., 83.

27. Marie-Thérèse d'Alverny, "Translations and Translators," in *Renaissance and Renewal in the Twelfth Century*, ed. Robert L. Benson and Giles Constable (Cambridge, MA: Harvard University Press, 1982), 440.

28. Hermann of Carinthia, *De essentiis*, trans. and ed. Charles Burnett (Leiden, Netherlands: E. J. Brill, 1982), 70.

29. Robert of Ketton, quoted in Charles Burnett, "A Group of Arabic-Latin Translators Working in Northern Spain in the Mid-Twelfth Century," *Journal of the Royal Asiatic Society* 63, no. 14 (1977): 63, n. 14. The Latin original is in Haskins, *Studies*, 121 (see chap. 5, n. 3).

30. James Kritzeck, *Peter the Venerable and Islam* (Princeton: Princeton University Press 1964), 3.

31. Peter the Venerable, *Patrologia Latina*, 671c, quoted in James Kritzeck, "Peter the Venerable and the Toledan Collection," in *Petrus Venerabilis 1156–1956: Studies and Texts Commemorating the Eighth Centenary of his Death*, ed. Giles Constable and James Kritzeck (Rome: Herder, 1956), 180. For a more recent study, see Thomas E. Burman, *Reading the Qur'an in Latin Christendom, 1140–1560* (Philadelphia: University of Pennsylvania Press, 2007).

32. Ibid., 177.

33. Peter the Venerable, *Liber contra sectum sive haeresim saracenorum*, quoted in Jolivet, "Arabic Inheritance," 113 (see chap. 5, n. 38).

34. Kritzeck, *Peter the Venerable*, 137–44.

35. Jacques Le Goff, *Intellectuals in the Middle Ages*, trans. Teresa Lavender Fagan (Cambridge, MA: Blackwell, 1993), 16.

36. Robert of Ketton, quoted in Kritzeck, *Peter the Venerable*, 62.

37. Pym, *Negotiating the Frontier*, 52.

38. *Ptolemy's Almagest*, trans. and ed. G. J. Toomer (New York: Springer-Verlag, 1984), 3.

39. Eulogy quoted in David C. Lindberg, "Transmission of Greek and Arabic Learning," in *Science in the Middle Ages*, ed. Lindberg (Chicago: University of Chicago Press, 1978), 66, n. 61. The eulogy was attached to Gerard's translation of Galen's *Tegni*. For the full eulogy text, see *A Source Book in Medieval Science*, ed. Edward Grant (Cambridge, MA: Harvard University Press, 1974), 35.

40. D'Alverny, "Translations and Translators," 453.

41. Avendauth, *De anima*, quoted in Jolivet, "Arabic Inheritance," 141.

42. Daniel of Morley, *Philosophia*, quoted in Pym, *Negotiating the Frontier*, 41.

43. Theodore Silverstein, "Daniel of Morley, English Cosmologist and Student of Arabic Science," *Mediaeval Studies* 10 (1948): 179.

44. Ibid., 185–89.

45. Burnett, *Introduction of Arabic Learning*, 63 (see chap. 2, n. 18).

46. Daniel of Morley, *Philosophia*, quoted in Pym, *Negotiating the Frontier*, 52.

47. Hugh of Santalla, quoted in Burnett, "Group of Arabic-Latin Translators," 90.

48. Burnett, *Introduction of Arabic Learning*, 60.

49. Oliverus Brito, *Philosophia*, quoted in McCluskey, *Astronomies and Cultures*, 191.

50. For the few sketchy details of Michael Scot's background, see Haskins, *Studies*, 272–73, and Lynn Thorndike, *Michael Scot*, 11–12 (see chap. 2, n. 34).

51. Michael Scot, *Liber particularis*, quoted in Thorndike, *Michael Scot*, 15.

52. Thorndike, *Michael Scot*, 72.

53. J. Wood Brown, *An Enquiry into the Life and Legend of Michael Scot* (Edinburgh: D. Douglas, 1897), 154.

54. Thorndike, *Michael Scot*, 39.

55. Sir Walter Scott, *The Lay of the Last Minstrel* (New York: C. S. Francis and Co.: 1845), 68.

56. Grant, *Foundations of Modern Science*, 34.

57. Charles Homer Haskins, *The Rise of Universities* (Ithaca, NY: Cornell Paperbacks, 1957), 9. See also Grant, *Foundations of Modern Science*, 34.

58. Le Goff, *Intellectuals*, 5–6.

59. Haskins, *Rise of Universities*, 82–83.

60. Thorndike, *Michael Scot*, 12.

Chapter 8: On the Eternity of the World

1. Ernst Kantorowicz, *Frederick the Second: 1194–1250*, trans. E. O. Lorimer (London: Constable and Co., 1931), 4–5.

2. Menocal, *Ornament of the World*, 192 (see chap. 6, n. 8).

3. Thomas Curtis van Cleve, *The Emperor Frederick II of Hohenstaufen*: Immutator Mundi (Oxford: Clarendon Press, 1972), 225.

4. Ibid., 224–25.

5. Charles Homer Haskins, "Science at the Court of the Emperor Frederick II," *American Historical Review* 27, no. 4 (1922), 680.

6. Quoted in van Cleve, *Emperor Frederick II*, xxx.

7. Van Cleve, *Emperor Frederick II*, 217.

8. Al-Maqrizi, quoted in van Cleve, *Emperor Frederick II*, 219.

9. Van Cleve, *Emperor Frederick II*, 158–60.

10. Haskins, *Studies*, 251 (see chap. 5, n. 3).

11. David Abulafia, *Frederick II: A Medieval Emperor* (London: Allen Lane, 1988), 257.

12. Ibid., 263.

13. Haskins, "Science at the Court," 672.

14. Thorndike, *Michael Scot*, 1 and 28 (see chap. 2, n. 34).

15. Haskins, "Science at the Court," 672.

16. Michael Scot, *Secrets of Nature*, quoted in Thorndike, *Michael Scot*, 3.

17. Frank J. Swetz, *Capitalism and Arithmetic: The New Mathematics of the 15th Century* (La Salle, IL: Open Court, 1987), 12–13.

18. Charles King, "Leonardo Fibonacci," in *From Five Fingers to Infinity: A Journey Through the History of Mathematics*, ed. Frank J. Swetz (Chicago: Open Court, 1994), 252. See also R. B. McClenan, "Leonardo of Pisa and His *Liber quadratorium*," in *From Five Fingers*, Swetz, 255.

19. *Fibonacci's Liber Abaci: A Translation into Modern English of Leonardo Pisano's Book of Calculation*, trans. and ed. L. E. Sigler (New York: Springer, 2002), 17.

20. Ibid., 15.

21. See King, "Leonardo Fibonacci," 252–54, and Swetz, *Capitalism and Arithmetic*, 234.

22. *Fibonacci's Liber Abaci*, 291.

23. Ibid., 404–05.

24. Haskins, *Studies*, 268.

25. Charles Homer Haskins, "The 'De arte venandi cum avibus' of the Emperor Frederick II," *English Historical Review* 36, no. 143 (1921), 342.

26. Charles Homer Haskins, "Some Early Treatises on Falconry," *Romanic Review* 13, no. 1 (1922), 18–22.

27. Van Cleve, *Emperor Frederick II*, 304.

28. Kantorowicz, *Frederick the Second*, 69.

29. Haskins, *Studies*, 268.

30. Michael Scot, *Liber particularis* quoted in Haskins, *Studies*, 266.

31. Haskins, "Science at the Court," 688.

32. *Confessions of St. Augustine*, 241 (see chap. 2, n. 45).

33. Richard C. Dales, *Medieval Discussions of the Eternity of the World* (Leiden, Netherlands: E. J. Brill, 1990), 18.

34. Al-Kindi, *Metaphysics*, quoted in Richard Walzer, "Arabic Transmission of Greek Thought to Medieval Europe," *Bulletin of the John Rylands Library* 29 (1945–46), 175–76.

35. Aristotle, *Metaphysics*, trans. Thomas Taylor (Frome, UK: Prometheus Trust, 2003), 238.

36. Dales, *Medieval Discussions*, 35–36.

37. Richard C. Dales, "The Origin of the Doctrine of the Double Truth," *Viator* 15 (1984), 170.

38. *Confessions of St. Augustine*, 242.

39. Dag Nikolaus Hasse, *Avicenna's De Anima in the Latin West: The Formation of a Peripatetic Philosophy of the Soul, 1160–1300* (London: Warburg Institute, 2000), 1.

40. Marenbon, *Later Medieval Philosophy*, 57 (see chap. 6, n. 36).

41. Avicenna, "The Autobiography," in *Avicenna and the Aristotelian Tradition: Introduction to Reading Avicenna's Philosophical Works*, trans. and ed. Dimitri Gutas (Leiden, Netherlands: E. J. Brill, 1988), 28.

42. Avicenna, "The Autobiography," *Avicenna*, 252.

43. Oliver Leaman, *An Introduction to Medieval Islamic Philosophy* (Cambridge: Cambridge University Press, 1985), 34.

44. Hasse, *Avicenna's De Anima*, 29.

45. A. C. Crombie, *Science, Optics and Music in Medieval and Early Modern Thought* (London: Hambledon Press, 1990), 100–03.

46. Ibid., 92–93.

47. Marenbon, *Later Medieval Philosophy*, 60–62.

48. Oliver Leaman, *A Brief Introduction to Islamic Philosophy* (Cambridge: Polity Press, 1999), 4.

49. Dales, *Medieval Discussions*, 43.

50. *Averroes: On the Harmony of Religion and Philosophy*, trans. and ed. George F. Hourani (London: Luzac, 1967), 12.

51. Ibid., 7.

52. Ibid., 9.

53. Leaman, *Brief Introduction*, 21. See also Majid Fakhry, *Averroes (Ibn Rushd): His Life, Works and Influence* (Oxford: Oneworld, 2001), xii–xiv.

54. Averroes, *On the Harmony*, 13.

55. Ibid.

56. Harry A. Wolfson, "Revised Plan for Publication of a Corpus Commentariorum Averrois in Aristotelem," *Speculum* 38 (1963): 90ff.

57. Leaman, *Brief Introduction*, 154–55.

58. Alfred L. Ivry, "Averroes and the West," in *A Straight Path: Studies in Medieval Philosophy and Culture*, ed. Ruth Link-Salinger and others (Washington, DC: Catholic University of America Press, 1988), 153.

59. Averroes, *The Incoherence of the Incoherence*, trans. and ed. Simon van den Bergh (London: Luzac, 1964), 319.

60. Ibid., 468.

61. Ibid., 425.

62. Fakhry, *Averroes*, xvi.

63. Averroes, *On the Harmony*, 23.

64. The full Arabic title has been translated as *The book of the decision [or distinction] of the discourse, and a determination of what there is of connection between religion and philosophy.* See Averroes, *On the Harmony*, 1.

65. Averroes, *On the Harmony*, 44.

66. Ibid., 22.

67. Marenbon, *Later Medieval Philosophy*, 52.

68. Van Steenberghen, *Aristotle in the West*, 82 (see chap. 6, n. 35).

69. Frederick II, quoted in van Cleve, *Emperor Frederick II*, 303. Some scholars have attributed this letter to Frederick's son, Manfred. For the view that the letter was almost certainly written by Frederick, see van Cleve, 303, n. 2.

Chapter 9: The Invention of the West

1. Edward Grant, "Science and Theology in the Middle Ages," in *God and Nature: Historical Essays on the Encounter Between Christianity and Science*, ed. David C. Lindberg and Ronald L. Numbers (Berkeley: University of California Press, 1986), 49–53.

2. Van Steenberghen, *Aristotle in the West*, 79–80 (see chap. 6, n. 35).

3. *Chartularium universitatis Paresiensis*, in Thorndike, *University Records*, 34 (see chap. 6, n. 32).

4. French and Cunningham, *Before Science*, 63 (see chap. 5, n. 44).

5. Grant, *Foundations of Modern Science*, 54 (see chap. 7, n. 1). See also Marenbon, *Later Medieval Philosophy*, 64 (see chap. 6, n. 36).

6. Friedrich Heer, *The Medieval World: Europe, 1100–1350*, trans. Janet Sondheimer (New York: World Publishing Company, 1961), 200.

7. Grant, *Foundations of Modern Science*, 37.

8. John of Fidanza, *Collationes de septem donis Spiritus Sancti* quoted in Tony Dodd, *The Life and Thought of Siger of Brabant, Twelfth-century Parisian Philosopher* (Lewiston, NY: Edwin Mellen Press, 1998), 71.

9. William of Baglione, *De Aeternitate Mundi*, quoted in Dales, *Medieval Discussions*, 112 (see chap. 8, n. 33).

10. On Thomas's teacher, see Jean-Pierre Tarrell, *Saint Thomas Aquinas: The Person and His Work*, trans. Robert Royal (Washington, DC: Catholic University of America, 1996), 7. On Michael's translations, see Thorndike, *Michael Scot*, 28 (see chap. 2, n. 34).

11. Marcia L. Colish, "Avicenna's Theory of Efficient Causation and Its Influence on Thomas Aquinas," in *Studies in Scholasticism* (Burlington, VT: Ashgate, 2006), 2–3.

12. Barry S. Kogan, "The Problem of Creation in Late Medieval Jewish Philosophy," in *A Straight Path*, 161 (see chap. 8, n. 58). Also see Dales, *Medieval Discussions*, 45–47 (see chap. 8, n. 33).

13. Averroes, *Incoherence of the Incoherence*, 65 (see chap. 8, n. 59).

14. Thomas Aquinas, *De aeternitate mundi*, in St. Thomas Aquinas, Siger of Brabant, and St. Bonaventure, *On the Eternity of the World*, trans. and ed. Cyril Vollert, Lottie H. Kendzierski, and Paul M. Byrne (Milwaukee, WI: Marquette University Press, 1964), 21.

15. Ibid., 22.

16. Vollert, Kendzierski, and Byrne, *On the Eternity*, 14.

17. Thomas Aquinas, *De aeternitate mundi*, in *On the Eternity*, 25.

18. Fernand van Steenberghen, *Thomas Aquinas and Radical Aristotelianism* (Washington, DC: Catholic University of America Press, 1978), 22.

19. Thomas Aquinas, *De aeternitate mundi*, in *An Aquinas Reader*, trans. and ed. Mary T. Clark (New York: Fordham University Press, 1972), 181.

20. Thomas Aquinas, *Responsio de 43 articulis*, quoted in Tarrell, *Saint Thomas Aquinas*, 169.

21. Ibid.

22. Richard E. Rubenstein, *Aristotle's Children: How Christians, Muslims and Jews Rediscovered Ancient Wisdom and Illuminated the Dark Ages* (Orlando, FL: Harcourt, 2003), 198.

23. Thomas Aquinas, *Summa theologiae*, quoted in *On the Eternity*, 66.

24. Dodd, *Life and Thought*, 73–76.

25. "Condemnations of 219 Propositions," in *Medieval Political Philosophy: A Sourcebook*, ed. Ralph Lerner and Muhsin Mahdi (New York: Free Press of Glencoe, 1963), 337.

26. Ibid., 338.

27. Mary M. McLaughlin, "Paris Masters of the Thirteenth and Fourteenth Centuries and Ideas of Intellectual Freedom," *Church History* 24, no. 3 (1955): 196.

28. Dodd, *Life and Thought*, 361.

29. Thomas S. Kuhn, *Copernican Revolution*, 2–3 (see chap. 6, n. 26).

30. Saliba, *Islamic Science*, 78–84 (see Prologue, n. 12).

31. Ibid., 88.

32. A. I. Sabra, "The Andalusian Revolt Against Ptolemaic Astronomy: Averroes and al-Bitruj," in *Transformation and Tradition in the Sciences*, ed. Everett Mendelsohn (London: Cambridge University Press, 1984), 133–34.

33. Ibid., 135–37.

34. Saliba, *Islamic Science*, 95.

35. Averroes, *Tafsir ma ba'd al-tabia*, quoted in Saliba, *Islamic Science*, 179.

36. Saliba, *Islamic Science*, 236.

37. Ibid., 183.

38. E. S. Kennedy and Victor Roberts, "The Planetary Theory of Ibn al-Shatir," *Isis* 50, no. 3 (1959): 227–35.

39. See Will Hartner, "Copernicus, the Man, the Work, and Its History," *Proceedings of the American Philosophical Society* 117, no. 3 (1973): 413–22.

40. Saliba, *Islamic Science*, 164.

41. Arthur Koestler once referred to Copernicus's work as "the book nobody read." For a lively but thoroughly serious response, see Owen Gingrich, *The Book Nobody Read: Chasing the Revolutions of Nicolaus Copernicus* (New York: Walker and Co., 2004).

42. Adelard of Bath, *Questions of Natural Science*, quoted in Gibson, "Adelard of Bath," 16 (see chap. 5, n. 56).

SELECTED BIBLIOGRAPHY

The following selections are provided for those readers who would like to explore further the topics, developments, and personalities presented in *The House of Wisdom*. A special effort has been made to include voices and viewpoints, particularly those from the Arab world, that are seldom heard in the standard Western narrative of the history of ideas. More detailed sources and specialist literature are addressed in the endnotes.

Abdo, Geneive. *No God but God: Egypt and the Triumph of Islam.* New York: Oxford University Press, 2001.

Abdo, Geneive, and Jonathan Lyons. *Answering Only to God: Faith and Freedom in Twenty-first Century Iran.* New York: Henry Holt, 2003.

Abulafia, David. *Frederick II: A Medieval Emperor.* London: Allen Lane, 1988.

Adelard of Bath. *Adelard of Bath, Conversations with His Nephew: On the Same and the Different, Questions on Natural Science and On Birds.* Translated and edited by Charles Burnett. Cambridge: Cambridge University Press, 1998.

Agius, Dionisius A., and Richard Hitchcock, ed. *The Arab Influence in Medieval Europe.* Reading, UK: Ithaca Press, 1994.

Ahmad, Nafis. *Muslims and the Science of Geography.* Dacca: University Press, 1980.

Al-Andalusi, Said. *Science in the Medieval World: "Book of the Categories of Nations."* Translated and edited by Semaan I. Salem and Alok Kumar. Austin: University of Texas Press, 1991.

Atiya, Aziz S. *Crusade, Commerce, and Culture.* Bloomington: Indiana University Press, 1962.

Attiyeh, George N., ed. *The Book in the Islamic World: The Written Word and Communication in the Middle East.* New York: New York University Press, 1995.

Averroes. *Averroes: On the Harmony of Religion and Philosophy.* Translated and edited by George F. Hourani. London: Luzac, 1967.

——. *Averroes' Tahafut al-Tahafut.* Translated and edited by Simon van den Bergh. 2 vols. Oxford: Oxford University Press, 1954.

Aziz, Ahmad. *A History of Islamic Sicily.* New York: Columbia University Press, 1979.

Al-Azmeh, A. "Barbarians in Arab Eyes." *Past and Present* 134 (1992): 3–18.

Bello, Iysa A. *The Medieval Islamic Controversy Between Philosophy and Orthodoxy.* Leiden, Netherlands: E. J. Brill, 1989.

Benson, Robert L., and Giles Constable, eds. *Renaissance and Renewal in the Twelfth Century.* Cambridge, MA: Harvard University Press, 1982.

Berggren, J. J. *Episodes in the Mathematics of Medieval Islam.* New York: Springer-Verlag, 2003.

Al-Biruni. *The Determination of the Coordinates of Cities: Al-Biruni's* Tahid al-Amakin. Translated and edited by Jamil Ali. Beirut: Centennial Publications, 1967.

Bloom, Jonathan. *Paper Before Print: The History and Impact of Paper in the Islamic World.* New Haven, CT: Yale University Press, 2001.

Bulmer-Thomas, Ivor. "Euclid and Medieval Architecture." *Archaeological Journal* 136 (1979): 136–50.

Burnett, Charles, ed. *Adelard of Bath: An English Scientist and Arabist of the Early Twelfth Century.* London: Warburg Institute, 1987.

———. *The Introduction of Arabic Learning into England.* London: British Library, 1997.

Butterworth, Charles E., and Blake Andree Kessel, eds. *The Introduction of Arabic Philosophy into Europe.* Leiden, Netherlands: E. J. Brill, 1994.

Cochrane, Louise. *Adelard of Bath: The First English Scientist.* London: British Museum Press, 1994.

Cooperson, Michael. *Al Ma'mun.* Oxford: Oneworld, 2005.

Crombie, A. C. *Augustine to Galileo.* Cambridge, MA: Harvard University Press, 1979.

———. *Science, Optics and Music in Medieval and Early Modern Thought.* London: Hambledon Press, 1990.

Crossley, John N., and Alan S. Henry. "Thus Spake al-Khwarizmi: A Translation of the Text of Cambridge University Library Ms. Ii.vi.5." *Historia Mathematica* 17 (1990): 103–31.

Curry, Patrick, ed. *Astrology, Science, and Society: Historical Essays.* Woodbridge, UK: Boydell Press, 1987.

Dales, Richard C. *Medieval Discussions of the Eternity of the World.* Leiden, Netherlands: E. J. Brill, 1990.

Daniel, Norman. *The Arabs and Medieval Europe.* London: Longman, 1979.

———. "Crusade Propaganda." In *A History of the Crusades,* vol. 6, *The Impact of the Crusades on Europe,* edited by Harry W. Hazard and Norman P. Zacour, 39–97. Madison: University of Wisconsin Press, 1989.

———. *Islam and the West: The Making of an Image.* Oxford: Oneworld, 1993.

Dohrn-van Rossum, Gerhard. *History of the Hour: Clocks and Modern Temporal Orders.* Translated by Thomas Dunlap. Chicago: University of Chicago Press, 1996.

Donini, Pier Giovanni. *Arab Travelers and Geographers.* London: Immel, 1991.

Dronke, Peter, ed. *A History of Twelfth-Century Western Philosophy.* Cambridge: Cambridge University Press, 1988.

Eidelberg, Shlomo, trans. and ed. *The Jews and the Crusaders: The Hebrew Chronicles of the First and Second Crusades.* Madison: University of Wisconsin Press, 1977.

Evans, James. *The History and Practice of Ancient Astronomy.* New York: Oxford University Press, 1998.

Fakhry, Majid. *Averroes, Aquinas and the Rediscovery of Aristotle in Western Europe.* Washington, DC: Center for Muslim-Christian Understanding, Georgetown University, 1997.

——. *Averroes (Ibn Rushd): His Life, Works and Influence.* Oxford: Oneworld, 2001.

——. *A History of Islamic Philosophy.* New York: Columbia University Press, 2004.

Fletcher, Richard. *Moorish Spain.* New York: Henry Holt, 1992.

Gabrieli, Francesco. *Arab Historians of the Crusades.* Translated by E. J. Costello. London: Routledge and Kegan Paul, 1969.

Gilson, Etienne. *Reason and Revelation in the Middle Ages.* New York: Charles Scribner's Sons, 1938.

Gingerich, Owen. "Islamic Astronomy." *Scientific American* 254 (April 1986): 68–75.

Goldstein, Bernard R. "The Making of Astronomy in Early Islam." *Nuncius: Annali di Storia Della Scienza* 1 (1986): 79–92.

Goss, Vladimir P., ed. *The Meeting of Two Worlds: Cultural Exchange Between East and West During the Period of the Crusades.* Kalamazoo, MI: Medieval Institute Publications, Western Michigan University, 1986.

Gutas, Dimitri. *Avicenna and the Aristotelian Tradition: Introduction to Reading Avicenna's Philosophical Works.* Leiden, Netherlands: E. J. Brill, 1988.

——. *Greek Thought, Arabic Culture: The Graeco-Arabic Translation Movement in Baghdad and Early Abbasid Society.* London: Routledge, 1998.

Harvey, John H. "Geometry and Gothic Design." *Transactions of the Ancient Monuments Society* 30 (1986): 43–56.

——. *The Medieval Architect.* London: Wayland, 1972.

Haskins, Charles Homer. "Michael Scot and Frederick II." *Isis* 4, no. 2 (1921): 250–75.

——. *The Rise of Universities.* Ithaca, NY: Cornell Paperbacks, 1957.

——. *Studies in the History of Mediaeval Science.* Cambridge, MA: Harvard University Press, 1927.

Al-Hassan, Ahmad Y. "Factors Behind the Decline of Islamic Science After the Sixteenth Century." In *Islam and the Challenge of Modernity: Historical and Contemporary Contexts,* edited by Sharifah Shifa Al-Attas, 351–89. Kuala Lumpur: International Institute of Islamic Thought and Civilisation, 1996.

Hasse, Dag Nikolaus. *Avicenna's* De Anima *in the Latin West: The Formation of a Peripatetic Philosophy of the Soul, 1160–1300.* London: Warburg Institute, 2000.

Hill, Donald R. *Studies in Medieval Islamic Technology.* Brookfield, VT: Ashgate, 1998.

Hillenbrand, Carole. *The Crusades: Islamic Perspectives.* Chicago: Fitzroy Dearborn, 1999.

Houben, Hubert. *Roger II of Sicily: A Ruler Between East and West.* Translated by Graham A. Lound and Diane Milburn. Cambridge: Cambridge University Press, 2002.

Hourani, George F. *Arab Seafaring in the Indian Ocean in Ancient and Early Medieval Times.* Princeton, NJ: Princeton University Press, 1995.

Huff, Toby. *The Rise of Early Modern Science: Islam, China, and the West.* Cambridge: Cambridge University Press, 1993.

Ibn Jubayr. *The Travels of Ibn Jubayr.* Translated by R. J. C. Broadhurst. London: J. Cape, 1952.

Ibn Khaldun. *The Muqaddimah: An Introduction to History.* Translated and edited by Franz Rosenthal. 3 vols. Princeton, NJ: Princeton University Press, 1967.

Ibn Munqidh, Usama. *The Book of Contemplation: Islam and the Crusades*. Translated by Paul M. Cobb. Hardmondsworth, UK: Penguin Classics, 2008.

Ibn al-Nadim. *The Fihrist of al-Nadim*. Translated and edited by Bayard Dodge. 2 vols. New York: Columbia University Press, 1970.

Ibn al-Qalanisi. *The Damascus Chronicle of the Crusades*. Translated and edited by H. A. R. Gibb. Mineola, NY: Dover Publications, 2002.

Jayyusi, Salma Khadra, ed. *The Legacy of Muslim Spain*. Leiden, Netherlands: E. J. Brill, 1994.

Kennedy, Hugh. *When Baghdad Ruled the Muslim World: The Rise and Fall of Islam's Greatest Dynasty*. New York: De Capo Press, 2004.

Khair, Tabish, and others, eds. *Other Routes: 1500 Years of African and Asian Travel Writing*. Bloomington: Indiana University Press, 2005.

Al-Khwarizmi. *The Algebra of Mohammad ben Musa*. Translated and edited by Frederic Rosen. Hildesheim, Germany: George Olms Verlag, 1986.

Kieckhefer, Richard. *Magic in the Middle Ages*. Cambridge: Cambridge University Press, 1990.

Kimble, George H. T. *Geography in the Middle Ages*. London: Methuen and Co., 1938.

Kimerling, A. Jon. "Cartographic Methods for Determining the Qibla." *Journal of Geography* 101 (2002): 20–26.

King, Charles. "Leonardo Fibonacci." In *From Five Fingers to Infinity: A Journey Through the History of Mathematics*, edited by Frank J. Swetz, 252–54. Chicago: Open Court, 1994.

King, David A. *In Synchrony with the Heavens: Studies in Astronomical Timekeeping and Instrumentation in Medieval Islamic Civilization*. Leiden, Netherlands: E. J. Brill, 2004.

——. *Astronomy in the Service of Islam*. Brookfield, VT: Variorum, 1993.

King, David A., and Richard P. Lorch. "Qibla Charts, Qibla Maps, and Related Instruments." In *The History of Cartography*, vol. 2, bk. 1, *Cartography in the Traditional Islamic and South Asian Societies*, edited by J. B. Harley and David Woodward. Chicago: University of Chicago Press, 1987.

Koestler, Arthur. *The Sleepwalkers: A History of Man's Changing Vision of the Universe*. London: Arkana, 1989.

Krey, August C., trans. and ed. *The First Crusades: The Accounts of Eyewitnesses and Participants*. Princeton, NJ: Princeton University Press, 1921.

Kuhn, Thomas S. *The Copernican Revolution: Planetary Astronomy in the Development of Western Thought*. Cambridge, MA: Harvard University Press, 1957.

Leaman, Oliver. *Averroes and His Philosophy*. Oxford: Clarendon Press, 1988.

——. *A Brief Introduction to Islamic Philosophy*. Cambridge: Polity Press, 1999.

Le Goff, Jacques. *Intellectuals in the Middle Ages*. Translated by Teresa Lavender Fagan. Cambridge, MA: Blackwell, 1993.

——. *Time, Work, & Culture in the Middle Ages*. Translated by Arthur Goldhammer. Chicago: University of Chicago Press, 1980.

Leonardo of Pisa. *Fibonacci's Liber Abaci: A Translation into Modern English of Leonardo Pisano's Book of Calculation*. Translated and edited by L. E. Sigler. New York: Springer, 2002.

Le Strange, Guy. *Baghdad During the Abbasid Caliphate*. Westport, CT: Greenwood Press, 1983.

Lindberg, David C. *The Beginnings of Western Science: The European Scientific Tradition in Philosophical, Religious, and Institutional Context, 660 B.C. to A.D. 1450*. Chicago: University of Chicago Press, 1992.

———. ed. *Science in the Middle Ages*. Chicago: University of Chicago Press, 1978.

Maalouf, Amin. *The Crusades Through Arab Eyes*. Translated by Jon Rothschild. New York: Schocken Books, 1984.

Mallette, Karla. *The Kingdom of Sicily, 1100–1250: A Literary History*. Philadelphia: University of Pennsylvania Press, 2005.

Marenbon, John. *Later Medieval Philosophy (1150–1350)*. London: Routledge and Kegan Paul, 1987.

Al-Masudi. *The Meadows of Gold*. Translated and edited by Paul Lunde and Caroline Stone. London: Kegan Paul, 1989.

McClenan, R. B. "Leonardo of Pisa and His *Liber quadratorium*." In *From Five Fingers to Infinity: A Journey Through the History of Mathematics*, edited by Frank J. Swetz, 255–60. Chicago: Open Court, 1994.

McCluskey, Stephen C. *Astronomies and Cultures in Early Medieval Europe*. New York: Cambridge University Press, 1998.

Menocal, María Rosa. *The Ornament of the World: How Muslims, Jews, and Christians Created a Culture of Tolerance in Medieval Spain*. Boston: Little, Brown, 2002.

Moran, Bruce T. *Distilling Knowledge: Alchemy, Chemistry, and the Scientific Revolution*. Cambridge, MA: Harvard University Press, 2005.

Mumford, Lewis. *Technics and Civilization*. New York: Harcourt, Brace and World, 1963.

Al-Muqaddasi. *The Best Divisions for Knowledge of the Regions*. Translated and edited by Basil Anthony Collins. Reading, UK: Garnet Publishing, 1994.

Nadvi, Syed Sulaiman. *The Arab Navigation*. Translated by Syed Sabahuddin Abdu Rahman. Lahore, Pakistan: Sh. Muhammad Ashraf, 1966.

Al-Najdi, Ahmad bin Majid. *Arab Navigation in the Indian Ocean Before the Coming of the Portuguese*. Translated and edited by G. G. Tibbetts. London: Royal Asiatic Society of Great Britain and Ireland, 1971.

Nasr, Seyyed Hossein. "Islamic Alchemy and the Birth of Chemistry." *Journal for the History of Arabic Science* 3, no. 1 (1979): 40–45.

Nasr, Seyyed Hossein, and Oliver Leaman, ed. *History of Islamic Philosophy*. New York: Routledge, 1996.

Newman, William R., and Anthony Grafton, ed. *Secrets of Nature: Astrology and Alchemy in Early Modern Europe*. Cambridge, MA: MIT Press, 2001.

Pedersen, Johannes. *The Arabic Book*. Translated by Geoffrey French. Princeton, NJ: Princeton University Press, 1984.

Peters, Francis E. *Aristotle and the Arabs*. New York: New York University Press, 1968.

Phillips, Jonathan. *Defenders of the Holy Land: Relations Between the Latin East and the West, 1119–1187*. Oxford: Clarendon Press, 1996.

Pickthall, Marmaduke. *The Meaning of the Glorious Koran: An Explanatory Translation*. New York: Alfred A. Knopf, 1909.

Pym, Anthony. *Negotiating the Frontier: Translators and Intercultures in Hispanic History*. Manchester, UK: St. Jerome Publishing, 2000.

Rashed, Roshdi. *The Development of Arabic Mathematics: Between Arithmetic and Algebra*. Translated by A. F. W. Armstrong. Dordrecht, Netherlands: Kluwer Academic Publishers, 1994.

Riley-Smith, Jonathan. *The First Crusade and the Idea of Crusading*. Philadelphia: University of Pennsylvania Press, 1986.

Rodinson, Maxime. *Europe and the Mystique of Islam*. Translated by Roger Veinus. Seattle: University of Washington Press, 1987.

Rubenstein, Richard E. *Aristotle's Children: How Christians, Muslims and Jews Rediscovered Ancient Wisdom and Illuminated the Dark Ages*. Orlando, FL: Harcourt, 2003.

Sabra, A. I. "The Andalusian Revolt Against Ptolemaic Astronomy: Averroes and al-Bitruj." In *Transformation and Tradition in the Sciences*, edited by Everett Mendelsohn. London: Cambridge University Press, 1984.

———. "An Eleventh-Century Refutation of Ptolemy's Planetary Theory." *Studia Copernicana* 16 (1978): 117–31.

Saliba, George. *Islamic Science and the Making of the European Renaissance*. Cambridge, MA: MIT Press, 2007.

Savage-Smith, Emilie, ed. *Magic and Divination in Early Islam*. Burlington, VT: Ashgate, 2004.

Sayili, Aydin. *The Observatory in Islam*. Ankara: Turk Tarih Kurumu Basimevi, 1960.

Sezgin, Fuat. *Mathematical Geography and Cartography in Islam and Their Continuation on the Occident*, vol. 1. Frankfurt am Main: Institute for the History of Arabic-Islamic Science, 2005.

Shatzmiller, Maya, ed. *Crusaders and Muslims in Twelfth-Century Syria*. Leiden, Netherlands: E. J. Brill, 1993.

Silverstein, Theodore. "Daniel of Morley, English Cosmologist and Student of Arabic Science." *Mediaeval Studies* 10 (1948): 179–96.

Southern, Richard W. *Medieval Humanism*. New York: Harper and Row, 1970.

Van Steenberghen, Fernand. *Aristotle in the West: The Origins of Latin Aristotelianism*. Translated by Leonard Johnston. Louvain, Belgium: E. Nauwelaerts, 1955.

———. *Thomas Aquinas and Radical Aristotelianism*. Washington, DC: Catholic University of America Press, 1978.

Swetz, Frank J. *Capitalism and Arithmetic: The New Mathematics of the 15th Century*. La Salle, IL: Open Court, 1987.

Tester, S. J. *A History of Western Astrology*. Woodbridge, UK: Boydell Press, 1987.

Thijssen, J. M. M. H. *Censure and Heresy at the University of Paris*. Philadelphia: University of Pennsylvania Press, 1998.

Thorndike, Lynn. *History of Magic and Experimental Science*. 8 vols. New York: Macmillan, 1923–58.

———. *Michael Scot*. London: Thomas Nelson and Sons, 1965.

———. *The Place of Magic in the Intellectual History of Europe*. New York: AMS Press, 1967.

Tyerman, Christopher. *God's War: A New History of the Crusades*. Cambridge, MA: Harvard University Press, 2006.

———. *The Invention of the Crusades*. Toronto: University of Toronto Press, 1998.

Van Cleve, Thomas Curtis. *The Emperor Frederick II of Hohenstaufen*: Immutator Mundi. Oxford: Clarendon Press, 1972.

Walzer, Richard. *Greek into Arabic: Essays on Islamic Philosophy*. Cambridge, MA: Harvard University Press, 1962.

Watson, Andrew M. *Agricultural Innovation in the Early Islamic World: The Diffusion of Crops and Farming Techniques, 700–1100*. Cambridge: Cambridge University Press, 1983.

Wiet, Gaston. *Baghdad: Metropolis of the Abbasid Caliphate*. Translated by Seymour Feiler. Norman: University of Oklahoma Press, 1971.

INDEX

A NOTE ON THE AUTHOR

Jonathan Lyons served as editor and foreign correspondent—mostly in the Muslim world—for Reuters for more than twenty years. He is now a researcher at the Global Terrorism Research Center and a Ph.D. candidate in the sociology of religion, both at Monash University in Melbourne, Australia.

A NOTE ON THE TYPE

The text of this book is set in Centaur. Centaur was designed by Bruce Rogers in 1914 as a titling fount only for the Metropolitan Museum of New York. It was modelled on Jenson's roman.

Copie de la Carte de L'EDRISI, tirée de l'Ouvrage du Docteur Vincent sur le Periple d'Arrien.

N.

S.

Montagnes de la Lune.

Lacs et Sources du Nil.

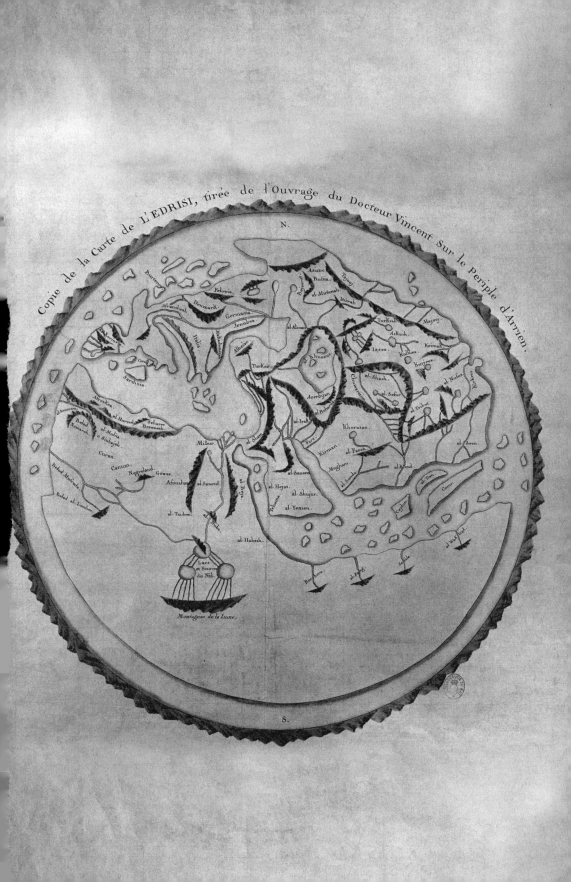

Copie de la Carte de L'EDRISI, tirée de l'Ouvrage du Docteur Vincent sur le periple d'Arrien.

N.

Burenos
Felows
Afraubeah
DenmarK
Germania
Jennbes
Italia
Batabanes
TurKeronen
Albeine
Corsi
TurKer
Sardinia
Afrechen
al-Hurreal
Seharre
Berenech
Abroens
Belad
Neurasah
al-Mahia
n Sinhajeh
Curan
Canum
Misur
Nigreland
Gowas
Afoushat
al-Saueed
al-Taidem
al-Nube
al-Habah
al-Beya
al-Hejaz
al-Shujur
al-Yemen
al-Sham

Berenes
Rubia
al-Murensh
Asiane
Yeiuoj
Iturah
TurKeth
AsKush
Izxes
Kulhoa
Keimak
Kunjbea
Kemah
al-Khuzzut
Azerbjun
al-Bolwah
al-Shash
Cluworain
al-Sehir
al-Treibet
al-Nubei
KirKan
al-Iraki
al-Sham
Fars
Kirman
al-Fazeh
Mughran
al-Saueed
al-Sauba
al-Kind
al-Dai
Comr
Khoratan
al-Seen
Ceylon

al-Sham

Azerbjun

Biseban
al-Fenj
Sofala
al-Wak Wak

Lacs et Sources du Nil.

Montagnes de la Lune.

S.